Subliminal

LEONARD MLODINOW

Subliminal

*The Revolution of the New Unconscious
and What it Teaches Us about Ourselves*

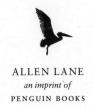

ALLEN LANE
an imprint of
PENGUIN BOOKS

ALLEN LANE

Published by the Penguin Group
Penguin Books Ltd, 80 Strand, London WC2R ORL, England
Penguin Group (USA) Inc., 375 Hudson Street, New York, New York 10014, USA
Penguin Group (Canada), 90 Eglinton Avenue East, Suite 700, Toronto, Ontario,
Canada M4P 2Y3 (a division of Pearson Penguin Canada Inc.)
Penguin Ireland, 25 St Stephen's Green, Dublin 2, Ireland (a division of Penguin Books Ltd)
Penguin Group (Australia), 250 Camberwell Road, Camberwell, Victoria 3124, Australia
(a division of Pearson Australia Group Pty Ltd)
Penguin Books India Pvt Ltd, 11 Community Centre, Panchsheel Park, New Delhi – 110 017, India
Penguin Group (NZ), 67 Apollo Drive, Rosedale, Auckland 0632, New Zealand
(a division of Pearson New Zealand Ltd)
Penguin Books (South Africa) (Pty) Ltd, Block D, Rosebank Office Park, 181 Jan Smuts Avenue, Parktown North,
Gauteng 2193, South Africa

Penguin Books Ltd, Registered Offices: 80 Strand, London WC2R ORL, England

www.penguin.com

First published in the United States of America by Pantheon Books,
a division of Random House, Inc., New York 2012
First published in Great Britain by Allen Lane 2012
001

Copyright © Leonard Mlodinow, 2012

The moral right of the author has been asserted

Printed in Great Britain by Clays Ltd, St Ives plc

A CIP catalogue record for this book is available from the British Library

Hardback ISBN: 978-1-846-14596-4
Trade paperback ISBN: 978-1-846-14598-8

www.greenpenguin.co.uk

Penguin Books is committed to a sustainable
future for our business, our readers and our planet.
This book is made from Forest Stewardship
Council™ certified paper.

ALWAYS LEARNING   **PEARSON**

To Christof Koch, K-lab,
and all those who have dedicated their careers
to understanding the human mind

Contents

Contents

Subliminal

Prologue

These subliminal aspects of everything that happens to us may seem to play very little part in our daily lives. But they are the almost invisible roots of our conscious thoughts.   —CARL JUNG

IN JUNE 1879, the American philosopher and scientist Charles Sanders Peirce was on a steamship journey from Boston to New York when his gold watch was stolen from his stateroom.[1] Peirce reported the theft and insisted that each member of the ship's crew line up on deck. He interviewed them all, but got nowhere. Then, after a short walk, he did something odd. He decided to guess who the perpetrator was, even though he had nothing to base his suspicions on, like a poker player going all in with a pair of deuces. As soon as Peirce made his guess, he found himself convinced that he had fingered the right man. "I made a little loop in my walk," he would later write, "which had not taken a minute, and as I turned toward them, all shadow of doubt had vanished."[2]

Peirce confidently approached his suspect, but the man called his bluff and denied the accusation. With no evidence or logical reason to back his claim, there was nothing Peirce could do—until the ship docked. When it did, Peirce immediately took a cab to the local Pinkerton office and hired a detective to investigate. The detective found Peirce's watch at a pawnshop the next day. Peirce asked the proprietor to describe the man who'd pawned it. According to Peirce, the pawnbroker described the suspect "so graphically that no doubt was possible that it had been my man." Peirce wondered how he had guessed the identity of the thief. He concluded that some kind of instinctual perception had guided him, something operating beneath the level of his conscious mind.

If mere speculation were the end of the story, a scientist would consider Peirce's explanation about as convincing as someone saying, "A little birdie told me." But five years later Peirce found a way to translate his ideas about unconscious perception into a laboratory experiment by adapting a procedure that had first been carried out by the physiologist E. H. Weber in 1834. Weber had placed small weights of varying degrees of heaviness, one at a time, at a spot on a subject's skin, in order to determine the minimum weight difference that could be detected by the subject.[3] In the experiment performed by Peirce and his prize student, Joseph Jastrow, the subjects of the study were given weights whose difference was just below that minimum detectable threshold (those subjects were actually Peirce and Jastrow themselves, with Jastrow experimenting on Peirce, and Peirce on Jastrow). Then, although they could not consciously discriminate between the weights, they asked each other to try to identify the heavier weight anyway, and to indicate on a scale running from 0 to 3 the degree of confidence they had in each guess. Naturally, on almost all trials both men chose 0. But despite their lack of confidence, they in fact chose the correct object on more than 60 percent of the trials, significantly more than would have been expected by chance. And when Peirce and Jastrow repeated the experiment in other contexts, such as judging surfaces that differed slightly in brightness, they obtained a comparable result—they could often correctly guess the answer even though they did not have conscious access to the information that would allow them to come to that conclusion. This was the first scientific demonstration that the unconscious mind possesses knowledge that escapes the conscious mind.

Peirce would later compare the ability to pick up on unconscious cues with some considerable degree of accuracy to "a bird's musical and aeronautic powers . . . it is to us, as those are to them, the loftiest of our merely instinctive powers." He elsewhere referred to it as that "inward light . . . a light without which the human race would long ago have been extirpated for its utter incapacity in the struggles for existence." In other words, the work done by the unconscious is a critical part of our evolutionary survival mechanism.[4] For over a century now, research and clinical psychologists have been cognizant of the fact that we all possess a rich and active unconscious life that plays out in parallel to our conscious thoughts and feelings and has a powerful effect on them, in ways we are only now beginning to be able to measure with some degree of accuracy.

Carl Jung wrote, "There are certain events of which we have not consciously taken note; they have remained, so to speak, below the threshold of consciousness. They have happened, but they have been absorbed subliminally."[5] The Latin root of the word "subliminal" translates to "below threshold." Psychologists employ the term to mean below the threshold of consciousness. This book is about subliminal effects in that broad sense—about the processes of the unconscious mind and how they influence us. To gain a true understanding of human experience, we must understand both our conscious and our unconscious selves, and how they interact. Our subliminal brain is invisible to us, yet it influences our conscious experience of the world in the most fundamental of ways: how we view ourselves and others, the meanings we attach to the everyday events of our lives, our ability to make the quick judgment calls and decisions that can sometimes mean the difference between life and death, and the actions we engage in as a result of all these instinctual experiences.

Though the unconscious aspects of human behavior were actively speculated about by Jung, Freud, and many others over the past century, the methods they employed—introspection, observations of overt behavior, the study of people with brain deficits, the implanting of electrodes into the brains of animals—provided only fuzzy and indirect knowledge. Meanwhile, the true origins of human behavior remained obscure. Things are different today. Sophisticated new technologies have revolutionized our understanding of the part of the brain that operates below our conscious mind—what I'm referring to here as the subliminal world. These technologies have made it possible, for the first time in human history, for there to be an actual science of the unconscious. That new science of the unconscious is the subject of this book.

PRIOR TO THE twentieth century, the science of physics described, very successfully, the physical universe as it was perceived through everyday human experience. People noticed that what goes up usually comes back down, and they eventually measured how quickly the turnaround occurs. In 1687 Isaac Newton put this working understanding of everyday reality into mathematical form in his book *Philosophiae Naturalis Principia Mathematica*; the title is Latin for *Mathematical Principles of Natural Philosophy*. The laws Newton formulated were so powerful that they could be used to accurately calculate the orbits of the moon and faraway planets. But around 1900, this neat and comfortable worldview was shaken. Scientists discovered that underlying Newton's everyday picture is a different reality, the deeper truth we now call quantum theory and relativity.

Scientists form theories of the physical world; we all, as social beings, form personal "theories" of our social world. These theories are part of the adventure of participating in human society. They cause us to interpret the behavior of others, to predict their actions, to make guesses about how to get what we want from them, and to decide, ultimately, on how we feel toward them. Do we trust them with our money, our health, our cars, our careers, our children—or our hearts? As was true in the physical world, in the social universe, too, there is a very different reality underlying the one we naively experience. The revolution in physics occurred when, in the nineteenth and early twentieth centuries, new technologies exposed the exotic behavior of atoms and newly discovered subatomic particles, like the photon and electron; analogously, the new technologies of neuroscience are today enabling scientists to expose a deeper mental reality, a reality that for all of prior human history has been hidden from view.

The science of the mind has been remade by one new technology in particular. Functional magnetic resonance imaging, or fMRI, emerged in the 1990s. It is related to the ordinary MRI that your doctor employs, except fMRI maps the activity of the brain's different structures by detecting the blood flow that waxes and wanes, just slightly, as that activity varies. In this way fMRI offers three-dimensional pictures of the working brain, inside and out, mapping, to a resolution of about a millimeter, the level of activity throughout the organ. To get an idea of what fMRI can do, consider this: scientists can now use data collected from your brain to reconstruct an image of what you are looking at.[6]

Prologue

Have a look at the pictures below. In each case, the image on the left is the actual image a subject was gazing at, and the image on the right is the computer's reconstruction. The reconstruction was created from the

The actual image: The computer's guess:

Courtesy of Jack Gallant

fMRI's electromagnetic readings of the subject's brain activity, without any reference to the actual image. It was accomplished by combining data from areas of the brain that respond to particular regions in a person's field of vision together with data from other parts of the brain that respond to different themes. A computer then sorted through a database of six million images and picked the one that best corresponded to those readings.

The result of applications like this has been an upheaval as radical as that of the quantum revolution: a new understanding of how the brain operates, and who we are as human beings. This revolution has a name, or at least the new field that it spawned has one. It is called social neuroscience. The first official meeting ever devoted to that field took place in April 2001.[7]

CARL JUNG BELIEVED that to learn about the human experience, it was important to study dreams and mythology. History is the story of events that played out in civilization, but dreams and myths are expressions of the human heart. The themes and archetypes of our dreams and myths, Jung pointed out, transcend time and culture. They arise from unconscious instincts that governed our behavior long before civilization papered over and obscured them, and they therefore teach us about what it means to be human on the deepest level. Today, as we piece together how the brain works, we are able to study human instincts directly, to see their physiological origins within the brain. It is by uncovering the workings of the unconscious that we can best understand both how we are related to other species and what makes us uniquely human.

The upcoming chapters are an exploration of our evolutionary heritage, of the surprising and exotic forces at play beneath the surface of our own minds, and of the impact of those unconscious instincts on what is usually considered willed, rational behavior—an impact that is much more powerful than we have previously believed it to be. If you really want to understand the social world, if you really want to understand yourself and others, and, beyond that, if you really want to overcome many of the obstacles that prevent you from living your fullest, richest life, you need to understand the influence of the subliminal world that is hidden within each of us.

PART I

The Two-Tiered Brain

CHAPTER 1

The New Unconscious

The heart has its reasons of which reason knows nothing.
—BLAISE PASCAL

W HEN MY MOTHER was eighty-five she inherited, from my son, a pet Russian tortoise named Miss Dinnerman. It lived in her yard, in a large pen enclosing both shrubs and lawn, delineated by chicken wire. My mother's knees were starting to go, so she'd had to curtail her traditional two-hour walks around the neighborhood. She was looking for a new friend, one she could easily access, and the tortoise got the job. She decorated the pen with rocks and pieces of wood and visited the animal every day, just like she used to visit the bank teller and the cashiers at Big Lots. On occasion she even brought Miss Dinnerman flowers, which she thought made the pen look pretty, but which the tortoise treated like a delivery from the local Pizza Hut.

My mother didn't mind when the tortoise ate her bouquets. She thought it was cute. "Look how she enjoys it," she'd say. But despite the cushy existence, the free room and board, and the freshly cut flowers, Miss Dinnerman's main goal in life seemed to be escape. Whenever she wasn't eating or sleeping, Miss Dinnerman would walk the perimeter, poking around for a hole in the chicken wire. She would even try to climb it, as awkward as a skateboarder trying to scale a spiral staircase. My mother saw this behavior, too, in human terms. To her, it was a heroic effort, like POW Steve McQueen plotting his breakout from a Nazi camp in *The Great Escape*. "Every creature wants freedom," my mother told me. "Even if she has it good here, she doesn't like being confined." My mother believed that Miss Dinnerman recognized her voice and responded to it. She believed that Miss Dinnerman understood her. "You're reading too much into her behavior," I told my mother. "Tortoises are primitive creatures." I would even demonstrate my point, waving my hands and hollering like a crazy person, then pointing out how the tortoise just ignored me. "So what?" she'd say. "Your kids ignore you, and you don't call them primitive creatures."

It can be difficult to distinguish willed, conscious behavior from that which is habitual or automatic. Indeed, as humans, our tendency to believe in consciously motivated behavior is so powerful that we read consciousness into not only our own behaviors but those of the animal kingdom as well. We do this with our pets, of course. It's called anthropomorphizing. The tortoise is as brave as a POW, the cat peed on the suitcase because it was mad at us for going away, the dog must hate the mailman for some good reason. Simpler organisms, too, can *appear* to behave with human-like thoughtfulness and intentionality. The lowly fruit fly, for example, goes through an elaborate mating ritual, which the male initiates by tapping the female with his foreleg and vibrating his wing in order to play her a courtship song.[1] If the female accepts the advance, she will do nothing, and the male will take over from there. If she is not sexually receptive, she will either strike him with her wings or legs, or run away. Though I have elicited frighteningly similar responses from *human* females, this fruit fly mating ritual is completely programmed. Fruit flies don't worry about issues such as where their relationship is headed; they simply exercise a routine that is hardwired within them. In fact, their actions are so directly related to their biological constitution that scientists have discovered a chemical that, when applied to a male of the species, will, within hours, convert a heterosexual fruit fly into one that is gay.[2] Even the roundworm called *C. elegans*—a creature made of only about a thousand cells—can appear to act with conscious intent. For instance, it may slither past a bit of perfectly digestible bacteria and toward another tidbit that awaits

12

it elsewhere on the petri dish. One might be tempted to conclude that the roundworm is exercising its free will, as we ourselves might do when rejecting an unappealing vegetable or a high-calorie desert. But a round-worm does not think to itself, *I'd better watch my diameter*; it simply moves toward the nutrient it has been programmed to hunt down.[3]

Animals like fruit flies and tortoises are at the lower end on the brain-power scale, but the role of automatic processing is not limited to such primitive creatures. We humans also perform many automatic, unconscious behaviors. We tend to be unaware of them, however, because the interplay between our conscious and our unconscious minds is so complex. This complexity has its roots in the physiology of our brains. As mammals, we have new layers of cortex built upon the base of our more primitive reptilian brains; and as humans, we have yet more cerebral matter built upon those. We have an unconscious mind and, superimposed upon it, a conscious brain. How much of our feelings, judgments, and behavior is due to each can be very hard to say, as we are constantly shifting back and forth between them. For example, one morning we mean to stop at the post office on the way to work, but at the key intersection, we turn right, toward the office, because we are running on autopilot—that is, acting unconsciously. Then, when trying to explain to the police officer the reason for our subsequent illegal U-turn, our conscious mind calculates the optimal excuse, while our autopilot unconscious handles the proper use of gerunds, subjunctive verbs, and indefinite articles so that our plea is expressed in fine grammatical form. If asked to step out of the car, we will consciously obey, then instinctively stand about four feet from the officer, although when talking to friends we automatically adjust that separation to about two and a half feet. (Most of us follow these unspoken rules of interpersonal distance without ever thinking about them and can't help feeling uncomfortable when they are violated.)

Once attention is called to them, it is easy to accept many of our simple behaviors (like making that right turn) as being automatic. The real issue is the extent to which more complex and substantive behaviors, with the potential to have a much greater impact on our lives, are also automatic—even though we may feel sure that they are carefully thought through and totally rational. How does our unconscious affect our attitude about questions like *Which house should I buy? Which stock should I sell? Should I hire that person to take care of my child?* Or: *Are bright blue eyes into which I can't stop staring a sufficient basis for a long-term loving relationship?*

If it is difficult to recognize automatic behavior in animals, it is even more difficult to recognize habitual behavior in ourselves. When I was in graduate school, long before my mother's tortoise stage, I used to phone her around eight every Thursday night. Then, one Thursday, I didn't. Most parents would have concluded that I forgot, or maybe that I finally "got a life" and was out for the evening. But my mother had a different interpretation. Starting around nine she began to call my apartment, asking for me. My roommate apparently didn't mind the first four or five calls, but after that, as I discovered the next morning, her reservoir of good will had dried up. Especially when my mother started accusing her of hiding the fact that I had been severely injured and hence was not calling because I was under sedation in the local hospital. By midnight, my mother's imagination had goosed that scenario up a couple notches—she was now accusing my roommate of covering up my recent death. "Why lie about it?" my mother asked. "I am going to find out."

Most children would be embarrassed to learn that their mother, a person who has known them intimately their whole life, would think it more plausible that they had been killed than that they had been out on a date. But I had seen my mother exhibit such behavior before. To outsiders, she appeared to be a perfectly normal individual, except for a few quirks, like believing in evil spirits and enjoying accordion music. Those were to be expected, remnants of the culture she grew up with in the old country, Poland. But my mother's mind worked differently from that of anyone else I knew. Today I understand why, even though my mother herself does not recognize it: decades earlier, her psyche had been restructured to view situations within a context that most of us could never imagine. It all started in 1939, when my mother was sixteen. Her own mother had died from abdominal cancer after suffering at home in excruciating pain for an entire year. Then, a short while later, my mother came home from school one day and found that her father had been taken by the Nazis. My mother and her sister, Sabina, were soon also taken away, to a forced labor camp, which her sister did not survive. Virtually overnight, my mother's life had been transformed from that of a well-loved and well-cared-for teenager in a well-to-do family to that of an orphaned, hated, and starving slave laborer. After her liberation my mother emigrated, married, settled in a peaceful neighborhood in Chicago, and had a stable and safe lower-middle-class family existence. She no longer had any rational reason to fear the sudden loss of everything dear to her, and yet that fear has driven her interpretation of everyday events for the rest of her life.

My mother interpreted the meanings of actions through a dictionary that was different from the one most of us use, and via her own unique rules of grammar. Her interpretations had become automatic to her, not consciously arrived at. Just as we all understand spoken language without any conscious application of linguistic rules, so too did she understand the world's message to her without any awareness that her early experiences had forever reshaped her expectations. My mother never recognized that her perceptions were skewed by the ever-present fear that at any moment justice, probability, and logic could cease to have force or meaning. Whenever I'd suggest it to her, she'd scoff at the idea of seeing a psychologist and deny that her past had had any negative effect on her view of the present. "Oh no?" I'd reply. "How come none of my friends' parents accuse their roommates of conspiring to cover up their death?"

We all have implicit frames of reference—with luck, less extreme—that produce habitual thinking and behavior. Our experiences and actions always *seem* to be rooted in conscious thought, and like my mother, we can find it difficult to accept that there are hidden forces at work behind the scenes. But though those forces may be invisible, they still exert a powerful pull. In the past there was a lot of speculation about the unconscious mind, but the brain was like a black box, its workings inaccessible to our understanding. The current revolution in thinking about the unconscious came about because, with modern instruments, we can watch as different structures and substructures in the brain generate feelings and emotions. We can measure the electrical output of individual neurons. We can map the neural activity that forms a person's thoughts. Today scientists can go beyond talking to my mother and guessing how her experiences affected her; today they can actually pinpoint the brain alterations that result from traumatic early experiences like hers and understand how such experiences cause physical changes in stress-sensitive brain regions.[4]

The modern concept of the unconscious, based on such studies and measurements, is often called the "new unconscious," to distinguish it from the idea of the unconscious that was popularized by a neurologist-turned-clinician named Sigmund Freud. Early on, Freud made several notable contributions to the fields of neurology, neuropathology, and anesthesia.[5] For example, he introduced the use of gold chloride to stain nerve tissue and used the technique to study the neural interconnections between the medulla oblongata, in the brain stem, and the cerebellum. In that, Freud was far ahead of his time, because it would be many decades before scientists understood the importance of brain connectivity and developed the tools needed to study it in any depth. But Freud himself did not pursue that study for long. Instead, he became interested in clinical practice. In treating his patients, Freud came to the correct conclusion that much of their behavior was governed by mental processes of which they were unaware. Lacking the technical tools with which to explore that idea in any scientific way, however, he simply talked to his patients, tried to draw them out about what was going on in the furthest recesses of their minds, observed them, and made whatever inferences he deemed valid. As we'll see, however, such methods are unreliable, and many unconscious processes can *never* be directly revealed through the kind of self-reflection encouraged by therapy, because they transpire in areas of the brain not open to the conscious mind. As a result, Freud was mainly off the mark.

HUMAN BEHAVIOR IS the product of an endless stream of perceptions, feelings, and thoughts, at both the conscious and the unconscious levels. The idea that we are not aware of the cause of much of our behavior can be difficult to accept. Although Freud and his followers believed in it, among research psychologists—the scientists within the field—the idea that the unconscious is important to our behavior was, until recent years, shunned as pop psychology. As one researcher wrote, "Many psychologists were reluctant to use the word 'unconscious' out of fear that their colleagues would think they had gone soft in the head."[6] John Bargh, a psychologist at Yale, recounts that when he started as a graduate student at the University of Michigan, in the late 1970s, it was almost universally assumed that not only our social perceptions and our judgments but also our behaviors were conscious and deliberate.[7] Anything that threatened that assumption was greeted with derision, as when Bargh told a close relative, a successful professional, about some of the early studies showing that people did things for reasons they were unaware of. Using his own experience as evidence that the studies were wrong, Bargh's relative insisted that he was unaware of even a single instance in which he'd done something for reasons he wasn't aware of.[8] Says Bargh, "We all hold dear the idea that we're the captain of our own soul, and we're in charge, and it's a very scary feeling when we're not. In fact, that's what psychosis is—the feeling of detachment from reality and that you're not in control, and that's a very frightening feeling for anyone."

Though psychological science has now come to recognize the importance of the unconscious, the internal forces of the new unconscious have little to do with the innate drives described by Freud, such as a boy's desire to kill his father in order to marry his mom, or a woman's envy of the male sexual organ.[9] We should certainly credit Freud with understanding the immense power of the unconscious—this was an important achievement—but we also have to recognize that science has cast serious doubt on the existence of many of the specific unconscious emotional and motivational factors he identified as molding the conscious mind.[10] As the social psychologist Daniel Gilbert wrote, the "supernatural flavor of Freud's Unbewusst [unconscious] made the concept generally unpalatable."[11]

The unconscious envisioned by Freud was, in the words of a group of neuroscientists, "hot and wet; it seethed with lust and anger; it was hallucinatory, primitive, and irrational," while the new unconscious is "kinder and gentler than that and more reality bound."[12] In the new view, mental processes are thought to be unconscious because there are portions of the mind that are inaccessible to consciousness due to the architecture of the brain, rather than because they have been subject to motivational forces like repression. The inaccessibility of the new unconscious is not considered to be a defense mechanism, or unhealthy. It is considered normal.

If there are times when a phenomenon I discuss sounds vaguely Freudian, the modern understanding of that phenomenon and its causes won't be. The new unconscious plays a far more important role than protecting us from inappropriate sexual desires (for our mothers or fathers) or from painful memories. Instead, it is a gift of evolution that is crucial to our survival as a species. Conscious thought is a great aid in designing a car or deciphering the mathematical laws of nature, but for avoiding snake bites or cars that swerve into your path or people who may mean to harm you, only the speed and efficiency of the unconscious can save you. As we'll see, to ensure our smooth functioning in both the physical and the social world, nature has dictated that many processes of perception, memory, attention, learning, and judgment are delegated to brain structures outside conscious awareness.

SUPPOSE YOUR FAMILY vacationed in Disneyland last summer. Looking back, you might question the rationality of having braved the crowds and ninety-five-degree heat to watch your little daughter spin in a giant teacup. But then you might remember that when you planned the trip, you assessed all the possibilities and concluded that her big smile would be all the payoff you needed. We are usually confident that we know the causes of our behavior. And sometimes that confidence is warranted. Yet if forces outside our awareness play a great role in our judgment and behavior, then we must not know ourselves as well as we think we do. *I took the job because I wanted a new challenge. I like that fellow because he has a great sense of humor. I trust my gastroenterologist because she lives and breathes intestines.* Each day we ask and answer many questions about our feelings and our choices. Our answers usually seem to make sense, but nonetheless they are often dead wrong.

How do I love thee? Elizabeth Barrett Browning felt she could count the ways, but chances are, she couldn't accurately list the reasons. Today we are beginning to be able to do just that, as you'll see when you have a look at the following table. It shows who has been marrying whom in three states of the southeastern United States.[13] One would think that both the who and the whom married for love, and no doubt they did. But what is love's source? It can be the beloved's smile, generosity, grace, charm, sensitivity—or the size of his biceps. The source of love has been pondered for eons by lovers, poets, and philosophers, but it is probably safe to say that none of them has ever waxed eloquent about this particular factor: the person's name. This table, however, shows that a person's name can subtly influence your heart—if the name matches your own.

Listed along the horizontal and vertical axes are the five most common U.S. surnames. The numbers in the table represent how many marriages occurred between a bride and a groom with the corresponding names. Note that the largest numbers, by far, occur along the diagonal—that is, Smiths marry other Smiths three to five times as often as they marry Johnsons, Williamses, Joneses, or Browns. In fact, Smiths marry other Smiths about as often as they marry people with all those other names, combined. And the Johnsons, Williamses, Joneses, and Browns behave similarly. What makes the effect even more striking is that these are the raw numbers—that is, since there are almost twice as many Smiths as Browns, if all else were equal, you'd expect Browns to marry the ubiquitous Smiths far more often than the rarer Browns—but even so, by far the greatest number of marriages among Browns is to other Browns.

GROOM SURNAME

		Smith	Johnson	Williams	Jones	Brown	Total
	Smith	**198**	55	43	62	44	402
	Johnson	55	**91**	49	49	31	275
BRIDE MAIDEN NAME	Williams	64	54	**99**	63	43	323
	Jones	48	40	57	**125**	25	295
	Brown	55	24	29	29	**82**	219
	Total	420	264	277	328	225	**1514**

What does this tell us? People have a basic desire to feel good about themselves, and we therefore have a tendency to be unconsciously biased in favor of traits similar to our own, even such seemingly meaningless traits as our names. Scientists have even identified a discrete area of the brain, called the dorsal striatum, as the structure that mediates much of this bias.[14]

Research suggests that when it comes to understanding our feelings, we humans have an odd mix of low ability and high confidence. You might feel certain you took a job because it presented a challenge, but perhaps you were really more interested in the greater prestige. You might swear you like that fellow for his sense of humor, but you might really like him for his smile, which reminds you of your mother's. You might think you trust your gastroenterologist because she is a great expert, but you might really trust her because she is a good listener. Most of us are satisfied with our theories about ourselves and accept them with confidence, but we rarely see those theories tested. Scientists, however, are now able to test those theories in the laboratory, and they have proven astonishingly inaccurate.

An example: Imagine you are on your way into a movie theater when a person who appears to be an employee of the theater comes up to you and asks if you will answer a few questions about the theater and its concessions in exchange for a free tub of popcorn and a drink. What that person doesn't tell you is that the popcorn you will be given comes in two sizes, one smaller than the other, but both so huge that you could not possibly finish the contents—and in two "flavors," one that subjects will later describe as "good" and "high quality," and another that will be described as "stale," "soggy," and "terrible." Nor will you be told that you are actually participating in a scientific study to measure how much you eat of the popcorn and why. Now, here's the question the researchers were studying: What will have a greater influence on the amount of popcorn you eat, its taste or the amount you are given? To address that question, they handed out four different popcorn-and-box combinations. Moviegoers were given either good popcorn in the smaller box, good popcorn in the larger box, bad popcorn in the smaller box, or bad popcorn in the larger box. The result? People seemed to "decide" how much to eat based on box size as much as taste. Other studies support this result, showing that doubling the size of a container of snack food increases consumption by 30 to 45 percent.[15]

I put quotation marks around "decide" above because that word often connotes a conscious action. It's unlikely that these decisions fit that description. The subjects did not say to themselves, *This free popcorn tastes awful, but there's plenty of it, so I may as well gorge.* Instead, research such as this supports what advertisers have long suspected—that "environmental factors" such as package design, package or portion size, and menu descriptions unconsciously influence us. What is most surprising is the magnitude of the effect—and of people's resistance to the idea that they could have been manipulated. While we sometimes acknowledge that such factors can influence other people, we usually believe—wrongly—that they cannot possibly affect *us*.[16]

In truth, environmental factors have a powerful—and unconscious— influence not only on how much we choose to eat but also on how the food tastes. For example, suppose you don't eat just in movie theaters but sometimes go to restaurants, sometimes even restaurants that provide more than just a menu board listing various types of hamburgers. These more elegant restaurants commonly offer menus peppered with terms like "crispy cucumbers," "velvety mashed potatoes," and "slow-roasted beets on a bed of arugula," as if at other restaurants the cucumbers are limp, the mashed potatoes have the texture of wool, and the beets are flash-fried, then made to sit up in an uncomfortable chair. Would a crispy cucumber, by any other name, taste as crisp? Would a bacon cheeseburger, presented in Spanish, become Mexican food? Could poetic description convert macaroni and cheese from a limerick to a haiku? Studies show that flowery modifiers not only tempt people to order the lyrically described foods but also lead them to rate those foods as *tasting better* than the *identical* foods given only a generic listing.[17] If someone were to ask about your taste in fine dining and you were to say, "I lean toward food served with vivid adjectives," you'd probably get a pretty strange look; yet a dish's description turns out to be an important factor in how it tastes. So the next time you have friends over for dinner, don't serve them salad from the store down the street; go for the subliminal effect and serve them a mélange of local greens.

Let's go a step further. Which would you enjoy more, velvety mashed potatoes or *velvety mashed potatoes*? Nobody has yet done a study on the effect of fonts on the taste of mashed potatoes, but a study has been done on the effects of font on attitudes toward *preparing* food. In that study participants were asked to read a recipe for creating a Japanese lunch dish, then to rate the amount of effort and skill they thought the recipe would require and how likely they were to prepare the dish at home. Subjects who were presented with the recipe in a difficult-to-read font rated the recipe as more difficult and said they were less likely to attempt to make the dish. The researchers repeated the experiment, showing other subjects a one-page description of an exercise routine instead of a recipe, and found similar results: subjects rated the exercise as harder and said they were less likely to try it when the instructions were printed in a font that was hard to read. Psychologists call this the "fluency effect." If the *form* of information is difficult to assimilate, that affects our judgments about the *substance* of that information.[18]

The science of the new unconscious is full of reports about phenomena such as these, quirks in our judgment and perception of people and events, artifacts that arise from the usually beneficial ways in which our brains automatically process information. The point is that we are not like computers that crunch data in a relatively straightforward manner and calculate results. Instead, our brains are made up of a collection of many modules that work in parallel, with complex interactions, most of which operate outside of our consciousness. As a consequence, the real reasons behind our judgments, feelings, and behavior can surprise us.

IF UNTIL RECENTLY academic psychologists have been reluctant to accept the power of the unconscious, so have others in the social sciences. Economists, for example, built their textbook theories on the assumption that people make decisions in their own best interests, by consciously weighing the relevant factors. If the new unconscious is as powerful as modern psychologists and neuroscientists believe it to be, economists are going to have to rethink that assumption. Indeed, in recent years a growing minority of maverick economists have had great success questioning the theories of their more traditional colleagues. Today, behavioral economists like Caltech's Antonio Rangel are changing the way economists think by presenting strong evidence that the textbook theories are flawed.

Rangel is nothing like what most people think of when they picture economists—theorists who pore over data and build complex computer models to describe market dynamics. A portly Spaniard who is himself a great lover of the good things in life, Rangel works with real people, often student volunteers, whom he drags into his lab to study while they taste wine or stare at candy bars after having fasted all morning. In a recent experiment, he and his colleagues showed that people would pay 40 to 61 percent more for an item of junk food if, rather than choosing from a text or image display, they were presented with the actual item.[19] The study also found that if the item is presented behind Plexiglas, rather than being available for you to simply grab, your willingness to pay sinks back down to the text and image levels. Sound weird? How about rating one detergent as being superior to another because it comes in a blue-and-yellow box? Or would you buy German wine rather than French because German beer hall music was playing in the background as you walked down the liquor aisle? Would you rate the quality of silk stockings as higher because you liked their scent?

In each of these studies, people were strongly influenced by the irrelevant factors—the ones that speak to our unconscious desires and motivations, which traditional economists ignore. Moreover, when quizzed about the reasons for their decisions, the subjects proved completely unaware that those factors had influenced them. For example, in the detergent study, subjects were given three different boxes of detergent and asked to try them all out for a few weeks, then report on which they liked best and why. One box was predominantly yellow, another blue, and the third was blue with splashes of yellow. In their reports, the subjects overwhelmingly favored the detergent in the box with mixed colors. Their comments included much about the relative merits of the detergents, but none mentioned the box. Why should they? A pretty box doesn't make the detergent work better. But in reality it was *just* the box that differed—the detergents inside were all identical.[20] We judge products by their boxes, books by their covers, and even corporations' annual reports by their glossy finish. That's why doctors instinctively "package" themselves in nice shirts and ties and it's not advisable for attorneys to greet clients in Budweiser T-shirts.

In the wine study, four French and four German wines, matched for price and dryness, were placed on the shelves of a supermarket in England. French and German music were played on alternate days from a tape deck on the top shelf of the display. On days when the French music played, 77 percent of the wine purchased was French, while on the days of German music, 73 percent of the wine purchased was German. Clearly, the music was a crucial factor in which type of wine shoppers chose to buy, but when asked whether the music had influenced their choice, only one shopper in seven said it had.[21] In the stocking study, subjects inspected four pairs of silk stockings that, unbeknownst to them, were absolutely identical, except that each had had a different and very faint scent applied to it. The subjects "found no difficulty in telling why one pair was the best" and reported perceiving differences in texture, weave, feel, sheen, and weight. Everything but scent. Stockings with one particular scent *were* rated highest much more often than the others, but the subjects denied using scent as a criterion, and only 6 of the 250 subjects even noticed that the stockings had been perfumed.[22]

"People think that their enjoyment of a product is based on the qualities of the product, but their experience of it is also very much based on the product's marketing," says Rangel. "For example, the same beer, described in different ways, or labeled as different brands, or with a different price, can taste very different. The same is true for wine, even though people like to believe it's all in the grapes, and the winemaker's expertise." Studies have indeed shown that when wines are tasted blind, there is little correlation between a wine's taste and its cost, but that there is a strong correlation when the wines are not sampled blind.[23] Since people generally expect higher-priced wine to taste better, Rangel was not surprised when volunteers he recruited to sip a series of wines labeled only by price rated a $90 bottle as better than another wine in the series that was marked as costing just $10.[24] But Rangel had cheated: those two wines, perceived as disparate, were actually identical—they were both from the $90 bottle. More important, the study had another twist: the wine tasting was conducted while the subjects were having their brains scanned in an fMRI machine. The resulting images showed that the price of the wine increased activity in an area of the brain behind the eyes called the orbitofrontal cortex, a region that has been associated with the experience of pleasure.[25] So though the two wines were not different, their taste difference was real, or at least the subjects' relative enjoyment of the taste was.

How can a brain conclude that one beverage tastes better than another when they are physically the same? The naive view is that sensory signals, such as taste, travel from the sense organ to the region of the brain where they are experienced in a more or less straightforward fashion. But as we'll see, brain architecture is not that simple. Though you are unaware of it, when you run cool wine over your tongue, you don't just taste its chemical composition; you also taste its price. The same effect has been demonstrated in the Coke-Pepsi wars, only with regard to brand. The effect was long ago dubbed the "Pepsi paradox," referring to the fact that Pepsi consistently beats Coke in blind taste tests, although people seem to prefer Coke when they know what they are drinking. Over the years, various theories have been proposed to explain this. One obvious explanation is the effect of the brand name, but if you ask people whether it is all those uplifting Coke ads they've seen that they are *really* tasting when they slurp their beverage, they almost always deny it. In the early 2000s, however, new brain-imaging studies found evidence that an area of the brain that neighbors the orbitofrontal cortex, called the ventromedial prefrontal cortex, or VMPC, is the seat of warm, fuzzy feelings such as those we experience when we contemplate a familiar brand-name product.[26] In 2007, researchers recruited a group of participants whose brain scans showed significant VMPC damage, and also a group whose VMPCs were healthy. As expected, both the normal and the brain-damaged volunteers preferred Pepsi to Coke when they did not know what they were drinking. And, as expected, those with healthy brains switched their preference when they knew what they were drinking. But those who had damage to their VMPC—their brain's "brand-appreciation" module—did *not* change preferences. They liked Pepsi better whether or not they knew what they were drinking. Without the ability to unconsciously experience a warm and fuzzy feeling toward a brand name, there is no Pepsi paradox.

The real lesson here has nothing to do with either wine or Pepsi. It is that what is true of beverages and brands is also true of the other ways we experience the world. Both direct, explicit aspects of life (the drink, in this case) and indirect, implicit aspects (the price or brand) conspire to create our mental experience (the taste). They key word here is "create." Our brains are not simply recording a taste or other experience, they are *creating* it. That's a theme we'll come back to again and again. We'd like to think that, when we pass up one guacamole in favor of another, it is because we have made a conscious choice based on taste, caloric content, price, our mood, the principle that guacamole should not contain mayonnaise, or any of a hundred other factors under our control. We believe that when we choose a laptop or a laundry detergent, plan a vacation, pick a stock, take a job, assess a sports star, make a friend, judge a stranger, and even fall in love, we understand the principal factors that influenced us.

Very often nothing could be further from the truth. As a result, many of our most basic assumptions about ourselves, and society, are false.

IF THE INFLUENCE of the unconscious is so great, it shouldn't just make itself known in the isolated situations of our private lives; it ought to have a demonstrable collective effect on our society as a whole. And it does—for instance, in the financial world. Since money is very important to us, each individual should be motivated to make financial decisions based exclusively on conscious and rational deliberation. That's why the foundations of classical economic theory are built on the idea that people do just that—that they behave rationally, in accordance with the guiding principle of their self-interest. While no one has yet figured out how to devise a general economic theory that takes into account the fact that "rationally" is not how people act, plenty of economic studies have demonstrated the societal implications of our collective deviation from the cold calculations of the conscious mind.

Consider the fluency effect I mentioned earlier. If you were debating whether to invest in a stock, you'd certainly take a look at the industry, the business climate, and the financial details of a company before deciding if you should put your money behind it. Low on any rational thinker's list, we probably agree, would be the ease with which you can pronounce the company's name. If you let *that* affect your investment decision, you probably have relatives scheming to seize control of your nest egg on the grounds that you are mentally incompetent. Still, as we saw with typefaces, the ease with which a person can process information (such as the name of a stock) does exert an *unconscious* effect on people's assessment of that information. While you may find it plausible that the fluency of information might affect people's judgment of a recipe for a Japanese dish, could it really affect a decision as important as choosing an investment? Do companies with simple names do better than companies whose names are tongue twisters?

Think about a firm preparing for an initial public offering (IPO). Its leaders will make a pitch regarding the company's wonderful future prospects, and they will back up that pitch with data. But privately held companies are usually far less familiar to prospective investors than companies that are already on the exchange, and since the newcomers have no long public track record, there is even more guessing than usual involved in this type of investment. To see whether savvy Wall Street traders making real investments are unconsciously prejudiced against companies with hard-to-pronounce names, researchers turned to data concerning actual IPOs. As the graph below indicates, they found that investors were indeed more likely to invest in the initial public offerings of companies whose name or ticker symbols were easy to pronounce than in companies with complicated names or symbols. Notice how the effect fades over time, which is to be expected, because with time firms develop both a track record and a reputation. (In case the effect also applies to books and authors, please take note of how easy it is to pronounce my name: Ma-lah-DI-nov.)

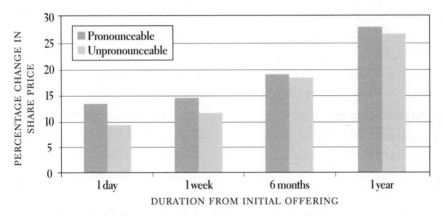

Performance of shares with pronounceable and unpronounceable ticker codes in the NYSE 1 day, 1 week, 6 months, and 1 year after entry into the market, from 1990 to 2004. A similar effect was found concerning IPOs on the American exchange.

Researchers have found other factors irrelevant to finance (but relevant to the human psyche) that affect stock performance. Take sunshine. Psychologists have long known that sunshine exerts subtly positive effects on human behavior. For example, one researcher recruited six waitresses at a restaurant in a shopping center in Chicago to keep track of their tips and the weather over thirteen randomly chosen spring days. Customers were probably unaware that the weather influenced them, but when it was sunny outside, they were significantly more generous.[27] Another study produced a similar result concerning the gratuities received by a waiter delivering meals to guests' rooms in an Atlantic City casino.[28] Could the same effect that induces customers to give an extra buck to a waiter for bringing them curly fries also apply to sophisticated traders evaluating the future earnings prospects of General Motors? Again, the idea can be tested. Much of the trading on Wall Street is, of course, done on behalf of people who reside far from New York, and investors are located across the country, but the trading patterns of agents in New York City have a significant effect on overall New York Stock Exchange performance. For example, at least before the global financial crisis of 2007–8, much of Wall Street's activity was due to proprietary trading—that is, big firms trading for their own accounts. As a result, plenty of money was traded by people who had occasion to know whether the sun was shining in New York—because they lived there. And so a finance professor at the University of Massachusetts decided to look into the relationship between local New York City weather and daily changes in the indices of stocks traded on Wall Street.[29] Analyzing data from between 1927 and 1990, he found that both very sunny and totally cloudy weather influenced stock prices.

You would be right to be skeptical of this. There are inherent dangers in what is called data mining, the wholesale sifting through data in the hope of discovering previously unrecognized patterns. According to the laws of chance, if you look around enough, you are bound to find something interesting. That "something interesting" may be an artifact of randomness or a real trend, and telling the difference between the two can require considerable expertise. The fool's gold in data mining is the statistical correlation that appears surprising and profound, even though it is meaningless. In the case of the sunshine study, if the connection between stock price and weather were a coincidence, one would probably find no such correlation in the data regarding stock markets in other cities. And so another pair of researchers repeated the earlier study, looking at stock market indices in twenty-six countries from 1982 through 1997.[30] They confirmed the correlation. According to their statistics, if a year had included only perfectly sunny days, the market return of the New York Stock Exchange would have averaged 24.8 percent, while if a year had been made up of completely overcast days, it would have averaged only 8.7

percent. (Unfortunately, they also found that there is little or nothing to be gained from buying and selling according to this observation, because the large number of trades required to keep up with the changing weather would eat up your profits in transaction costs.)

We all make personal, financial, and business decisions, confident that we have properly weighed all the important factors and acted accordingly— and that we know how we came to those decisions. But we are aware of only our conscious influences, and so have only partial information. As a result, our view of ourselves and our motivations, and of society, is like a jigsaw puzzle with most of the pieces missing. We fill in blanks and make guesses, but the truth about us is far more complex and subtle than that which can be understood as the straightforward calculation of conscious and rational minds.

WE PERCEIVE, WE remember our experiences, we make judgments, we act—and in all of these endeavors we are influenced by factors we aren't aware of. We'll run into many more examples of this in the pages that follow, as I describe the different aspects of the unconscious brain. We'll see how our brains process information through two parallel tiers, one conscious, the other unconscious, and we'll begin to recognize the power of the unconscious. The truth is that our unconscious minds are active, purposeful, and independent. Hidden they may be, but their effects are anything but, for they play a critical role in shaping the way our conscious minds experience and respond to the world.

To begin our tour of the hidden areas of the mind, let's consider the way we receive sensory input, the conscious and unconscious pathways through which we absorb information about the physical world.

CHAPTER 2

Senses Plus Mind Equals Reality

The eye that sees is not a mere physical organ but a means of perception conditioned by the tradition in which its possessor has been reared. —RUTH BENEDICT

THE DISTINCTION BETWEEN the conscious and the unconscious has been made in one form or another since the time of the Greeks.[1] Among the most influential of the thinkers delving into the psychology of consciousness was the eighteenth-century German philosopher Immanuel Kant. During his time, psychology was not an independent subject but merely a catchall category for what philosophers and physiologists discussed when they speculated about the mind.[2] Their laws concerning human thought processes were not scientific laws but philosophical pronouncements. Since these thinkers required little empirical basis for their theorizing, each one was free to favor his own purely speculative theory over his rival's purely speculative theory. Kant's theory was that we actively construct a picture of the world rather than merely documenting objective events, that our perceptions are not based just on what exists but, rather, are somehow created—and constrained—by the general features of the mind. That belief was surprisingly near the modern perspective, though today scholars generally take a more expansive view than Kant's of the mind's general features, especially with regard to biases arising from our desires, needs, beliefs, and past experiences. Today we believe that when you look at your mother-in-law, the image you see is based not only on her optical qualities but also on what is going on in your head—for example, your thoughts about her bizarre child-rearing practices or whether it was a good idea to agree to live next door.

Kant felt that empirical psychology could not become a science because you cannot weigh or otherwise measure the events that occur in your brain. In the nineteenth century, however, scientists took a stab at it. One of the first practitioners was the physiologist E. H. Weber, the man who, in 1834, performed the simple experiment on the sense of touch that involved placing a small reference weight at a spot on his subjects' skin, then asking them to judge whether a second weight was heavier or lighter than the first.[3] The interesting thing Weber discovered was that the smallest difference a person could detect was proportional to the magnitude of the reference weight. For example, if you were just barely able to sense that a six-gram weight was heavier than a reference object that weighed five grams, one gram would be the smallest detectible difference. But if the reference weight were ten times heavier, the smallest difference you'd be able to detect would be ten times as great—in this case, ten grams. This doesn't sound like an earth-shattering result, but it was crucial to the development of psychology because it made a point: through experimentation one *can* uncover mathematical and scientific laws of mental processing.

In 1879 another German psychologist, Wilhelm Wundt, petitioned the Royal Saxon Ministry of Education for money to start the world's first psychology laboratory.[4] Though his request was denied, he established the laboratory anyway, in a small classroom he had already been using, informally, since 1875. That same year, a Harvard MD and professor named William James, who had taught Comparative Anatomy and Physiology, started teaching a new course called The Relations Between Physiology and Psychology. He also set up an informal psychology laboratory in two basement rooms of Lawrence Hall. In 1891 it attained official status as the Harvard Psychological Laboratory. In recognition of their pathbreaking efforts, a Berlin newspaper referred to Wundt as "the psychological Pope of the Old World" and James as "the psychological Pope of the

New World."[5] It was through their experimental work, and that of others inspired by Weber, that psychology was finally put on a scientific footing. The field that emerged was called the "New Psychology." For a while, it was the hottest field in science.[6]

The pioneers of the New Psychology each had his own views about the function and importance of the unconscious. The British physiologist and psychologist William Carpenter was one of the most prescient. In his 1874 book *Principles of Mental Physiology,* he wrote that "two distinct trains of Mental action are carried on simultaneously, one consciously, the other unconsciously," and that the more thoroughly we examine the mechanisms of the mind, the clearer it becomes "that not only an automatic, but an unconscious action enters largely into all its processes."[7] This was a profound insight, one we continue to build on to this day.

Despite all the provocative ideas brewing in European intellectual circles after the publication of Carpenter's book, the next big step in understanding the brain along the lines of Carpenter's two-trains concept came from across the ocean, from the American philosopher and scientist Charles Sanders Peirce—the man who did the studies of the mind's ability to detect what should have been undetectable differences in weight and brightness. A friend of William James's at Harvard, Peirce had founded the philosophical doctrine of pragmatism (though it was James who elaborated on the idea and made it famous). The name was inspired by the belief that philosophical ideas or theories should be viewed as instruments, not absolute truths, and their validity judged by their practical consequences in our lives.

Peirce had been a child prodigy.[8] He wrote a history of chemistry when he was eleven. He had his own laboratory when he was twelve. At thirteen, he studied formal logic from his older brother's textbook. He could write with both hands and enjoyed inventing card tricks. He was also, in later life, a regular user of opium, which was prescribed to relieve a painful neurological disorder. Still, he managed to turn out twelve thousand printed pages of published works, on topics ranging from the physical sciences to the social sciences. His discovery of the fact that the unconscious mind has knowledge unknown to the conscious mind—which had its unlikely origin in the incident in which he was able to form an accurate hunch about the identity of the man who stole his gold watch—was the forerunner of many other such experiments. The process of arriving seemingly by chance at a correct answer you aren't aware of knowing is now used in what is called a "forced choice" experiment, which has become a standard tool in probing the unconscious mind. Although Freud is the cultural hero associated with popularizing the unconscious, it is really to pioneers like Wundt, Carpenter, Peirce, Jastrow, and William James that we can trace the roots of modern scientific methodology and thought about the unconscious mind.

TODAY WE KNOW that Carpenter's "two distinct trains of Mental action" are actually more like two entire railway systems. To update Carpenter's metaphor, we would say that the conscious and unconscious railways each comprise a myriad of densely interconnected lines, and that the two systems are also connected to each other at various points. The human mental system is thus far more complex than Carpenter's original picture, but we're making progress in deciphering its map of routes and stations.

What has become abundantly clear is that within this two-tier system, it is the unconscious tier that is the more fundamental. It developed early in our evolution, to deal with the basic necessities of function and survival, sensing and safely responding to the external world. It is the standard infrastructure in all vertebrate brains, while the conscious can be considered an optional feature. In fact, while most nonhuman species of animals can and do survive with little or no capacity for conscious symbolic thought, no animal can exist without an unconscious.

According to a textbook on human physiology, the human sensory system sends the brain about eleven million bits of information each second.[9] However, anyone who has ever taken care of a few children who are all trying to talk to you at once can testify that your conscious mind cannot process anywhere near that amount. The actual amount of information we can handle has been estimated to be somewhere between sixteen and fifty bits per second. So if your conscious mind were left to process all that incoming information, your brain would freeze like an overtaxed computer. Also, though we don't realize it, we are making many decisions each second. Should I spit out my mouthful of food because I detect a strange odor? How shall I adjust my muscles so that I remain standing and don't tip over? What is the meaning of the words that person across the table from me is uttering? And what kind of person is he, anyway?

Evolution has provided us with an unconscious mind because our unconscious is what allows us to survive in a world requiring such massive information intake and processing. Our sensory perception, our memory recall, our everyday decisions, judgments, and activities all seem effortless—but that is only because the effort they demand is expended mainly in parts of the brain that function outside awareness.

Take speech. Most people who read the sentence "The cooking teacher said the children made good snacks" instantly understand a certain meaning for the word "made." But if you read, "The cannibal said the children made good snacks," you automatically interpret the word "made" in a more alarming sense. Though we think that making these distinctions is easy, the difficulty in making sense of even simple speech is well appreciated by computer scientists who struggle to create machines that can respond to natural language. Their frustration is illustrated by a possibly apocryphal story of the early computer that was given the task of translating the homily "The spirit is willing but the flesh is weak" into Russian and then back into English. According to the story, it came out: "The vodka is strong but the meat is rotten." Luckily, our unconscious does a far better job, and handles language, sense perception, and a teeming multitude of other tasks with great speed and accuracy, leaving our deliberative conscious mind time to focus on more important things, like complaining to the person who programmed the translation software. Some scientists estimate that we are conscious of only about 5 percent of our cognitive function. The other 95 percent goes on beyond our awareness and exerts a huge influence on our lives—beginning with making our lives possible.

One sign that there is a lot of activity going on in our brains of which we are not aware comes from a simple analysis of energy consumption.[10] Imagine yourself sprawled on the couch watching television; you are subject to few demands on your body. Then imagine yourself doing something physically demanding—say, racing down a street. When you run fast, the energy consumption in your muscles is multiplied by a factor of one hundred compared to the energy you use as a couch potato. That's because, despite what you might tell your significant other, your body is working a lot harder—one hundred times so—when you're running than when you're stretched out on the sofa. Let's contrast this energy multiplier with the multiplier that is applicable when you compare two forms of mental activity: vegging out, in which your conscious mind is basically idle, and playing chess. Assuming that you are a good player with an excellent knowledge of all the possible moves and strategies and are concentrating deeply, does all that conscious thought tax your conscious mind to the same degree that running taxed your muscles? No. Not remotely. Deep concentration causes the energy consumption in your brain to go up by only about 1 percent. No matter what you are doing with your conscious mind, it is your unconscious that dominates your mental activity—and therefore uses up most of the energy consumed by the brain. Regardless of whether your conscious mind is idle or engaged, your unconscious mind is hard at work doing the mental equivalent of push-ups, squats, and wind sprints.

ONE OF THE most important functions of your unconscious is the processing of data delivered by your eyes. That's because, whether hunting or gathering, an animal that sees better eats better and avoids danger more effectively, and hence lives longer. As a result, evolution has arranged it so that about a third of your brain is devoted to processing vision: to interpreting color, detecting edges and motion, perceiving depth and distance, deciding the identity of objects, recognizing faces, and many other tasks. Think of it—a third of your brain is busy doing all those things, yet you have little knowledge of or access to the processing. All that hard work proceeds outside your awareness, and then the result is offered to your conscious mind in a neat report, with the data digested and interpreted. As a result, you never have to bother figuring out what it means if these rods or those cones in your retinas absorb this or that number of photons, or to translate optic nerve data into a spatial distribution of light intensities and frequencies, and then into shapes, spatial positions, and meaning. Instead, while your unconscious mind is working feverishly to do all those things, you can relax in bed, recognizing, seemingly without effort, the lighting fixture on the ceiling—or the words in this book. Our visual system is not only one of the most important systems within our brain, it is also among the most studied areas in neuroscience. Understanding its workings can shed a lot of light on the way the two tiers of the human mind function together—and apart.

One of the most fascinating of the studies that neuroscientists have done on the visual system involved a fifty-two-year-old African man referred to in the literature as TN. A tall, strong-looking man, a doctor who, as fate would have it, was destined to become renowned as a patient, TN took the first step on his path to pain and fame one day in 2004 when, while living in Switzerland, he had a stroke that knocked out the left side of a part of his brain called the visual cortex.

The main part of the human brain is divided into two cerebral hemispheres, which are almost mirror images of each other. Each hemisphere is divided into four lobes, a division originally motivated by the bones of the skull that overlie them. The lobes, in turn, are covered by a convoluted outer layer about the thickness of a formal dinner napkin. In humans, this outer covering, the neocortex, forms the largest part of the brain. It consists of six thinner layers, five of which contain nerve cells, and the projections that connect the layers to one another. There are also input and output connections from the neocortex to other parts of the brain and nervous system. Though thin, the neocortex is folded in a manner that allows almost three square feet of neural tissue—about the size of a large pizza—to be packed into your skull.[11] Different parts of the neocortex perform different functions. The occipital lobe is located at the very back of your head, and its cortex—the visual cortex—contains the main visual processing center of the brain.

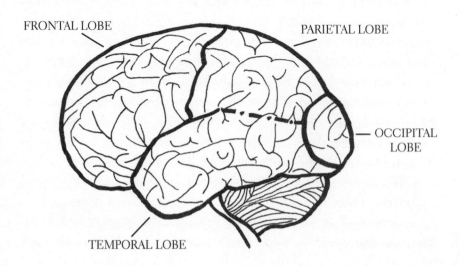

FRONTAL LOBE

PARIETAL LOBE

OCCIPITAL LOBE

TEMPORAL LOBE

A lot of what we know about the function of the occipital lobe comes from creatures in which that lobe has been damaged. You might look askance at someone who seeks to understand the function of the brakes on a car by driving one that doesn't have any—but scientists selectively destroy parts of animals' brains on the theory that one can learn what those parts do by studying animals in which they no longer do it. Since university ethics committees would frown on killing off parts of the brain in human subjects, researchers also comb hospitals seeking unfortunate people whom nature or an accident has rendered suitable for their study. This can be a tedious search because Mother Nature doesn't care about the scientific usefulness of the injuries she inflicts. TN's stroke was note-worthy in that it pretty cleanly took out just the visual center of his brain. The only drawback—from the research point of view—was that it affected only the left side, meaning that TN could still see in half his field of vision. Unfortunately for TN, that situation lasted for just thirty-six days. Then a tragic second hemorrhage occurred, freakishly destroying what was almost the mirror image of the first region.

After the second stroke, doctors did tests to see whether it had ren-dered TN completely blind, for some of the blind have a small measure of residual sight. They can see light and dark, for example, or read a word if it covers the side of a barn. TN, though, could not even see the barn. The doctors who examined him after his second stroke noted that he could not discern shapes or detect movement or colors, or even the presence of an intense source of light. An exam confirmed that the visual areas in his occipital lobe were not functioning. Though the optical part of TN's visual system was still fully functional, meaning his eyes could gather and record light, his visual cortex lacked the ability to process the information that his retinas were sending it. Because of this state of affairs—an intact optical system, but a completely destroyed visual cortex—TN became a tempting subject for scientific research, and, sure enough, while he was still in the hospital a group of doctors and researchers recruited him.

There are many experiments one can imagine performing on a blind subject like TN. One could test for an enhanced sense of hearing, for example, or memory for past visual experiences. But of all possible ques-tions, one that would probably not make your list would be whether a blind man can sense your mood by staring at your face. Yet that is what these researchers chose to study.[12]

They began by placing a laptop computer a couple feet in front of TN and showing him a series of black shapes—either circles or squares—presented on a white background. Then, in the tradition of Charles Sanders Peirce, they presented him with a forced choice: when each shape appeared, they asked him to identify it. Just take a stab at it, the researchers pleaded. TN obliged. He was correct about half the time, just what one would expect if he truly had no idea what he was seeing. Now comes the interesting part. The scientists displayed a new series of images—this time, a series of angry and happy faces. The game was essentially the same: to guess, when prompted, whether the face on the screen was angry or happy. But identifying a facial expression is a far different task from perceiving a geometric shape, because faces are much more important to us than black shapes.

Faces play a special role in human behavior.[13] That's why, despite men's usual preoccupation, Helen of Troy was said to have "the face that launched a thousand ships," not "the breasts that launched a thousand ships." And it's why, when you tell your dinner guests that the tasty dish they are savoring is cow pancreas, you pay attention to their faces and not their elbows—or their words—to get a quick and accurate report of their attitudes toward organ meat. We look to faces to quickly judge whether someone is happy or sad, content or dissatisfied, friendly or dangerous. And our honest reactions to events are reflected in facial expressions controlled in large part by our unconscious minds. Expressions, as we'll see in Chapter 5, are a key way we communicate and are difficult to suppress or fake, which is why great actors are hard to find. The importance of faces is reflected in the fact that, no matter how strongly men are drawn to the female form, or women to a man's physique, we know of no part of the human brain dedicated to analyzing the nuances of bulging biceps or the curves of firm buttocks or breasts. But there is a discrete part of the brain that is used to analyze faces. It is called the fusiform face area. To illustrate the brain's special treatment of faces, look at the photos of President Barack Obama on page 39.[14]

The photo on the left of the right-side-up pair looks horribly distorted, while the left member of the upside-down pair does not look very unusual.

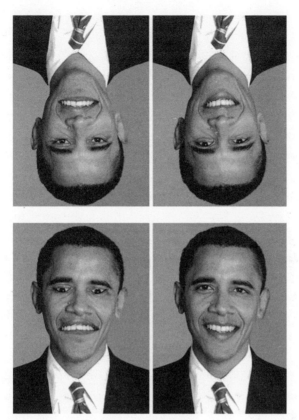

www.moillusions.com. Used with permission.

In reality the bottom pair is identical to the top pair, except that the top photos have been flipped. I know because I flipped them, but if you don't trust me just rotate this book 180 degrees, and you'll see that what is now the top pair will appear to have the bad photo, and what is now the bottom pair will look pretty good. Your brain devotes a lot more attention (and neural real estate) to faces than to many other kinds of visual phenomena because faces are more important—but not upside-down faces, since we rarely encounter those, except when performing headstands in a yoga class. That's why we are far better at detecting the distortion on the face that is right side up than on the one that is flipped over.

The researchers studying TN chose faces as their second series of images in the belief that the brain's special and largely unconscious focus on faces might allow TN to improve his performance, even though he'd have no conscious awareness of seeing anything. Whether he was looking at faces, geometric shapes, or ripe peaches ought to have been a moot point, given that TN was, after all, blind. But on this test TN identified the faces as happy or angry correctly almost two times out of three. Though the part of his brain responsible for the conscious sensation of vision had obviously been destroyed, his fusiform face area was receiving the images. It was influencing the conscious choices he made in the forced-choice experiment, but TN didn't know it.

Having heard about the first experiment involving TN, a few months later another group of researchers asked him if he would participate in a different test. Reading faces may be a special human talent, but not falling on your face is even more special. If you suddenly notice that you are about to trip over a sleeping cat, you don't consciously ponder strategies for stepping out of the way; you just do it.[15] That avoidance is governed by your unconscious, and it is the skill the researchers wanted to test in TN. They proposed to watch as he walked, without his cane, down a cluttered hallway.[16]

The idea excited all those involved except the person not guaranteed to remain vertical. TN refused to participate.[17] He may have had some success in the face test, but what blind man would consent to navigating an obstacle course? The researchers implored him, in effect, to just do it. And they kindly offered to have an escort trail him to make sure he didn't fall. After some prodding, he changed his mind. Then, to the amazement of everyone, including himself, he zigged and zagged his way perfectly down the corridor, sidestepping a garbage can, a stack of paper, and several boxes. He didn't stumble once, or even collide with any objects. When asked how he'd accomplished this, TN had no explanation and, one presumes, requested the return of his cane.

The phenomenon exhibited by TN—in which individuals with intact eyes have no conscious sensation of seeing but can nevertheless respond in some way to what their eyes register—is called "blindsight." This important discovery "elicited disbelief and howls of derision" when first reported and has only recently come to be accepted.[18] But in a sense it shouldn't have been surprising: it makes perfect sense that blindsight would result when the conscious visual system is rendered nonfunctional but a person's eyes and unconscious system remain intact. Blindsight is a strange syndrome—a particularly dramatic illustration of the two tiers of the brain operating independently of each other.

THE FIRST PHYSICAL indication that vision occurs through multiple pathways came from a British Army doctor named George Riddoch in 1917.[19] In the late nineteenth century, scientists had begun to study the importance of the occipital lobe in vision by creating lesions in dogs and monkeys. But data on humans was scarce. Then came World War I. Suddenly the Germans were turning British soldiers into promising research subjects at an alarming pace. This was partly because British helmets tended to dance atop the soldiers' heads, which might have looked fashionable but didn't cover them very well, especially in the back. Also, the standard in that conflict was trench warfare. As it was practiced, a soldier's job was to keep all of his body protected by the solid earth except for his head, which he was instructed to stick up into the line of fire. As a result, 25 percent of all penetrating wounds suffered by British soldiers were head wounds, especially of the lower occipital lobe and its neighbor the cerebellum.

The same path of bullet penetration today would turn a huge swath of the brain into sausage meat and almost certainly kill the victim. But in those days bullets were slower and more discrete in their effects. They tended to bore neat tunnels through the gray matter without disturbing the surrounding tissue very much. This left the victims alive and in better condition than you might imagine given that their heads now had the topology of a doughnut. One Japanese doctor who worked under similar conditions in the Russo-Japanese War saw so many patients injured in that manner that he devised a method for mapping the precise internal brain injury—and the deficits expected—based on the relation of the bullet holes to various external landmarks on the skull. (His official job had been to determine the size of the pension owed the brain-damaged soldiers.)[20]

Dr. Riddoch's most interesting patient was a Lieutenant Colonel T., who had a bullet sail through his right occipital lobe while he was leading his men into battle. After taking the hit he bravely brushed himself off and proceeded to continue leading his men. When asked how he felt, he reported being dazed but said he was otherwise just fine. He was wrong.

Fifteen minutes later, he collapsed. When he woke up it was eleven days later, and he was in a hospital in India.

Although he was now conscious again, one of the first signs that something was amiss came at dinner, when Lieutenant Colonel T. noted that he had a hard time seeing bits of meat residing on the left side of his plate. In humans, the eyes are wired to the brain in such a way that visual information from the left side of your field of vision is transmitted to the right side of your brain, and vice versa, no matter which eye that information comes from. In other words, if you stare straight ahead, everything to your left is transmitted to the right hemisphere of your brain, which is where Lieutenant Colonel T. took the bullet. After he was transferred to a hospital in England, it was established that Lieutenant Colonel T. was totally blind on the left side of his visual field, with one bizarre exception. He could detect motion there. That is, he couldn't see in the usual sense—the "moving things" had no shape or color—but he did know if something was moving. It was partial information, and of little use. In fact, it annoyed him, especially during train rides, when he would sense that things were moving past at his left but he couldn't see anything there.

Since Lieutenant Colonel T. was consciously aware of the motion he detected, his wasn't a case of true blindsight, as TN's was, but still, the case was groundbreaking for its suggestion that vision is the cumulative effect of information traveling along multiple pathways, both conscious and unconscious. George Riddoch published a paper on Lieutenant Colonel T. and others like him, but unfortunately another British Army doctor, one far better known, derided Riddoch's work. With that it virtually disappeared from the literature, not to resurface for many decades.

UNTIL RECENTLY, UNCONSCIOUS vision was difficult to investigate because patients with blindsight are exceedingly rare.[21] But in 2005, Antonio Rangel's Caltech colleague Christof Koch and a coworker came up with a powerful new way to explore unconscious vision in healthy subjects. Koch arrived at this discovery about the unconscious because of his interest in its flip side—the meaning of consciousness. If studying the unconscious was, until recently, not a good career move, Koch says that studying consciousness was, at least until the 1990s, "considered a sign of cognitive decline." Today, however, scientists study the two subjects hand in hand, and one of the advantages of research on the visual system is that it is in some sense simpler than, say, memory or social perception.

The technique Koch's group discovered exploits a visual phenomenon called binocular rivalry. Under the right circumstances, if one image is presented to your left eye while a different image is presented to your right eye, you won't see both of them, somehow superimposed. Instead, you'll perceive just one of the two images. Then, after a while, you'll see the other image, and then the first again. The two images will alternate in that manner indefinitely. What Koch's group found, however, was that if they present a *changing* image to one eye and a static one to the other, people will see *only* the changing image, and never the static one.[22] In other words, if your right eye were exposed to a film of two monkeys playing Ping-Pong and your left to a photo of a hundred-dollar bill, you'd be unaware of the static photo even though your left eye had recorded the data and transmitted it to your brain. The technique provides a powerful tool for creating, in a sense, artificial blindsight—a new way to study unconscious vision without destroying any part of the brain.

Employing the new technique, another group of scientists performed an experiment on normal people analogous to the one the facial expression researchers performed on patient TN.[23] They exposed each subject's right eye to a colorful and rapidly changing mosaic-like image, and each subject's left eye to a static photograph that pictured an object. That object was positioned near either the right edge of the photograph or the left, and it was their subjects' task to guess where the object was, even though they did not consciously perceive the static photo. The researchers expected that, as in the case of TN, the subjects' unconscious cues would be powerful only if the object pictured was of vital interest to the human brain. This led to an obvious category. And so when the researchers performed this experiment, they selected, for one of the static images, pornography—or, in their scientific jargon, a "highly arousing erotic image." You can get erotica at almost any newsstand, but where do you get scientifically controlled erotica? It turns out that psychologists have a database for that. It is called the International Affective Picture System, a collection of 480 images ranging from sexually explicit material to mutilated bodies to pleasant images of children and wildlife, each categorized according to the level of arousal it produces.

As the researchers expected, when presented with unprovocative static images and asked whether the object was on the left- or the right-hand side of the photo, the subjects' answers were correct about half the time, which is what you would expect from completely random, uninformed guesses, a rate comparable to TN's when he was making guesses about circles versus squares. But when heterosexual male subjects were shown an image of a naked woman, they gained a significant ability to discern on which side of the image she was located, as did females who were shown images of naked men. That didn't happen when men were shown naked men, or when women were shown naked women—with one exception, of course. When the experiment was repeated on homosexual subjects, the results flipped in the manner you might expect. The results mirrored the subjects' sexual preferences.

Despite their successes, when asked afterward what they had seen, all the subjects described just the tedious progression of rapidly chang- ing mosaic images the researchers had presented to their right eye. The subjects were clueless that while their conscious minds were looking at a series of snoozers, their unconscious minds were feasting on *Girls (or Boys) Gone Wild*. This means that while the processing of the erotic image was never delivered to the consciousness, it did register powerfully enough in the unconscious that the subjects had a subliminal awareness of it. We are reminded again of the lesson Peirce learned: We don't consciously perceive everything that registers in our brain, so our unconscious mind may notice things that our conscious mind doesn't. When that happens we may get a funny feeling about a business associate or a hunch about a stranger and, like Peirce, not know the source.

I learned long ago that it is often best to follow those hunches. I was twenty, in Israel just after the Yom Kippur War, and went up to visit the Golan Heights, in Israeli-occupied Syria. While hiking along a deserted road I spotted an interesting bird in a farmer's field, and being a bird-watcher, I resolved to get a closer look. The field was ringed by a fence, which doesn't normally deter bird-watchers, but this fence had a curious sign on it. I pondered what the sign might say. It was in Hebrew, and my Hebrew wasn't quite good enough to decipher it. The usual message would have been "No Trespassing," but somehow this sign seemed different. Should I stay out? Something told me yes, a something I now imagine was very much like the something that told Peirce who had stolen his watch. But my intellect, my conscious deliberative mind, said, *Go ahead. Just be quick.* And so I climbed the fence and walked into the field, toward the bird. Soon I heard some yelling in Hebrew, and I turned to see a man down the road on a tractor, gesturing at me in a very animated fashion. I returned to the road. It was hard to understand the man's loud jabbering, but between my broken Hebrew and his hand gestures, I soon figured out the issue. I turned to the sign, and now realized that I did recognize those Hebrew words. The sign said, "Danger, Minefield!" My unconscious had gotten the message, but I had let my conscious mind overrule it.

It used to be difficult for me to trust my instincts when I couldn't produce a concrete, logical basis for them, but that experience cured me. We are all a bit like patient TN, blind to certain things, being advised by our unconscious to dodge to the left and right. That advice can often save us, if we are willing to open ourselves to the input.

PHILOSOPHERS HAVE FOR centuries debated the nature of "reality," and whether the world we experience is real or an illusion. But modern neuroscience teaches us that, in a way, all our perceptions must be considered illusions. That's because we perceive the world only indirectly, by processing and interpreting the raw data of our senses. That's what our unconscious processing does for us—it creates a model of the world. Or as Kant said, there is *Das Ding an sich*, a thing as it is, and there is *Das Ding für uns*, a thing as we know it. For example, when you look around, you have the feeling that you are looking into three-dimensional space. But you don't directly sense those three dimensions. Instead, your brain reads a flat, two-dimensional array of data from your retinas and creates the sensation of three dimensions. Your unconscious mind is so good at processing images that if you were fitted with glasses that turn the images in your eyes upside down, after a short while you would see things right side up again. If the glasses were then removed, you would see the world upside down again, but just for a while.[24] Because of all that processing, when we say, "I see a chair," what we really mean is that our brain has created a mental model of a chair.

Our unconscious doesn't just interpret sensory data, it enhances it. It has to, because the data our senses deliver is of rather poor quality and must be fixed up in order to be useful. For example, one flaw in the data your eyes supply comes from the so-called blind spot, a spot on the back of your eyeball where the wire connecting your retina and your brain is attached. This creates a dead region in each eye's field of vision. Normally you don't even notice it because your brain fills in the picture based on the data it gets from the surrounding area. But it is possible to design an artificial situation in which the hole becomes visible. For example, close your right eye, look at the number 1 on the right side of the line below, and move the book toward you (or away from you) until the sad face disappears—it will then be in your blind spot. Keeping your head still, now look at the 2, the 3, and so on, still with your left eye. The sad face will reappear, probably around the number 4.

To help compensate for their imperfections, your eyes change position a tiny bit several times each second. These jiggling motions are called microsaccades, to distinguish them from ordinary saccades, the larger, more rapid patterns your eyes ceaselessly follow when you study a scene. These happen to be the fastest movements executed by the human body, so rapid that they cannot be observed without special instruments. For example, as you read this text your eye is making a series of saccades along the line. And if I were talking to you, your gaze would bounce around my face, mostly near my eyes. All told, the six muscles controlling your eyeball move it some 100,000 times each day, about as many times as your heart beats.

If your eyes were a simple video camera, all that motion would make the video unwatchable. But your brain compensates by editing out the period during which your eye is in transit and filling in your perception in a way that you don't notice. You can illustrate that edit quite dramatically, but you'll need to enlist as your partner a good friend, or perhaps an acquaintance who has had a few glasses of wine. Here is what you do: Stand facing your partner, with about four inches separating your noses, then ask your partner to fixate midway between your eyes. Next, have your partner look toward your left ear and back. Repeat this a couple of times. Meanwhile, your job is to observe your partner's eyes and note that you have no difficulty seeing them move back and forth. The question is, If you could stand nose to nose with yourself and repeat the procedure, would you see *your own* eyes move? If it is true that your brain edits out visual information received during eye movements, you would not. How can you perform this test? Stand facing a mirror, with your nose two inches from the mirror's surface (this corresponds to four inches from a real person). Look first right between your eyes, then at your left ear, then back. Repeat a couple of times. Miraculously, you get the two views but never see your eye move between them.

Another gap in the raw data delivered by your eyes has to do with your peripheral vision, which is quite poor. In fact, if you hold your arm out and gaze at your thumbnail, the only part of your field of vision with good resolution will be the area within, and perhaps just bordering, your nail. Even if you have twenty-twenty vision, your visual acuity outside that central region will be roughly comparable to that experienced by a person who needs thick glasses and doesn't have them. You can get a taste for that if you look at this page from a distance of a couple feet and stare at the central asterisk in the first line below (try not to cheat—it isn't easy!). The F's in that line are a thumbnail apart. You'll probably be able to recognize the A and F just fine, but not much of the other letters at all. Now go down to the second line. Here, the increasing size of the letters gives you some help. But if you're like me, you won't be able to clearly read all the letters

P Z L E F A ✳ A F E Q C A

G C D E F A ✳ A F E Z P O

P G L E F A ✳ A F E D C R

unless they are as large as they appear in the third line. The size of the magnification required for you to be able to see the letters at the periphery is an indication of the poor quality of your peripheral vision.

The blind spot, saccades, poor peripheral vision—all these issues should cause you severe problems. When you look at your boss, for example, the true retinal image would show a fuzzy, quivering person with a black hole in the middle of his or her face. However emotionally appropriate that may seem, it is not an image you'll ever perceive, because your brain automatically processes the data, combining the input from both eyes, removing the effects of the jiggling, and filling in gaps on the assumption that the visual properties of neighboring locations are similar. The images below illustrate some of the processing your brain does for you. On the left is the scene as recorded by a camera. On the right is the same image as it would appear if recorded by a human retina with no additional processing. Fortunately for you, that processing gets done in the unconscious, making the images you see as polished and refined as those picked up by the camera.

Our hearing works in an analogous manner. For example, we unconsciously fill in gaps in auditory data. To demonstrate this, in one study experimenters recorded the sentence "The state governors met with their respective legislatures convening in the capital city," then erased the 120-millisecond portion of the sentence containing the first "s" sound in "legislatures" and replaced it with a cough. They told twenty experimental

 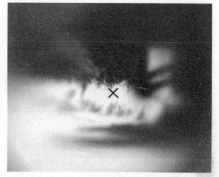

Original image, made by a camera. The same image seen by a retina (right eye, fixation at the X.) Courtesy of Laurent Itti.

subjects that they would hear a recording containing a cough and would be given printed text so they could circle the exact position in the text at which the cough occurred. The subjects were also asked if the cough had masked any of the circled sounds. All of the volunteers reported hearing the cough, but nineteen of the twenty said that there was no missing text. The only subject who reported that the cough had obscured any phonemes named the wrong one.[25] What's more, in follow-up work the researchers found that even practiced listeners couldn't identify the missing sound. Not only could they not pinpoint the exact location of the cough—they couldn't even come close. The cough didn't seem to occur at any clear point within the sentence; rather, it seemed to coexist with the speech sounds without affecting their intelligibility.

Even when the entire syllable "gis" in "legislatures" was obliterated by the cough, subjects could not identify the missing sound.[26] The effect is called phonemic restoration, and it's conceptually analogous to the filling in that your brain does when it papers over your retinal blind spot, and enhances the low resolution in your peripheral vision—or fills holes in your knowledge of someone's character by employing clues based on their appearance, their ethnic group, or the fact that they remind you of your uncle Jerry. (About that, more later.)

Phonemic restoration has a striking property: because it is based on the context in which you hear words, what you think you heard at the beginning of a sentence can be affected by the words that come *at the end*. For example, letting an asterisk denote the cough, listeners in another famous study reported hearing the word "wheel" in the sentence "It was found that the *eel was on the axle." But they heard "heel" when they listened to the sentence "It was found that the *eel was on the shoe." Similarly, when the final word in the sentence was "orange" they heard "peel," and when it was "table," they heard "meal."[27] In each case the data provided to each subject's brain included the same sound, "*eel." Each brain patiently held the information, awaiting more clues as to the context. Then, after hearing the word "axle," "shoe," "orange," or "table," the brain filled in the appropriate consonant. Only at that time did it pass to the subject's conscious mind, leaving the subject unaware of the alteration and quite confident of having accurately heard the word that the cough had partially obscured.

IN PHYSICS, SCIENTISTS invent models, or theories, to describe and predict the data we observe about the universe. Newton's theory of gravity is one example; Einstein's theory of gravity is another. Those theories, though they describe the same phenomenon, constitute very different versions of reality. Newton, for example, imagined that masses affect each other by exerting a force, while in Einstein's theory the effects occur through a bending of space and time and there is no concept of gravity as a force. Either theory could be employed to describe, with great accuracy, the falling of an apple, but Newton's would be much easier to use. On the other hand, for the calculations necessary for the satellite-based global positioning system (GPS) that helps you navigate while driving, Newton's theory would give the wrong answer, and so Einstein's must be used. Today we know that actually both theories are wrong, in the sense that both are only approximations of what really happens in nature. But they are also both correct, in that they each provide a very accurate and useful description of nature in the realms in which they do apply.

As I said, in a way, every human mind is a scientist, creating a model of the world around us, the everyday world that our brains detect through our senses. Like our theories of gravity, our model of the sensory world is only approximate and is based on concepts invented by our minds. And like our theories of gravity, though our mental models of our surroundings are not perfect, they usually work quite well.

The world we perceive is an artificially constructed environment whose character and properties are as much a result of unconscious mental processing as they are a product of real data. Nature helps us overcome gaps in information by supplying a brain that smooths over the imperfections, at an unconscious level, before we are even aware of any perception. Our brains do all of this without conscious effort, as we sit in a high chair enjoying a jar of strained peas or, later in life, on a couch, sipping a beer. We accept the visions concocted by our unconscious minds without question, and without realizing that they are only an interpretation, one constructed to maximize our overall chances of survival, but not one that is in all cases the most accurate picture possible.

That brings up a question to which we will return again and again, in contexts ranging from vision to memory to the way we judge the people we meet: If a central function of the unconscious is to fill in the blanks when there is incomplete information in order to construct a useful picture of reality, how much of that picture is accurate? For example, suppose you meet someone new. You have a quick conversation, and on the basis of that person's looks, manner of dress, ethnicity, accent, gestures—and perhaps some wishful thinking on your part—you form an assessment. But how confident can you be that your picture is a true one?

In this chapter I focused on the realm of visual and auditory perception to illustrate the brain's two-tier system of data processing and the ways in which it supplies information that does not come directly from the raw data in front of it. But sensory perception is just one of many arenas of mental processing in which portions of the brain that operate at the unconscious level perform tricks to fill in missing data. Memory is another, for the unconscious mind is actively involved in shaping your memory. As we are about to see, the unconscious tricks that our brains employ to create memories of events—feats of imagination, really—are as drastic as the alterations they make to the raw data received by our eyes and ears. And the way the tricks conjured up by our imaginations supplement the rudiments of memory can have far-reaching—and not always positive—effects.

CHAPTER 3

Remembering and Forgetting

A man sets himself the task of portraying the world. Through the years
he peoples a space with images of provinces, kingdoms, mountains,
bays, ships, islands, fishes, rooms, instruments, stars, horses, and people. Shortly before his death, he discovers that the patient labyrinth of
lines traces the image of his face. —JORGE LUIS BORGES

JUST SOUTH OF the Haw River in central North Carolina lies the old
mill town of Burlington. It's a part of the country that is home to blue her-
ons, tobacco, and hot, humid summer nights. The Brookwood Garden
Apartments is a typical Burlington complex. A pleasant single-story building made of gray brick, it is situated a few miles east of Elon College,
now Elon University, a private school that, with the decline of the mills,
came to dominate the town. On one of those hot nights in July 1984, a
twenty-two-year-old Elon student named Jennifer Thompson was asleep
in bed when a man snuck up to her back door.[1] It was three o'clock in the
morning. As her air conditioner hummed and rattled, the man cut Jennifer Thompson's phone line, busted the lightbulb outside her door, and
broke in. The noise was not enough to rouse her from her sleep, but the
man's footsteps inside her apartment eventually did. She opened her eyes
and made out the form of someone crouching in the darkness at her side.

A moment later the man jumped on her, put a knife to her throat, and threatened to kill her if she resisted. Then, as the intruder raped her, she studied his face, focusing on being able to identify him if she survived.

Thompson eventually tricked the rapist into allowing her to turn on a light and fix him a drink, at which point she escaped, naked, out the back door. She frantically pounded on the door of the next unit. The sleeping occupants didn't hear her, but the rapist did, and he came after her. Thompson raced across the lawn toward a brick house that had a light on. The rapist gave up and moved on to a nearby building, where he again broke in, and raped another woman. Thompson, meanwhile, was taken to Memorial Hospital, where the police obtained samples of her hair and vaginal fluid. Afterward, they took her to the station, where Thompson recounted her study of the rapist's face for the police sketch artist.

The next day the tips started pouring in. One pointed to a man named Ronald Cotton, twenty-two, who worked at a restaurant near Thompson's apartment. Cotton had a record. He had previously pleaded guilty to a charge of breaking and entering and, while a teenager, to sexual assault. Three days after the incident, Detective Mike Gauldin summoned Thompson to headquarters to look at six photos, which he lined up on a table. According to the police report, Thompson studied the photos for five minutes. "I can almost remember feeling like I was at an SAT test," she said. One of the photos was a shot of Cotton. She picked him out. A few days later, Gauldin presented Thompson with a physical lineup of five men. Each man was asked to step forward, utter a line, then turn and step back. At first unsure whether the rapist was the fourth man or the fifth, Thompson eventually settled on the fifth. Cotton again. According to Thompson, when informed that this was the same man she had identified from the photo lineup, she thought to herself, "Bingo, I did it right." In court Thompson pointed her finger at Cotton and once more identified him as her rapist. The jury reached a verdict in forty minutes, and the judge sentenced Cotton to life plus fifty years. Thompson said it was the happiest day of her life. She celebrated with champagne.

The first sign that something was amiss, other than the defendant's denials, came after Cotton, working in the prison kitchen, encountered a man named Bobby Poole. Poole bore a resemblance to Cotton and, therefore, also to the face in the police sketch based on Thompson's description. What's more, Poole was in prison for the same crime, rape. Cotton confronted Poole about the Thompson case, but Poole denied any involvement. Luckily for Cotton, Bobby Poole blabbed to another inmate that he had indeed raped Thompson and the other woman. Ronald Cotton had by pure chance run into the actual rapist. As a result of the prison confession, Cotton won a new trial.

At the second trial Jennifer Thompson was asked again if she could identify her rapist. She stood fifteen feet from both Poole and Cotton and looked them over. Then she pointed at Cotton and reaffirmed that he was her rapist. Poole looked something like Cotton, but thanks to the experiences that she had had during the time *after* the rape—her identifying Cotton in a photo, then in a lineup, then in the courtroom—Cotton's was the face forever burned into her memory of that night. Instead of becoming a free man, Cotton emerged from his second trial with an even harsher punishment: he got two life sentences.

Seven more years passed. What was left of the evidence from the ten-year-old crime, including a fragment of a single sperm from the perpetrator, languished on a shelf in the Burlington Police Department. Meanwhile, the new technology of DNA testing was making the news, thanks to the double-murder trial of O. J. Simpson. Cotton prodded his attorney to request that the sperm fragment be tested. Eventually, his attorney was able to get the test done. The result proved that Bobby Poole, not Ronald Cotton, had raped Jennifer Thompson.

In the Thompson case, all we know is that the victim misremembered her attacker. We'll never know how accurately or inaccurately Thompson remembered the other details of her attack because no objective record of the crime exists. But it is difficult to imagine a witness more reliable than Jennifer Thompson. She was bright. She stayed relatively calm during the assault. She studied her attacker's face. She focused on remembering it. She had no prior knowledge of or bias against Cotton. Yet she fingered the wrong man. That has to be disturbing, for if Jennifer Thompson was mistaken in her identification, perhaps no eyewitness can be trusted to reliably identify an unknown assailant. There's plenty of evidence to suggest that this is the case—some of it from the very people who organize lineups like the one that resulted in Cotton's arrest.

About seventy-five thousand police lineups take place each year, and statistics on those show that 20 to 25 percent of the time witnesses make a choice that the police *know* is incorrect. They can be sure of this because the witnesses have chosen one of the "known innocents" or "fillers" that the police inserted into the lineup simply to fill it out.[2] These are often police detectives themselves, or inmates plucked from the local jail. Such false identifications don't get anyone in trouble, but think about the implications: the police know that a fifth to a quarter of the time a witness will identify an individual who they are certain did not commit the crime, yet when a witness fingers the person who is their *suspect*, the police—and the courts—assume that *that* identification is reliable. As the above statistics reveal, it's not. In fact, experimental studies in which people are exposed to mock crimes suggest that when the true culprit is *not* in the lineup, more than half the time eyewitnesses will do exactly what Jennifer Thompson did: they will choose someone anyway, selecting the person who best matches their memory of the criminal.[3] As a result, false eyewitness identification seems to be the leading cause of wrongful conviction. An organization called the Innocence Project, for example, found that of the hundreds of people exonerated on the basis of postconviction DNA testing, 75 percent had been imprisoned because of inaccurate eyewitness identification.[4]

You would think that such findings would result in a massive overhaul of the process and the use of eyewitness identification. Unfortunately, the legal system is resistant to change, especially when the changes are fundamental—and inconvenient. As a result, to this day the magnitude and probability of memory error has gone virtually unnoticed. Certainly the law occasionally pays lip service to the fact that eyewitnesses can be mistaken, but most police departments still rely heavily on lineups, and you can still convict someone in court solely on the eyewitness testimony of a stranger. In fact, judges often prohibit the defense from introducing testimony about the scientific research on the flaws of eyewitness identification. "Judges say it's either too complicated, abstract, and unconnected for jurors to understand, and other times they say it's too simplistic," says Brandon Garrett, the author of a book called *Convicting the Innocent*.[5] The courts even discourage jurors who are deliberating from using the trial transcript to aid their memory of the testimony they heard in court. The state of California, for example, recommends that judges inform juries that "their memories should prevail over the written transcript."[6] Lawyers will tell you there are practical reasons for that policy—for instance, that deliberations would take too long if jurors pored over the trial transcripts. But to me, that seems outrageous, like saying we should believe someone's testimony about an incident rather than a film of the incident itself. We'd never settle for such thinking in other areas of life. Imagine the American Medical Association telling doctors not to rely on patients' charts. "Heart murmur? I don't remember any heart murmur. Let's take you off that medication."

IT'S RARE TO have proof of what actually happened, so in most cases we'll never know how accurate our memories really are. But there are exceptions. In fact, there is one example in which those who study memory distortion were provided with a record that couldn't have been surpassed had they orchestrated the incident themselves. I'm referring to the Watergate scandal of the 1970s. That scandal concerned a break-in by Republican operatives at the headquarters of the Democratic National Committee and the subsequent cover-up by the administration of President Richard Nixon. A fellow named John Dean, the White House counsel to Nixon, was deeply involved in orchestrating the cover-up, which eventually led to Nixon's resignation. Dean was said to have an extraordinary memory, and as millions around the world watched on live television, he testified at hearings held by the United States Senate. In his testimony, Dean recalled incriminating conversations with Nixon and other principals in such great detail that he became known as the "human tape recorder." What endows Dean's testimony with scientific importance is the fact that the Senate committee later discovered that there was also a *real* tape recorder listening in on the president: Nixon was secretly recording his conversations for his own later use. The human tape recorder could be checked against reality.

The psychologist Ulric Neisser did the checking. He painstakingly compared Dean's testimony to the actual transcripts and cataloged his findings.[7] John Dean, it turns out, was more like a historical novelist than a tape recorder. He was almost never right in his recollections of the content of the conversations, and he was usually not even close.

For example, on September 15, 1972—before the scandal engulfed the White House—a grand jury concluded its investigation by handing down indictments against seven men. They included the five Watergate burglars but only two of the people involved in planning the crime, and they were the "small fish"—Howard Hunt and Gordon Liddy. The Justice Department said it had no evidence on which to indict anyone higher up. That seemed to be a victory for Nixon. In his testimony, Dean had this to say about the president's reaction:

> Late that afternoon I received a call requesting me to come to the President's Oval Office. When I arrived at the Oval Office I found Haldeman [Nixon's chief of staff] and the President. The President asked me to sit down. Both men appeared to be in very good spirits and my reception was very warm and cordial. The President then told me that Bob—referring to Haldeman—had kept him posted on my handling of the Watergate case. The President told me I had done a good job and he appreciated how difficult a task it had been and the President was pleased that the case had stopped with Liddy. I responded that I could not take credit because others had done much more difficult things than I had done. As the President discussed the present status of the situation I told him that all I had been able to do was to contain the case and assist in keeping it out of the White House. I also told him there was a long way to go before this matter would end and that I certainly could make no assurances that the day would not come when this matter would start to unravel.

On comparing this meticulous account of the meeting to the transcript, Neisser found that hardly a word of it was true. Nixon didn't make any of the statements Dean attributed to him. He didn't ask Dean to sit down; he didn't say that Haldeman had kept him posted; he didn't say that Dean had done a good job; and he didn't say anything about Liddy or the indictments. Nor did Dean say any of the things he attributed to himself. In fact, not only did Dean not say that he "could make no assurances" that the matter wouldn't start to unravel, he actually said pretty much the opposite, reassuring Nixon that "nothing is going to come crashing down."

Of course, Dean's testimony sounds self-serving, and he might have been intentionally lying about his role. But if he was lying, he did a poor job of it, because, on the whole, his Senate testimony is just as self-incriminating as the actual, though very different, conversations revealed by the transcripts. And in any case, what is most interesting are the little details, neither incriminating nor exonerating, about which Dean seemed so certain, and was so wrong.

Perhaps you are thinking that the distortions so frequent in the memories of those who were the victims of serious crimes (or those who, like Dean, were trying to cover up such crimes) don't have much to do with your everyday life, with how well you remember the details of your personal interactions. But memory distortions occur in everyone's life. Think, for example, about a business negotiation. The various parties to the negotiation go back and forth, over the course of some days, and you are sure that you remember both what you and what the others said. In constructing your memory, however, there is what you said, but there is also what you communicated, what the other participants in the process interpreted as your message, and, finally, what they recalled about those interpretations. It's quite a chain, and so people often strongly disagree in their recollections of events. That's why when they are having important conversations, lawyers take notes. Though this doesn't eliminate the potential for memory lapses, it does minimize it. Unfortunately, if you go through life taking notes on all your interpersonal interactions, chances are you won't have many.

Cases like those of John Dean and Jennifer Thompson raise the same questions that have been raised, over the years, in thousands of other court cases: What is it about the way human memory works that produces such distortions? And how much can we trust our own memories of day-to-day life?

THE TRADITIONAL VIEW of memory, and the one that persists among most of us, is that it is something like a storehouse of movies on a computer's hard drive. This is a concept of memory analogous to the simple video camera model of vision I described in the last chapter, and it is just as misguided. In the traditional view, your brain records an accurate and complete record of events, and if you have trouble remembering, it is because you can't find the right movie file (or don't really want to) or because the hard drive has been corrupted in some way. As late as 1991, in a survey conducted by the psychologist Elizabeth Loftus, most people, including the great majority of psychologists, still held this traditional view of memory: that whether accessible or repressed, clear or faded, our memory is a literal recorder of events.[8] Yet if memories were indeed like what a camera records, they could be forgotten or they could fade so that they were no longer clear and vivid, but it would be difficult to explain how people—like Thompson and Dean—could have memories that are both clear and vivid while also being wrong.

One of the first scientists to realize that the traditional view does not accurately describe the way human memory operates had his epiphany after a case of false testimony—his own. Hugo Münsterberg was a German psychologist.[9] He hadn't started out intending to study the human mind, but when he was a student at the University of Leipzig he attended a series of lectures by Wilhelm Wundt. That was in 1883, just a few years after Wundt had started his famous psychology lab. Wundt's lectures not only moved Münsterberg, they changed his life. Two years later Münsterberg completed a PhD under Wundt in physiological psychology, and in 1891 he was appointed assistant professor at the University of Freiburg. That same year, while attending the First International Congress in Paris, Münsterberg met William James, who had been impressed by his work. James was then officially the director of the new Harvard Psychological Laboratory, but he wanted to resign from the post to focus on his interests in philosophy. He lured Münsterberg across the Atlantic as his replacement, despite the fact that although Münsterberg could read English he could not speak it.

The incident that inspired Münsterberg's particular interest in memory occurred a decade and a half later, in 1907.[10] While he was vacationing with his family at the seashore, his home in the city was burglarized. Informed of this by the police, Münsterberg rushed back and took stock of the condition of his house. Later, he was called to testify under oath about what he had found. He gave the court a detailed account of his survey, which included the trail of candle wax he had seen on the second floor, a large mantel clock the burglar had wrapped in paper for transport but then left on the dining room table, and evidence that the burglar had entered through a cellar window. Münsterberg testified with great certainty, for as a scientist and a psychologist, he was trained in careful observation, and he was known to have a good memory, at least for dry intellectual facts. "During the last eighteen years," Münsterberg once wrote, "I have delivered about three thousand university lectures. For those three thousand coherent addresses I had not once a single written or printed line or any notes whatever on the platform. . . . My memory serves me therefore rather generously." But this was no university lecture. In this case, each of the above statements proved to be false. His confident testimony, like Dean's, was riddled with errors.

Those errors alarmed Münsterberg. If *his* memory could mislead him, others must be having the same problem. Maybe his errors were not unusual but the norm. He began to delve into reams of eyewitness reports, as well as some early pioneering studies of memory, in order to investigate more generally how human memory functions. In one case Münsterberg studied, after a talk on criminology in Berlin, a student stood up and shouted a challenge to the distinguished speaker, one Professor Franz von Liszt, a cousin of the composer Franz Liszt. Another student jumped to his feet to defend von Liszt. An argument ensued. The first student pulled a gun. The other student rushed him. Then von Liszt joined the fray. Amid the chaos, the gun went off. The entire room erupted into bedlam. Finally von Liszt shouted for order, saying it was all a ruse. The two enraged students weren't really students at all but actors following a script. The altercation had been part of a grand experiment. The purpose of the exercise? To test everyone's powers of observation and memory. Nothing like a fake shootout in psych class to liven things up.

After the event, von Liszt divided the audience into groups. One group was asked to immediately write an account of what they had seen, another was cross-examined in person, and others were asked to write reports a little later. In order to quantify the accuracy of the reports, von Liszt divided the performance into fourteen bite-sized components, some referring to people's actions, others to what they said. He counted as errors omissions, alterations, and additions. The students' error rates varied from 26 to 80 percent. Actions that never occurred were attributed to the actors. Other important actions were missed. Words were put into the arguing students' mouths, and even into the mouths of students who had said nothing.

As you might imagine, the incident received a fair amount of publicity. Soon staged conflicts became the vogue among psychologists all over Germany. They often involved, as the original had, a revolver. In one copycat experiment, a clown rushed into a crowded scientific meeting, followed by a man wielding a gun. The man and the clown argued, then fought and, after the gun went off, ran out of the room—all in less than twenty seconds. Clowns are not unheard of in scientific meetings, but they rarely wear clown costumes, so it is probably safe to assume that the audience knew the incident was staged, and why. But although the observers were aware that a quiz would follow, their reports were grossly inaccurate. Among the inventions that appeared in the reports were a wide variety of different costumes attributed to the clown and many details describing the fine hat on the head of the man with the gun. Hats were common in those days, but the gunman had not worn one.

From the nature of these memory errors, and those documented in many other incidents he studied, Münsterberg fashioned a theory of memory. He believed that none of us can retain in memory the vast quantity of details we are confronted with at any moment in our lives and that our memory mistakes have a common origin: they are all artifacts of the techniques our minds employ to fill in the inevitable gaps. Those techniques include relying on our expectations and, more generally, on our belief systems and our prior knowledge. As a result, when our expectations, beliefs, and prior knowledge are at odds with the actual events, our brains can be fooled.

For example, in his own case, Münsterberg had overheard police conversations about the burglar entering through the cellar window and, without realizing it, incorporated that information into his memory of the crime scene. But there was no such evidence, for, as the police later discovered, their initial speculation had been wrong. The burglar had actually entered by removing the lock on the front door. The clock Münsterberg remembered packed in paper for transport had actually been packed in a tablecloth, but, as Münsterberg wrote, his "imagination gradually substituted the usual method of packing with wrapping paper." As for the candle wax he so clearly remembered having seen on the second floor, it was actually in the attic. When he spotted it, he wasn't aware of its importance, and by the time the issue came up, he was focused on the strewn papers and other disorder on the second floor, apparently causing him to recall having seen the candle wax there.

Münsterberg published his ideas about memory in a book that became a best seller, *On the Witness Stand: Essays on Psychology and Crime.*[11] In it, he elaborated on a number of key concepts that many researchers now believe correspond to the way memory really does work: first, people have a good memory for the general gist of events but a bad one for the details; second, when pressed for the unremembered details, even well-intentioned people making a sincere effort to be accurate will inadvertently fill in the gaps by making things up; and third, people will believe the memories they make up.

Hugo Münsterberg died on December 17, 1917, at age fifty-three, after suffering a cerebral hemorrhage and collapsing while delivering a lecture to a class at Radcliffe.[12] His ideas on memory, and his pioneering work in applying psychology to law, education, and business, had made him famous, and he'd counted as friends notables like President Theodore Roosevelt and the philosopher Bertrand Russell. But one person Münsterberg did not consider to be a friend in his later years was his onetime sponsor and mentor, William James.[13] For one, James had become fascinated with psychics, communication with the dead, and other mystical activities, which Münsterberg and many others considered to be pure quackery. For another, James, if not a convert to psychoanalysis, had at least followed Freud's work with interest and saw value in it. Münsterberg, on the other hand, was blunt about his view of the unconscious, writing, "The story of the subconscious mind can be told in three words: there is none."[14] In fact, when Freud visited Boston in 1909 to speak—in German—at Harvard, Münsterberg showed his disapproval by remaining conspicuously absent.

Between them, Freud and Münsterberg had come up with theories of mind and memory that were of great importance, but unfortunately the men had little impact on each other: Freud understood much better than Münsterberg did the immense power of the unconscious, but he thought that repression, rather than a dynamic act of creation on the part of the unconscious, was the reason for the gaps and inaccuracies in our memory;

while Münsterberg understood much better than Freud did the mechanics and the reasons for memory distortion and loss—but had no sense at all of the unconscious processes that created them.

HOW COULD A memory system that discards so much of our experience have survived the rigors of evolution? Though human memory is subject to the distortion of memory reconstruction, if those subliminal distortions had proved seriously detrimental to our ancestors' survival, our memory system, or perhaps our species, would not have survived. Though our memory system is far from perfect, it is, in most situations, exactly what evolution requires: it is good enough. In fact, in the big picture, human memory is wonderfully efficient and accurate—sufficient to have enabled our ancestors to generally recognize the creatures they should avoid and those they should hunt down, where the best trout streams are, and the safest way back to camp. In modern terms, the starting point in understanding how memory works is Münsterberg's realization that the mind is continuously bombarded by a quantity of data so vast that it cannot possibly handle all of it—the roughly eleven million bits per second I mentioned in the last chapter. And so we have traded perfect recall for the ability to handle and process that staggering amount of information.

When we hold a baby's birthday party in the park, we experience two intense hours of sights and sounds. If we crammed all of them into memory, we'd soon have a huge warehouse of smiles, frosting mustaches, and poopy diapers. Important aspects of the experience would be stored amid irrelevant clutter, such as the patterns of color on each mother's blouse, the small talk made by each dad, the cries and screams of every child present, and the steadily growing number of ants on the picnic table. The truth is, you don't care about the ants or the small talk, and you don't want to remember everything. The challenge that the mind faces, and that the unconscious meets, is to be able to sift through this inventory of data in order to retain the parts that actually do matter to you. If the sifting doesn't occur, you just get lost in the data dump. You see the trees but not the forest.

There is, in fact, a famous study that illustrates the downside of an unfiltered memory, a case study of an individual who had such a memory.

The study was performed over the course of thirty years, starting in the 1920s, by the Russian psychologist A. R. Luria.[15] The man who couldn't forget was a famed mnemonist named Solomon Shereshevsky. Shereshevsky apparently remembered in great detail everything that happened to him. Once Luria asked Shereshevsky to recount their initial meeting. Shereshevsky recalled that they were in Luria's apartment and described exactly what the furniture looked like and what Luria was wearing. Then he recited without error the list of seventy words that—fifteen years earlier—Luria had read aloud and asked him to repeat.

The downside of Shereshevsky's flawless memory was that the details often got in the way of understanding. For instance, Shereshevsky had great trouble recognizing faces. Most of us store in memory the general features of the faces we remember, and when we see someone we know, we identify the person by matching the face we're looking at to a face in that limited catalog. But Shereshevsky's memory housed a great many versions of every face he had ever seen. To Shereshevsky, each time a face changed its expression or was seen in different lighting, it was a new face, and he remembered them all. So any given person had not one face but dozens, and when Shereshevsky encountered someone he knew, matching that person's face to the faces stored in his memory meant performing a search of a vast inventory of images to try to find an exact equivalent to what he was seeing.

Shereshevsky had similar problems with language. If you spoke to him, though he could always play back your exact words, he had trouble understanding your point. The comparison with language is apt, because this is another trees-and-forest problem. Linguists recognize two types of language structure: surface structure and deep structure. Surface structure refers to the specific way an idea is expressed, such as the words used and their order. Deep structure refers to the gist of the idea.[16] Most of us avoid the problems of clutter by retaining the gist but freely discarding details. As a result, although we can retain deep structure—the meaning of what was said—for long periods of time, we can accurately remember surface structure—the words in which it was said—for just eight to ten seconds.[17] Shereshevsky apparently had an exact and long-lasting memory of all the details of the surface structure, but those details interfered with his ability to extract the gist of what was being said. His inability to forget the irrelevant became so frustrating that at times he would write things down on paper and then burn the page, hoping his memory of them would also go up in flames. It didn't work.

Read the following list of words, and please pay careful attention: candy, sour, sugar, bitter, good, taste, tooth, nice, honey, soda, chocolate, heart, cake, eat, and pie. If you read only the first few words carefully and then skimmed the rest because you lack patience and feel silly allowing yourself to be ordered around by a book, please reconsider—it is important. *Please* read through the list. Study it for half a minute. Now cover the list so you can't see the words, and keep it covered while you read the next paragraph.

If you are a Shereshevsky you'll have no trouble recalling all the words on the list, but chances are, your memory works a bit differently. In fact, I have given the little exercise I am about to give you to a dozen groups over the years, and the result is always the same. I'll tell you the punch line after I explain the exercise. It is simple: just identify which of the following three words appeared on the above list: taste, point, sweet. Your answer doesn't have to be just one word. Perhaps all of them were listed? Or none of them? Please give this some thought. Assess each word carefully. Can you picture seeing it on the list? Are you confident? Don't choose a word as being on the list unless you are sure of it and can picture it there. Please settle on your answer. Now please uncover the list in the previous paragraph and see how you did.

The vast majority of people recall with great confidence that "point" was not on the list. The majority also recall that "taste" was. The punch line of the exercise has to do with the other word: "sweet." If you recalled seeing that word, it is an illustration of the fact that your memory is based on your recollection of the *gist* of the list you saw and not the *actual* list: the word "sweet" was *not* on the list, but most of the words on the list *were* related thematically to the concept of sweetness. The memory researcher Daniel Schacter wrote that he gave tests like this to many audiences and the great majority of people claimed that "sweet" was on the list, even though it was not.[18] I have also given this test to many large groups, and while I did not find a great majority remembering that "sweet" was on the list, I did consistently get about half of my audience claiming it was— about the same number who correctly recalled that "taste" was on it. That result was consistent across many cities and countries. The difference between my results and Schacter's may stem from the way I phrase the question—for I always stress that people should not designate a word unless they are *sure*, unless they can picture the list and vividly see that the word is on it.

Our process of remembering can be said to be analogous to the way computers store images, except that our memories have the added complexity that the memory data we store changes over time—we'll get to that later. In computers, to save storage space, images are often highly "compressed," meaning that only certain key attributes of the original image are kept; this technique can reduce the file size from megabytes to kilobytes. When the image is viewed, the computer predicts, from the limited information in the compressed file, what the original image looked like. If we view a small "thumbnail"-sized image made from a highly compressed data file, it usually looks very much like the original. But if we blow the image up, if we look closely at the details, we see many errors—blocks and bands of solid color where the software guessed wrong and the missing details were incorrectly filled in.

That's how both Jennifer Thompson and John Dean got fooled, and it's essentially the process Münsterberg envisioned: remember the gist, fill in the details, believe the result. Thompson recalled the "gist" of her rapist's face, and when she saw a man in the lineup of photographs who fit the general parameters of what she remembered, she filled in the details of her memory with the face of the man in front of her, working off the expectation that the police wouldn't show her a set of pictures unless they had reason to believe the rapist's photo was among them (though as it turned out, it wasn't). Similarly, Dean remembered few of the details of his individual conversations, but when he was pressed, his mind filled them in, using his expectations about what Nixon would have said. Neither Thompson nor Dean was aware of those fabrications. And both had them reinforced by repeatedly being asked to relive the events they were remembering, for when we are repeatedly asked to re-create a memory, we reinforce it each time, so that in a way we are remembering the memory, not the event.

You can easily see how this happens in your own life. Your brain, for example, might have recorded in its neurons the feeling of being embarrassed when you were teased by a fourth-grade boy because you brought your favorite teddy bear to school. You probably wouldn't have retained a picture of the teddy bear, or the boy's face, or the look on that face when you threw your peanut butter sandwich at him (or was it ham and cheese?). But suppose that years later you had reason to relive the moment. Those details might then have come to mind, filled in by your unconscious. If, for some reason, you returned to the incident again and again—perhaps because in retrospect it had become a funny story about your childhood that people always enjoyed hearing—you most likely created a picture of the incident so indelibly vivid and clear to yourself that you would believe totally in the accuracy of all the details.

If this is so, you may be wondering, then why have you never noticed your memory mistakes? The problem is that we rarely find ourselves in the position that John Dean was in—the position of having an accurate recording of the events we claim to remember. And so we have no reason to doubt our memories. Those who have made it their business to investigate memory in a serious fashion, however, can provide you with plenty of reasons for doubting. For example, the psychologist Dan Simons, ever the scientist, became so curious about his own memory errors that he picked an episode from his own life—his experiences on September 11, 2001—and did something few of us would ever make the effort to do.[19] He investigated, ten years later, what had actually happened. His memory of that day seemed very clear. He was in his lab at Harvard with his three graduate students, all named Steve, when they heard the news, and they spent the rest of the day together, watching the coverage. But Simons's investigation revealed that only one of the Steves was actually present—another was out of town with friends, and the third was giving a talk elsewhere on campus. As Münsterberg might have predicted, the scene Simons remembered was the scene he'd have expected, based on prior experience, since those three students were usually in the lab—but it wasn't an accurate picture of what happened.

THROUGH HIS LOVE of case studies and real-life interactions, Hugo Münsterberg advanced the frontiers of our understanding of how we store and retrieve memories. But Münsterberg's work left open a major issue: How does memory change over time? As it turned out, at about the same period when Münsterberg was writing his book, another pioneer, a laboratory scientist who, like Münsterberg, swam against the Freudian tide, was studying the evolution of memory. The son of a shoemaker from the tiny country town of Stow-on-the-Wold in England, the young Frederic Bartlett had to take over his own education when the town's equivalent of a high school closed.[20] That was in 1900. He did the job well enough that he ended up an undergraduate at Cambridge University, where he remained for graduate school; he eventually became the institution's first professor in the new field of experimental psychology. Like Münsterberg, Bartlett did not go into academia planning to study memory. He came to it through an interest in anthropology.

Bartlett was curious about the way culture changes as it is passed from person to person, and through the generations. The process, he thought, must be similar to the evolution of an individual's personal memories. For example, you might remember a crucial high school basketball game in which you scored four points, but years later, you might remember that number as being fourteen. Meanwhile, your sister might swear you spent the game in a beaver costume, dressed as the team's mascot. Bartlett studied how time and social interactions among people with differing recollections of events change the memory of those events. He hoped, through that work, to gain an understanding of how "group memory," or culture, develops.

Bartlett imagined that the evolution of both cultural and personal memories resembles the whisper game (also called the telephone game). You probably recall the process: the first person in a chain whispers a sentence or two to the next person in the chain, who whispers it to the next person, and so on. By the end, the words bear little resemblance to what was said at the beginning. Bartlett used the whisper game paradigm to study how stories evolve as they pass from one person's memory to the next. But his real breakthrough was to adapt the procedure to study how the story can evolve over time within an individual's memory. Essentially, he had his subjects play the whisper game with themselves. In his most famous work, Bartlett read his subjects the Native American folktale "The War of the Ghosts." The story is about two boys who leave their village to hunt seals at the river. Five men in a canoe come along and ask the boys to accompany them in attacking some people in a town upriver. One of the boys goes along, and, during the attack, he hears one of the warriors remark that he—the boy—had been shot. But the boy doesn't feel anything, and he concludes that the warriors are ghosts. The boy returns to his village and tells his people about his adventure. The next day, when the sun rises, he falls over, dead.

After reading the story to his subjects, Bartlett asked them to remind themselves of the tale after fifteen minutes, and then at irregular intervals after that, sometimes over a period of weeks or months. Bartlett studied the way that his subjects recounted the stories over time, and he noted an important trend in the evolution of memory: there wasn't just memory loss; there were also memory additions. That is, as the original reading of the story faded into the past, new memory data was fabricated, and that fabrication proceeded according to certain general principles. The subjects maintained the story's general form but dropped some details and changed others. The story became shorter and simpler. With time, supernatural elements were eliminated. Other elements were added or reinterpreted so that "whenever anything appeared incomprehensible, it was either omitted or explained" by adding content.[21] Without realizing it, people seemed to be trying to alter the strange story into a more understandable and familiar form. They provided the story with their own organization, making it seem to them more coherent. Inaccuracy was the rule, and not the exception. The story, Bartlett wrote, "was robbed of all its surprising, jerky and inconsequential form."

This figurative "smoothing out" of memories is strikingly similar to a literal smoothing out that Gestalt psychologists in the 1920s had noted in studies of people's memory for geometric shapes: if you show someone a shape that is irregular and jagged, and quiz them about it later, they'll recall the shape as being far more regular and symmetrical than it actually was.[22] In 1932, after nineteen years of research, Bartlett published his results. The process of fitting memories into a comfortable form "is an active process," he wrote, and depends on the subject's own prior knowledge and beliefs about the world, the "preformed tendencies and bias which the subject brings to the task" of remembering.[23]

For many years Bartlett's work on memory was forgotten, though he went on to an illustrious career in which he helped train a generation of British researchers to work in experimental psychology. Today Bartlett's memory research has been rediscovered, and replicated in a modern setting. For example, the morning after the explosion of the space shuttle

Challenger, Ulric Neisser, the man who did the John Dean study, asked a group of Emory University students how they'd first heard the news. The students all wrote clear accounts of their experiences. Then, about three years later, he asked the forty-four students who were still on campus to again recall that experience.[24] Not one of the accounts was entirely correct, and about one-quarter of them were entirely wrong. The act of hearing the news became less random and more like the dramatic stories or clichés you might expect someone to tell, just as Bartlett might have predicted. For example, one subject, who'd heard the news while chatting with friends at the cafeteria, later reported how "some girl came running down the hall screaming 'the space shuttle just blew up.' " Another, who'd heard it from various classmates in her religion class, later remembered, "I was sitting in my freshman dorm room with my roommate and we were watching TV. It came on a news flash and we were both totally shocked." Even more striking than the distortions were the students' reactions to their original accounts. Many insisted that their later memories were more accurate. They were reluctant to accept their earlier description of the scene, even though it was in their own handwriting. Said one, "Yes, that's my handwriting—but I still remember it the other way!" Unless all these examples and studies are just strange statistical flukes, they ought to give us pause regarding our own memories, especially when they conflict with someone else's. Are we "often wrong but never in doubt"? We might all benefit from being less certain, even when a memory seems clear and vivid.

How good an eyewitness are you? The psychologists Raymond Nickerson and Marilyn Adams invented a neat challenge. Just think of—but don't look at—an American penny. It's an object you might have viewed thousands of times, but how well do you really know it? Can you draw one? Take a moment to try, or at least try to imagine one. What are the main features on each side? When you are done, have a look at the graphic on the following page and try this easier task: pick out the correct penny from among the beautiful sketches Nickerson and Adams kindly provided.[25]

If you picked A, you would have been in the minority of subjects who chose the correct coin in Nickerson and Adams's experiment. And if your drawings or imaginings have all eight features of the penny—features such

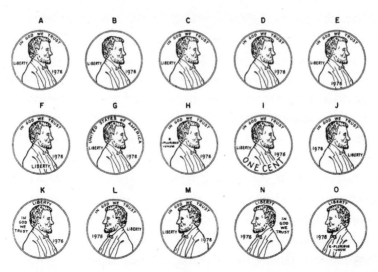

Reprinted from R. S. Nickerson and M. J. Adams, "Long-Term Memory for a Common Object,"
Cognitive Psychology 11, 287–307, copyright 1979, with permission from Elsevier

as the profile of Abraham Lincoln on one side, and phrases like IN GOD
WE TRUST and E PLURIBUS UNUM—then you are in the top 5 percent in
memory for detail. If you did poorly on this test, it doesn't mean you have a
bad memory. Your memory for *general* features might be excellent. In fact,
most people can remember previously viewed photographs surprisingly
well, even after a long interval. But they are remembering only general
content, not precise form.[26] To not store in memory the details of a penny
is for most of us an advantage; unless we have to answer a question on a
game show with a lot of money at stake, we have no need to remember
what's on a penny, and to do so could get in the way of our remembering
more important things.

One reason we don't retain details of the images that our eyes pick
up is that in order for us to remember them, the details first have to have
captured our conscious attention. But while the eye delivers a multitude
of details, our conscious mind doesn't register most of them. The disparity
between what we see and what we register and, therefore, remember, can
be dramatic.

The key to one experiment investigating that disparity was the fact that
when you study an image with many objects in it, your eye will shift among
the different objects displayed. For example, if an image shows two people

seated at a table with a vase on it, you might look at one person's face, then the vase, then the other person's face, then perhaps the vase again, then the tabletop, and so on, all in rapid succession. But remember the experiment in the last chapter, in which you stood facing a mirror and noted that there were blanks in your perception during the time your eyes were moving? The researchers who performed this study cleverly realized that if, during the split second their subjects' eyes were in motion, the image the subjects were looking at changed subtly, the subjects might not notice. Here is how it worked: Each subject started by looking at some initial image on a computer screen. The subject's eyes would move from object to object, bringing different aspects of the scene into focus. After a while, during one of the subject's numerous eye shifts, the experimenters would replace the image with one that was slightly altered. As a result, once the subject's eyes settled on the new target object, certain details of the image were different—for example, the hats the two men in the scene had been wearing were exchanged. The great majority of subjects didn't notice. In fact, only half the subjects noticed when the two people exchanged heads![27]

It's interesting to speculate how important a detail has to be to register with us. To test if memory gaps like this also happen when the objects that change from shot to shot are the focus of attention, Dan Simons and his fellow psychologist Daniel Levin created videos depicting simple events in which the actor playing a particular character changed from scene to scene.[28] Then they recruited sixty Cornell University students, who agreed to watch the videos in exchange for candy. In a typical video, as depicted by the sample frames below, a person sitting at a desk hears a phone ring,

Figure provided by Daniel Simons

gets up, and walks toward the door. The video then cuts to a view of the hallway, where a different actor walks to the telephone and answers it. The change is not as drastic as, say, replacing Brad Pitt with Meryl Streep. But neither were the two actors hard to tell apart. Would the students notice the switch?

After viewing the film, the students were asked to write a brief description of it. If they didn't mention the actors' change, they were asked directly, "Did you notice that the person who was sitting at the desk was a different person than the one who answered the phone?" About two-thirds of them admitted that they hadn't noticed. Surely during each shot they were aware of the actor and her actions. But they didn't retain in their memory the details of her identity. Emboldened by that startling find, the researchers decided to go a step further. They examined whether this phenomenon, called change blindness, also occurred in real-world interactions. This time they took their experiment outdoors, onto the Cornell University campus.[29] There, a researcher carrying a campus map approached unsuspecting pedestrians to ask for directions to a nearby building. After the

Figure provided by Daniel Simons

researcher and pedestrian had spoken for ten or fifteen seconds, two other men, each holding one end of a large door, rudely passed between them. As the door passed, it blocked the pedestrian's view of the experimenter for about one second. During that time, a new researcher with an identical map stepped in to continue the direction-asking interaction while the original researcher walked off behind the door. The substitute researcher was two inches shorter, wore different clothing, and had a noticeably different voice than the original. The pedestrian's conversational partner had suddenly morphed into someone else. Still, most of the pedestrians didn't notice, and were quite surprised when told of the switch.

IF WE'RE NOT very good at noticing or remembering the details of scenes that occurred, an even more serious issue is recalling something that never happened at all. Remember the people in my audiences who reported seeing in their mind's eye a vivid picture of the word "sweet" on the list I had presented to them? Those people were having a "false memory," a memory that *seemed* real but wasn't. False memories feel no different than memories that are based in reality. For example, in the many variations of the word list experiment researchers have performed over the years, people who "remembered" phantom words rarely felt they were taking a shot in the dark. They reported recalling them vividly, and with great confidence. In one of the more revealing experiments, two word lists were read to volunteers by two different readers, a man and a woman.[30] After the readings, the volunteers were presented with another list, this one containing words they both had and had not heard. They were asked to identify which were which. For each word they remembered hearing, they were also asked whether it had been uttered by the male or the female speaker. The subjects were pretty accurate in recalling whether the man or woman had said the words they'd actually heard. But to the researchers' surprise, the subjects almost always also expressed confidence in identifying whether it was the man or the woman who had spoken the words they were *wrong* about having heard. That is, even when the subjects were remembering a word that had not actually been uttered, their memory of its utterance was vivid and specific. In fact, when told in a postexperiment debriefing that they hadn't really heard a word they thought they had heard, the subjects frequently refused to believe it. In many cases the experimenters had to replay the videotape of the session to convince them, and even then, some of the subjects, like Jennifer Thompson in Ronald Cotton's second trial, refused to accept the evidence that they were mistaken—they accused the researchers of switching the tape.

The idea that we can remember events that never happened was a key plot element of the famous Philip K. Dick story "We Can Remember It for You Wholesale," which begins with a man approaching a company to have the memory of an exciting visit to Mars implanted in his brain. As it turns out, planting simple false memories is not that hard, and requires no high-tech solution like the one Dick envisioned. Memories of events that supposedly happened long ago are particularly easy to implant. You might not be able to convince anyone that they have been to Mars, but if your child's fantasy is a ride in a hot air balloon, research has shown that it *is* possible to supply that memory with none of the expense or bother of arranging the actual experience.[31]

In one study scientists recruited twenty subjects who had never been in a hot air balloon, as well as one accompanying family member. Each family member secretly provided the researchers with three photos depicting the subject in the midst of some moderately significant event that occurred when the subject was between four and eight years old. They also provided other shots, which the researchers used to create a bogus photo of the subject in a hot air balloon. The photos, both real and faked, were then presented to the subjects, who were not aware of the ruse. The subjects were asked to recall everything they could about the scene depicted by each photo and were given a few minutes to think about it, if needed. If nothing came to them, they were asked to close their eyes and try to picture themselves as they appeared in the photo. The process was repeated two more times, at intervals of three to seven days. When it was over, half the subjects recalled memories of the balloon trip. Some recounted sensory details of the ride. Said one subject after being told the photo was a phony, "I still feel in my head that I actually was there; I can sort of see images of it. . . ."

False memories and misinformation are so easy to plant that they have been induced in three-month-old infants, gorillas, and even pigeons and rats.[32] As humans, we are so prone to false memories that you can sometimes induce one simply by casually telling a person about an incident that didn't really happen. Over time, that person may "remember" the incident but forget the source of that memory. As a result, he or she will confuse the imagined event with his or her actual past. When psychologists employ this procedure, they are typically successful with between 15 and 50 percent of their subjects. For example, in a recent study, subjects who had actually been to Disneyland were asked to repeatedly read and think about a fake print advertisement for the amusement park.[33] The copy in the fake ad invited the reader to "imagine how you felt when you first saw Bugs Bunny with your own eyes up close. . . . Your mother pushing you in his direction so you would shake his hand, waiting to capture the moment with a picture. You needed no urging, but somehow the closer you got, the bigger he got. . . . He doesn't look that big on TV, you thought. . . . And it hits you hard. Bugs, the character you idolized on TV, is only several feet away. . . . Your heart stops but that doesn't stop your hands from sweating. You wipe them off just before reaching up to grab his hand. . . ." Later, when asked in a questionnaire about their personal memories of Disneyland, more than a quarter of the subjects reported having met Bugs Bunny there. Of those, 62 percent remembered shaking his hand, 46 percent recalled hugging him, and one recalled that he was holding a carrot. It was not possible that such encounters really occurred, because Bugs Bunny is a Warner Brothers property, and Disney inviting Bugs to roam Disneyland is something like the king of Saudi Arabia hosting a Passover Seder.

In other studies people have been led to believe that they had once gotten lost in a shopping mall, been rescued by a lifeguard, survived a vicious animal attack, and been uncomfortably licked on the ear by Pluto.[34] They have been made to believe that they once had a finger caught in a mousetrap,[35] spilled a punch bowl at a wedding reception,[36] and were hospitalized overnight for a high fever.[37] But even when memories are entirely fabricated, they are usually based on something true. Kids might be induced into believing they took a ride on a hot air balloon—but the details the child fills in to explain the bogus balloon ride photo percolate from the child's unconscious, from a body of stored sensory and psychological experiences and the expectations and beliefs that stem from those experiences.

THINK BACK ON your life. What do you remember? When I do that, I find that it is not enough. Of my father, for example, who died more than twenty years ago, my memory holds but meager scraps. Walking with him after his stroke, as he leans for the first time on a cane. Or his glittering eyes and warm smile at one of my then-infrequent visits home. Of my earlier years I recall even less. I remember his younger self beaming with joy at a new Chevrolet and erupting with anger when I threw away his cigarettes. And if I go back still further, trying to remember the earliest days of childhood, I have yet fewer, ever more out-of-focus snapshots: of my father hugging me sometimes, or my mother singing to me while she held me and stroked my hair.

I know, when I shower my children with my usual excess of hugs and kisses, that most of those scenes will not stay with them. They will forget, and for good reason. I would not wish upon them the unforgetting life of a Shereshevsky. But my hugs and kisses do not vanish without a trace. They remain, at least in aggregate, as fond feelings and emotional bonds. I know that my memory of my parents would overflow any tiny vessel formed from merely the concrete episodes that my consciousness recalls, and I hope that the same will be true of my children. Moments in time may be forever forgotten, or viewed through a hazy or distorting lens, yet something of them nonetheless survives within us, permeating our unconscious. From there, they impart to us a rich array of feelings that bubble up when we think about those who were dearest to our hearts—or when we think of others whom we've only met, or the exotic and ordinary places we've lived in and visited, or the events that shaped us. Though imperfectly, our brains still manage to communicate a coherent picture of our life experience.

In the last chapter we saw how our unconscious takes the incomplete data provided by our senses, fills in what's missing, and passes the perception to our conscious minds. When we look at a scene we think we are seeing a sharp, well-defined picture, like a photograph, but we really see only a small part of the picture clearly, and our subliminal brains paint in the rest. Our brains use the same trick in memory. If you were designing the system for human memory, you probably would not choose a process that tosses out data wholesale and then, when asked to retrieve it, makes things up. But for the vast majority of us, the method works well, most of the time. Our species would not have survived if that weren't so. Through evolution, perfection may be abandoned, but sufficiency must be achieved. The lesson that teaches me is to be both humble and grateful. Humble, because any great confidence I feel in any particular memory could well be misplaced; but grateful, both for the memories I retain and the ability to not retain all of them. Conscious memory and perception accomplish their miracles with a heavy reliance on the unconscious. In the chapter that follows, we'll see that this same two-tier system affects what is most important to us: the way we function in our complex human societies.

CHAPTER 4

The Importance of Being Social

Strange is our situation here on earth. Each of us comes for a short visit, not knowing why, yet sometimes seeming to a divine purpose. From the standpoint of daily life, however, there is one thing we do know: that we are here for the sake of others. —ALBERT EINSTEIN

I CAME HOME FROM work late one evening, hungry and frustrated, and popped into my mother's house, which was next door to mine. She was eating a frozen dinner and sipping from a mug of hot water. CNN blared on the TV in the background. She asked how my day had been. I said, "Oh, it was good." She looked up from her black plastic food tray and, after a moment, said, "No, it wasn't. What happened? Have some pot roast." My mother was eighty-eight, hard of hearing, and half blind in her right eye—which was her good eye. But when it came to perceiving her son's emotions, my mother's X-ray vision was unimpaired.

As she read my mood with such fluency, I thought about the man who had been my coworker and partner in frustration that day—the physicist Stephen Hawking, who could hardly move a muscle, thanks to a forty-five-year struggle with motor neuron disease. By this stage in the progression of his illness, he could communicate only by painstakingly twitching the cheek muscle under his right eye. That twitch was detected by a sensor on his glasses and communicated to a computer in his wheelchair. In this manner, with the help of some special software, he managed to select letters and words from a screen, and eventually to type out what he wanted to express. On his "good" days, it was as if he were playing a video game where the prize was the ability to communicate a thought. On his "bad" days, it was as if he were blinking in Morse code but had to look up the dot and dash sequence between each letter. On the bad days—and this had been one of them—our work was frustrating for both of us. And yet, even when he could not form words to express his ideas about the wave function of the universe, I had little trouble detecting when his attention shifted from the cosmos to thoughts of calling it quits and moving on to a nice curry dinner. I always knew when he was content, tired, excited, or displeased, just from a glance at his eyes. His personal assistant had this same ability. When I asked her about it, she described a catalog of expressions she'd learned to recognize over the years. My favorite was "the steely-faced glint of glee" he displayed when composing a potent rejoinder to someone with whom he strongly disagreed. Language is handy, but we humans have social and emotional connections that transcend words, and are communicated—and understood—without conscious thought.

The experience of feeling connected to others seems to start very early in life. Studies on infants show that even six-month-olds make judgments about what they observe of social behavior.[1] In one such study infants watched as a "climber," which was nothing more than a disk of wood with large eyes glued onto its circular "face," started at the bottom of a hill and repeatedly tried but failed to make its way to the top. After a while, a "helper," a triangle with similar eyes glued on, would sometimes approach from farther downhill and help the climber with an upward push. On other attempts, a square "hinderer" would approach from uphill and shove the circular disk back down.

The experimenters wanted to know if the infants, unaffected and uninvolved bystanders, would cop an attitude toward the hinderer square. How does a six-month-old show its disapproval of a wooden face? The same way six-year-olds (or sixty-year-olds) express social displeasure: by refusing to play with it. That is, when the experimenters gave the infants a chance to reach out and touch the figures, the infants showed a definite reluctance to reach for the hinderer square, as compared to the helper triangle. Moreover, when the experiment was repeated with either a helper and a neutral bystander block or a hinderer and a neutral block, the infants preferred the friendly triangle to the neutral block, and the neutral block to the nasty square. Squirrels don't set up foundations to cure rabies, and snakes don't help strange snakes cross the road, but humans place a high value on kindness. Scientists have even found that parts of our brain linked to reward processing are engaged when we participate in acts of mutual cooperation, so being nice can be its own reward.[2] Long before we can verbalize attraction or revulsion, we are attracted to the kind and repelled by the unkind.

One advantage of belonging to a cohesive society in which people help one another is that the group is often better equipped than an unconnected set of individuals to deal with threats from the outside. People intuitively realize that there is strength in numbers and take comfort in the company of others, especially in times of anxiety or need. Or, as Patrick Henry famously said, "United we stand, divided we fall." (Ironically, Henry collapsed and fell into the arms of bystanders shortly after uttering the phrase.)

Consider a study performed in the 1950s. About thirty female students at the University of Minnesota, none of whom had previously met, were ushered into a room and asked not to speak to each other.[3] In the room was a "gentleman of serious mien, horn-rimmed glasses, dressed in a white laboratory coat, stethoscope dribbling out of his pocket, behind him an array of formidable electrical junk." Seeking to induce anxiety, he melodramatically introduced himself as "Dr. Gregor Zilstein of the Medical School's Departments of Neurology and Psychiatry." Actually, he was Stanley Schachter, a harmless professor of social psychology. Schachter told the students he had asked them there to serve as subjects in an experiment on the effects of electric shocks. He would be shocking them, he said, and studying their reactions. After going on for seven or eight minutes about the importance of the research, he concluded by saying,

"These shocks will hurt, they will be painful. . . . It is necessary that our shocks be intense. . . . [We will] hook you into apparatus such as this [motioning toward the scary equipment behind him], give you a series of shocks, and take various measures such as your pulse rate, blood pressure, and so on."

Schachter then told the students that he needed them to leave the room for about ten minutes while he brought in still more equipment and set it all up. He noted that there were many rooms available, so they could wait either in a room by themselves or in one with other subjects. Later, Schachter repeated the scenario with a different group of about thirty students. But this time, he aimed to lull them into a state of relaxation. And so, instead of the scary part about intense shocks, he said,

"What we will ask each of you to do is very simple. We would like to give each of you a series of very mild electric shocks. I assure you that what you feel will not in any way be painful. It will resemble more a tickle or a tingle than anything unpleasant."

He then gave these students the same choice about waiting alone or with others. In reality, that choice was the climax of the experiment; there would be no electric shocks for either group.

The point of the ruse was to see if, because of their anxiety, the group expecting a painful shock would be more likely to seek the company of others than the group not expecting one. The result: about 63 percent of the students who were made anxious about the shocks wanted to wait with others, while only 33 percent of those expecting tickly, tingly shocks expressed that preference. The students had instinctively created their own support groups. It's a natural instinct. A quick look at a web directory of support groups in Los Angeles, for example, turned up groups focused on abusive behavior, acne, Adderall addiction, addiction, ADHD, adoption, agoraphobia, alcoholism, albinism, Alzheimer's, Ambien users, amputees, anemia, anger management, anorexia, anxiety, arthritis, Asperger's syndrome, asthma, Ativan addiction, and autism—and that's just the A's. Joining support groups is a reflection of the human need to associate with others, of our fundamental desire for support, approval, and friendship. We are, above all, a social species.

Social connection is such a basic feature of human experience that when we are deprived of it, we suffer. Many languages have expressions—

such as "hurt feelings"—that compare the pain of social rejection to the pain of physical injury. Those may be more than just metaphors. Brain-imaging studies show that there are two components to physical pain: an unpleasant emotional feeling and a feeling of sensory distress. Those two components of pain are associated with different structures in the brain. Scientists have discovered that social pain is also associated with a brain structure called the anterior cingulate cortex—the same structure involved in the emotional component of physical pain.[4]

It's fascinating that the pain of a stubbed toe and the sting of a snubbed advance share a space in your brain. The fact that they are roommates gave some scientists a seemingly wild idea: Could painkillers that reduce the brain's response to physical brain also subdue social pain?[5] To find out, researchers recruited twenty-five healthy subjects to take two tablets twice each day for three weeks. Half received extra-strength Tylenol (acetaminophen) tablets, the other half placebos. On the last day, the researchers invited the subjects, one by one, into the lab to play a computer-based virtual ball-tossing game. Each person was told they were playing with two other subjects located in another room, but in reality those roles were played by the computer, which interacted with the subjects in a carefully designed manner. In round 1, those reputedly human teammates played nicely with the subjects, but in round 2, after tossing the virtual ball to the subject a few times, the teammates started playing only with each other, rudely excluding the subject from the game, like soccer players who refuse to pass the ball to a peer. After the exercise, the subjects were asked to fill out a questionnaire designed to measure social distress. Compared to those who took the placebo, those who took the Tylenol reported a reduced level of hurt feelings.

There was also a twist. Remember Antonio Rangel's experiment in which the subjects tasted wine while having their brains scanned in an fMRI machine? These researchers employed the same technique—they had the subjects play the virtual ball game while lying in an fMRI machine. So while they were being snubbed by their teammates, their brains were being scanned by the machine. It showed that the subjects who'd taken Tylenol had reduced activity in the brain areas associated with social exclusion. Tylenol, it seems, really does reduce the neural response to social rejection.

When the Bee Gees long ago sang "How Can You Mend a Broken Heart?" they probably didn't foresee that the answer was to take two Tylenols. That Tylenol would help really does sound far-fetched, so the brain researchers also performed a clinical test to see if Tylenol had the same effect outside the lab, in the real world of social rejection. They asked five dozen volunteers to fill out a "hurt feelings" survey, a standard psychological tool, every day for three weeks. Again, half the volunteers took a dose of Tylenol twice a day, while the other half took a placebo. The result? The volunteers on Tylenol did indeed report significantly reduced social pain over that time period.

The connection between social pain and physical pain illustrates the links between our emotions and the physiological processes of the body. Social rejection doesn't just cause emotional pain; it affects our physical being. In fact, social relationships are so important to humans that a lack of social connection constitutes a major risk factor for health, rivaling even the effects of cigarette smoking, high blood pressure, obesity, and lack of physical activity. In one study, researchers surveyed 4,775 adults in Alameda County, near San Francisco.[6] The subjects completed a questionnaire asking about social ties such as marriage, contacts with extended family and friends, and group affiliation. Each individual's answers were translated into a number on a "social network index," with a high number meaning the person had many regular and close social contacts and a low number representing relative social isolation. The researchers then tracked the health of their subjects over the next nine years. Since the subjects had varying backgrounds, the scientists employed mathematical techniques to isolate the effects of social connectivity from risk factors such as smoking and the others I mentioned above, and also from factors like socioeconomic status and reported levels of life satisfaction. They found a striking result. Over the nine-year period, those who'd placed low on the index were twice as likely to die as individuals who were similar with regard to other factors but had placed high on the social network index. Apparently, hermits are bad bets for life insurance underwriters.

SOME SCIENTISTS BELIEVE that the need for social interaction was the driving force behind the evolution of superior human intelligence.[7]

After all, it is nice to have the mental capacity to realize that we live in a curved four-dimensional space-time manifold, but unless the lives of early humans depended on having a GPS unit to locate the nearest sushi restaurant, the capability to develop such knowledge was not important to the survival of our species and, hence, did not drive our cerebral evolution. On the other hand, social cooperation and the social intelligence it requires seem to have been crucial to our survival. Other primates also exhibit social intelligence, but not nearly to the extent that we do. They may be stronger and faster, but we have the superior ability to band together and coordinate complex activities. Do you need to be smart to be social? Could the need for innate skill at social interaction have been the reason we developed our "higher" intelligence—and could what we usually think of as the triumphs of our intelligence, such as science and literature, be just a by-product?

Eons ago, having a sushi dinner involved skills a bit more advanced than saying, "Pass the wasabi." It required catching a fish. Before about fifty thousand years ago, humans did not do that; nor did they eat other animals that were available but difficult to catch. Then, rather abruptly (on the evolutionary scale of time), humans changed their behavior.[8] According to evidence uncovered in Europe, within the span of just a few millennia people started fishing, catching birds, and hunting down dangerous but tasty and nutritious large animals. At about the same time, they also started building structures for shelter and creating symbolic art and complex burial sites. Suddenly they had both figured out how to gang up on woolly mammoths and begun to participate in the rituals and ceremonies that are the rudiments of what we now call culture. In a brief period of time, the archaeological record of human activity changed more than it had in the previous million years. The sudden manifestation of the modern capacity for culture, ideological complexity, and cooperative social structure—without any change in human anatomy to explain it—is evidence that an important mutation may have occurred within the human brain, a software upgrade, so to speak, that enabled social behavior and thereby bestowed on our species a survival advantage.

When we think of humans versus dogs and cats, or even monkeys, we usually assume that what distinguishes us is our IQ. But if human intelligence evolved for social purposes, then it is our social IQ that ought to be the principal quality that differentiates us from other animals. In particular, what seems special about humans is our desire and ability to understand what other people think and feel. Called "theory of mind," or "ToM," this ability gives humans a remarkable power to make sense of other people's past behavior and to predict how their behavior will unfold given their present or future circumstances. Though there is a conscious, reasoned component to ToM, much of our "theorizing" about what others think and feel occurs subliminally, accomplished through the quick and automatic processes of our unconscious mind. For example, if you see a woman racing toward a bus that pulls away before she can get on it, you know without giving it any thought that she was frustrated and possibly ticked off about not reaching the bus in time, and when you see a woman moving her fork toward and away from a piece of chocolate cake, you assume she's concerned about her weight. Our tendency to automatically infer mental states is so powerful that we apply it not only to other people but to animals and even, as the six-month-olds did in the wooden disk study I described above, to inanimate geometrical shapes.[9]

It is difficult to overestimate the importance to the human species of ToM. We take the operation of our societies for granted, but many of our activities in everyday life are possible only as a result of group efforts, of human cooperation on a large scale. Building a car, for example, requires the participation of thousands of people with diverse skills, in diverse lands, performing diverse tasks. Metals like iron must be extracted from the ground and processed; glass, rubber, and plastics must be created from numerous chemical precursors and molded; batteries, radiators, and countless other parts must be produced; electronic and mechanical systems must be designed; and it all must come together, coordinated from far and wide, in one factory so that the car can be assembled. Today, even the coffee and bagel you might consume while driving to work in the morning is the result of the activities of people all over the world—wheat farmers in one state, bakers most likely in another, dairy farmers yet elsewhere; coffee plantation workers in another country, and roasters hopefully closer to you; truckers and merchant marines to bring it all together; and all the people who make the roasters, tractors, trucks, ships, fertilizer, and whatever other devices and ingredients are involved. It is ToM that enables us to form the large and sophisticated social systems, from farming communities to large corporations, upon which our world is based.

Scientists are still debating whether *nonhuman* primates use ToM in their social activities, but if they do, it seems to be at only a very basic level.[10] Humans are the only animal whose relationships and social organization make high demands on an individual's ToM. Pure intelligence (and dexterity) aside, that's why fish can't build boats and monkeys don't set up fruit stands. Pulling off such feats makes human beings unique among the animals. In our species, rudimentary ToM develops in the first year. By age four, nearly all human children have gained the ability to assess other people's mental states.[11] When ToM breaks down, as in autism, people can have difficulty functioning in society. In his book *An Anthropologist on Mars*, the clinical neurologist Oliver Sacks profiled Temple Grandin, a high-functioning autistic woman. She had told him about what it was like to go to the playground when she was a child, observing the other children's responses to social signals she could not herself perceive. "Something was going on between the other kids," he described her as thinking, "something swift, subtle, constantly changing—an exchange of meanings, a negotiation, a swiftness of understanding so remarkable that sometimes she wondered if they were all telepathic."[12]

One measure of ToM is called intentionality.[13] An organism that is capable of reflecting about its own state of mind, about its own beliefs and desires, as in *I want a bite of my mother's pot roast*—is called "first-order intentional." Most mammals fit in that category. But knowing about yourself is a far different skill from knowing about someone else. A second-order intentional organism is one that can form a belief about *someone else's* state of mind, as in *I believe my son wants a bite of my pot roast*. Second-order intentionality is defined as the most rudimentary level of ToM, and all healthy humans have it, at least after their morning coffee. If you have third-order intentionality you can go a step further, reasoning about what a person thinks a second person thinks, as in *I believe my mom thinks that my son wants a bite of her pot roast*. And if you are capable of going a level beyond that, of thinking *I believe my friend Sanford thinks that my daughter Olivia thinks that his son Johnny thinks she is cute* or *I believe my boss, Ruth, knows that our CFO, Richard, thinks that my colleague John doesn't believe her budgets and revenue projections can be trusted*, then you're engaging in fourth-order intentionality, and so on. Fourth-order thinking makes for a pretty complicated sentence, but if you ponder these for a minute, you'll probably realize you engage in it quite frequently, for it is typical of what is involved in human social relationships.

Fourth-order intentionality is required to create literature, for writers must make judgments based on their own experiences of fourth-order intentionality, such as *I think that the cues in this scene will signal to the reader that Horace thinks that Mary intends to dump him.* It is also necessary for politicians and business executives, who could easily be outmaneuvered without that skill. For example, I knew a newly hired executive at a computer games company—call her Alice—who used her highly developed ToM to get out of a touchy situation. Alice felt certain that an outside company that had a long-term contract for programming services with her new employer was guilty of certain financial improprieties. Alice had no proof, and the outside company had an airtight long-term contract that required a $500,000 payment for early termination. But: *Alice knew that Bob (the CEO of the outside company) knew that Alice, being new on the job, was afraid to make a misstep.* That's third-order intentionality. Also: *Alice knew that Bob knew that she knew that Bob was not afraid of a fight.* That's fourth-order thinking. Understanding this, Alice considered a ploy: What if she made a bluff that she had proof of the impropriety and used that to force Bob to let them out of the contract? How would Bob react? She used her ToM analysis to look at the situation from Bob's point of view. Bob saw her as someone who was hesitant to take chances and who knew that he was a fighter. Would such a person make a grand claim she couldn't back up? Bob must have thought not, for he agreed to let Alice's employer out of the contract for a small fraction of the contractually obligated sum.

The evidence on nonhuman primates seems to show that they fall somewhere between first- and second-order thinking. A chimp may think to itself, *I want a banana* or even *I believe George wants my banana,* but it wouldn't go as far as thinking, *I believe George thinks that I want his banana.* Humans, on the other hand, commonly engage in third- and fourth-order intentionality and are said to be capable of sixth-order. Tackling those higher-order ToM sentences taxes the mind in a way that, to me, feels analogous to the thinking required when doing research in theoretical physics, in which one must be able to reason about long chains of interrelated concepts.

If ToM both enables social connection and requires extraordinary brain power, that may explain why scientists have discovered a curious connection between brain size and social group size among mammals. To be precise, the size of a species' neocortex—the most recently evolved part of the brain—*as a percentage of that species' whole brain* seems to be related to the size of the social group in which members of that species hang out.[14] Gorillas form groups of under ten, spider monkeys closer to twenty, and macaques more like forty—and these numbers accurately reflect the neocortex-to-whole-brain ratio of each of these species.

Suppose we use the mathematical relationship that describes the connection between group size and relative neocortex size in nonhuman primates to predict the size of human social networks. Does it work? Does the ratio of neocortex to overall brain size apply to calculating the size of human networks, too?

To answer that question, we first have to come up with a way of defining group size among humans. Group size in nonhuman primates is defined by the typical number of animals in what are called grooming cliques. These are social alliances like the cliques our kids form in school or those adults have been known to form at the PTA. In primates, clique members regularly clean each other, removing dirt, dead skin, insects, and other objects by stroking, scratching, and massaging. Individuals are particular about both whom they groom and whom they are groomed by, because these alliances act as coalitions to minimize harassment from others of their kind. Group size in humans is harder to define in any precise way because humans relate to one another in many different types of groups, with different sizes, different levels of mutual understanding, and different degrees of bonding. In addition, we have developed technologies designed specifically to aid large-scale social communication, and we have to be careful to exclude from group size measurements people such as e-mail contacts we hardly know. In the end, when scientists look at groups that seem to be the cognitive equivalent of nonhuman grooming cliques—the clans among Australian aboriginals, the hair-care networks of female bushmen, or the number of individuals to whom people send Christmas cards—the human group size comes out to about 150, just about what the neocortex size model predicts.[15]

Why should there be a connection between brain power and the number of members in a social network? Think about human social circles, circles consisting of friends and relatives and work associates. If these are to remain meaningful, they can't get too big for your cognitive capacities, or you won't be able to keep track of who is who, what they all want, how they relate to one another, who can be trusted, who can be counted on to help out with a favor, and so on.[16]

To explore just how connected we humans are, in the 1960s the psychologist Stanley Milgram selected about 300 people at random in Nebraska and Boston and asked each of them to start a chain letter.[17] The volunteers were sent a packet of materials with a description of the study, including the name of a "target person"—a randomly chosen man in Sharon, Massachusetts, who worked as a stockbroker in Boston. They were instructed to forward the packet to the target person if they knew him or, if they didn't, to send it to whichever of their acquaintances they deemed most likely to know him. The intention was that the acquaintance, upon receiving the packet, would also follow the instructions and send it along, until eventually someone would be found who did know the target person and would send it directly to him.

Many people along the way didn't bother, and broke the chain. But out of the initial 300 or so individuals, 64 did generate chains that ultimately found the man in Sharon, Massachusetts. How many intermediaries did it take until someone knew someone who knew someone who knew someone . . . who knew the target? The median number was only about 5. The study led to the coining of the term "six degrees of separation," based on the idea that six links of acquaintanceship are enough to connect any two people in the world. The same experiment, made much easier by the advent of e-mail, was repeated in 2003.[18] This time the researchers started with 24,000 e-mail users in more than 100 countries, and 18 different target people spread far and wide. Of the 24,000 e-mail chains those subjects started, only about 400 reached their target. But the result was similar: the target was contacted in a median of five to seven steps.

We give out Nobel Prizes in scientific fields like physics and chemistry, but the human brain also deserves a gold medallion for its extraordinary ability to create and maintain social networks, such as corporations, government agencies, and basketball teams, in which people work smoothly together to accomplish a common goal with a minimum of miscommunication and conflict. Perhaps 150 is the natural group size for humans in the wild, unaided by formal organizational structures or communications technology, but given those innovations of civilization, we have blasted through the natural barrier of 150 to accomplish feats that only thousands of humans working together could possibly attain. Sure, the physics behind the Large Hadron Collider, a particle accelerator in Switzerland, is a monument to the human mind. But so are the scale and complexity of the organization that built it—one LHC experiment alone required more than 2,500 scientists, engineers, and technicians in 37 countries to work together, solving problems cooperatively in an ever-changing and complex environment. The ability to form organizations that can create such achievements is as impressive as the achievements themselves.

THOUGH HUMAN SOCIAL behavior is clearly more complex than social behavior in other species, there are also striking commonalities in certain fundamental aspects of the way all mammals connect with others of their species. One of the interesting aspects of most nonhuman mammals is that they are "small-brained." By that, scientists mean the part of the brain that in humans is responsible for conscious thought is, in nonhuman mammals, relatively small compared to the part of the brain involved in unconscious processes.[19] Of course, no one is quite sure exactly how conscious thought arises, but it seems to be centered mainly in the frontal lobe of the neocortex, in particular in a region called the prefrontal cortex. In other animals, these regions of the brain are either much smaller or nonexistent. In other words, animals react more and think less, if at all. So a human's unconscious mind might raise an alarm at the sight of Uncle Matt stabbing his arm with a shish kebab skewer, only to have the conscious mind remind that human that Uncle Matt thinks it is funny to perform shocking magic tricks. Your pet rabbit's reaction, in contrast, would probably not be mitigated by such conscious, rational considerations. The rabbit's reaction would be automatic. It would follow its gut instincts and simply flee Uncle Matt and his skewer. But although a rabbit just can't take a joke, the brain regions responsible for a rabbit's *unconscious* processing are not that different from ours.

In fact, the organization and chemistry of the unconscious brain is shared across mammal species, and many automatic neural mechanisms in apes and monkeys and even lower mammals are similar to our own, and produce startlingly humanlike behavior.[20] So although other animals can't teach us much about ToM, they they can provide insights into some of the other automatic and unconscious aspects of our social tendencies. That's why, while other people read books like *Men Are from Mars, Women Are from Venus* to learn about male and female social roles, I turn to sources like "Mother-Infant Bonding and the Evolution of Mammalian Social Relationships"—which, some say, serves to minimize the mammalian social relationships in my own life.

Consider this quote from that work:

Reproductive success in males is generally determined by competing with other males to mate with as many females as possible. Hence, males rarely form strong social bonds and male coalitions are typically hierarchical with an emphasis on aggressive rather than affiliative behavior.[21]

That sounds like something you'd observe hanging out at a sports bar, but scientists are discussing the behavior of *nonhuman* mammals. Perhaps the difference between human males and bulls, tomcats, and male sheep is not that nonhuman mammals don't have sports bars but that, to nonhuman mammals, the whole world is a sports bar. Of females, those same researchers write:

The female reproductive strategy is one of investing in the production of a relatively few offspring . . . and success is determined by the quality of care and the ability to enable infant survival beyond the weaning age. Females therefore form strong social bonds with their infants and female-female relationships are also strongly affiliative.

That, too, sounds familiar. One has to be careful about reading too much into mammalian behavior "in general," but this does seem to explain why it is mostly women who have slumber parties and form book clubs, and why, despite my promises to be affiliative rather than aggressive, they have never let me into either. The fact that on some level human and nonhuman mammals seem to behave similarly does not mean that a cow would enjoy a candlelight dinner, that a mother sheep wants nothing more than to see her babies grow up happy and well-adjusted, or that rodents aspire to retiring in Tuscany with their soul mates. What it does suggest is that although human social behavior is far more complex than that of other animals, the evolutionary roots of our behaviors can be found in those animals, and we can learn something about ourselves by studying them.

Just how programmed *is* the social behavior of nonhuman mammals? Take sheep, for example.[22] A female sheep—a ewe—is by disposition rather nasty to baby sheep (or, as the meat industry likes us to call them, lambs). If a lamb approaches, wishing to suckle, the ewe will scream at it with a high-pitched bleat, and maybe throw in a head butt or two. However, the birthing process transforms the mother. It seems magical, that transformation from shrew to nurturer. But it doesn't seem to be due to conscious, maternal thoughts of her child's love. It's chemical, not magical. The process is instigated by the stretching of the birth canal, which causes a simple protein called oxytocin to be released in the ewe's brain. This opens a window of a couple hours' duration in which the ewe is open to bonding. If a lamb approaches her while that window is open, the ewe will bond with it, whether it is her baby, her neighbor's, or a baby from the farm down the street. Then, once the oxytocin window has closed, she'll stop bonding with new lambs. After that, if she has bonded with a lamb, she'll continue to suckle it and to speak soothingly to it—which in sheep talk means low-pitched bleats. But she'll be her nasty old self to all other lambs, even to her own if it didn't approach her during the bonding window. Scientists, however, can open and close this bonding window at will, by injecting the ewe with oxytocin or inhibiting her from producing it herself. It's like flicking a switch on a robot.

Another famous series of studies in which scientists have been able to program mammalian behavior by chemical manipulation concerns the vole, a small rodent that resembles a mouse and encompasses about 150 different species. One of those species, the prairie vole, would be a model citizen in human society. Prairie voles mate for life. They are loyal—among prairie voles whose partner disappears, for example, fewer than 30 percent will shack up with someone else.[23] And they make responsible fathers—the males stick around to guard the nest and share in the parenting. Scientists study prairie voles because they are a fascinating contrast with two related species of voles, the montane vole and the meadow vole. In contrast to prairie voles, montane and meadow voles form societies of sexually promiscuous loners.[24] The males of those species are, in human terms, ne'er-do-wells. They will mate with whatever female is around, then wander off and leave her to take care of the kids. If placed randomly in a large room, they avoid others of their species, preferring to crawl off to some isolated corner. (Prairie voles, on the other hand, will cluster in little chat groups.)

What is amazing about these creatures is that scientists have been able to identify the specific brain characteristic responsible for the behavioral differences among vole species, and to use that knowledge to change their behavior from that of one species to that of another. The chemical involved is again oxytocin. To have an effect on brain cells, oxytocin molecules first have to bind to receptors—specific molecules on the surface membrane of a cell. Monogamous prairie voles have many receptors for oxytocin and a related hormone called vasopressin in a particular region of the brain. A similarly high concentration of oxytocin and vasopressin receptors is found in that region of the brain in other monogamous mammals. But in promiscuous voles, there is a dearth of those receptors. And so, for example, when scientists manipulate a meadow vole's brain to increase the number of receptors, the loner meadow vole suddenly becomes outgoing and sociable like its cousin the prairie vole.[25]

Unless you're an exterminator, I've probably now supplied more than you need to know about prairie voles, and as for lambs, most of us never come into contact with them except those accompanied by mint jelly. But I've gone into detail about oxytocin and vasopressin because they play an important role in the modulation of social and reproductive behavior in mammals, including ourselves. In fact, related compounds have played a role in organisms for at least seven hundred million years, and are at work even in invertebrates such as worms and insects.[26] Human social behavior is obviously more advanced and more nuanced than that of voles and sheep. Unlike them, we have ToM, and we are far more capable of overruling unconscious impulses through conscious decisions. But in humans, too, oxytocin and vasopressin regulate bonding.[27] In human mothers, as in ewes, oxytocin is released during labor and delivery. It is also released in a woman when her nipples or cervix are stimulated during sexual intimacy and in both men and women when they reach sexual climax. And in both men and women, the oxytocin and vasopressin that are released into the brain after sex promote attraction and love. Oxytocin is even released during hugs, especially in women, which is why mere casual physical touch can lead to feelings of emotional closeness even in the absence of a conscious, intellectual connection between the participants.

In the broader social environment, oxytocin also promotes trust, and is produced when people have positive social contact with others.[28] In one experiment, two strangers played a game in which they could cooperate to earn money. But the game was designed so that each contestant could also gain at the expense of the other. As a result, trust was an issue, and as the game progressed the players gauged each other's character. Each assessed whether his or her partner tended to play fairly, so both players could benefit equally, or selfishly, to reap a greater benefit at his or her expense.

The unique aspect of this study was that the researchers monitored the players' oxytocin levels by taking blood samples after they made their decisions. They found that when a player's partner played in a manner that indicated trust, the player's brain responded to that show of trust by releasing oxytocin. In another study, in which subjects played an investment game, investors who inhaled an oxytocin nose spray were much more likely to *show* trust in their partners, by investing more money with them. And when asked to categorize faces based on their expression, volunteers who were given oxytocin rated strangers as appearing more trustworthy and attractive than did other subjects not administered the drug. (Not surprisingly, oxytocin sprays are now available over the Internet, though they are not very effective unless the oxytocin is sprayed directly into the target person's nostril.)

One of the most striking pieces of evidence of our automatic animal nature can be seen in a gene that governs vasopressin receptors in human brains. Scientists discovered that men who have two copies of a certain form of this gene have *fewer* vasopressin receptors, which makes them analogous to promiscuous voles. And, indeed, they exhibit the same sort of behavior: men with fewer vasopressin receptors are twice as likely to have experienced marital problems or the threat of divorce and half as likely to be married as men who have more vasopressin receptors.[29] So although we are much more complex in our behaviors than sheep and voles, people, too, are hardwired to certain unconscious social behaviors, a remnant of our animal past.

SOCIAL NEUROSCIENCE IS a new field, but the debate over the origin and nature of human social behavior is probably as old as human civilization itself. Philosophers of centuries past didn't have access to studies like those of the lambs and voles; however, as long as they have speculated about the mind, they have debated the degree to which we are in conscious control of our lives.[30] They used different conceptual frameworks, but observers of human behavior from Plato to Kant usually found it necessary to distinguish between direct causes of behavior—those motivations we can be in touch with through introspection—and hidden internal influences that could only be inferred.

In modern times, as I mentioned, it was Freud who popularized the unconscious. But though his theories had great prominence in clinical applications and popular culture, Freud influenced books and films more than he influenced experimental research in psychology. Through most of the twentieth century, empirical psychologists simply neglected the unconscious mind.[31] Odd as it may sound today, in the first half of that century, which was dominated by those in the behaviorist movement, psychologists even sought to do away with the concept of mind altogether. They not only likened the behavior of humans to that of animals, they considered both humans and animals to be merely complex machines that responded to stimuli in predictable ways. However, though the introspection elicited by Freud and his followers is unreliable, and the inner workings of the brain were, at the time, unobservable, the idea of completely disregarding the human mind and its thought processes struck many as absurd. By the end of the 1950s the behaviorist movement had faded, and two new movements grew in its place, and flourished. One was cognitive psychology, inspired by the computer revolution. Like behaviorism, cognitive psychology generally rejected introspection. But cognitive psychology did embrace the idea that we have internal mental states such as beliefs. It treated people as information systems that process those mental states much in the way a computer processes data. The other movement was social psychology, which aimed to understand how people's mental states are affected by the presence of others.

With these movements, psychology once again embraced the study of the mind, but both movements remained dubious about the mysterious unconscious. After all, if people are unaware of subliminal processes, and if one cannot trace them within the brain, what evidence do we have that such mental states are even real? In both cognitive and social psychology, the term "unconscious" was thus usually avoided. Still, like the therapist who doggedly brings you back again and again to the subject of your father, a handful of scientists kept doing experiments whose outcomes suggested that such processes *had* to be investigated, because they played such an important role in social interactions. By the 1980s, a number of now-classic experiments offered powerful evidence of the unconscious, automatic components of social behavior.

Some of those early studies of behavior drew directly on Frederic Bartlett's memory theories. Bartlett believed that the distortions he had observed in people's recall could be accounted for by assuming that their minds followed certain unconscious mental scripts, which were aimed at filling in gaps and making information consistent with the way they thought the world to be. Wondering whether our *social behavior* might also be influenced by some unconscious playbook, cognitive psychologists postulated the idea that many of our daily actions proceed according to predetermined mental "scripts"[32]—that they are, in fact, mindless.

In one test of that idea, an experimenter sat in a library and kept an eye on the copier. When someone approached it, the experimenter rushed up and tried to cut in front, saying, "Excuse me, I have five pages. May I use the Xerox machine?" Sure, sharing is caring, but unless the subject was making a great many more than five copies, the experimenter has provided no justification for the intrusion, so why yield? Apparently a good number of people felt that way: 40 percent of the subjects gave the equivalent of that answer, and refused. The obvious way to increase the likelihood of compliance is to offer a valid and compelling reason why someone should let you go first. And indeed, when the experimenter said, "Excuse me, I have five pages. May I use the Xerox machine, because I'm in a rush?" the rate of refusals fell radically, from 40 percent to just 6 percent. That makes sense, but the researchers suspected that something else might be going on; maybe people weren't consciously assessing the reason and deciding it was a worthy one. Maybe they were mindlessly—automatically—following a mental script.

That script might go something like this: Someone asks a small favor with zero justification: say no; someone asks a small favor but offers a reason, any reason: say yes. Sounds like a robot or computer program, but could it apply to people? The idea is easy to test. Just walk up to people approaching a photocopier and to each of them say something like "Excuse me, I have five pages. May I use the Xerox machine, because xxx," where "xxx" is a phrase that, though parading as the reason for the request, really provides no justification at all. The researchers chose as "xxx" the phrase "because I have to make some copies," which merely states the obvious and does not offer a legitimate reason for butting in. If the people making copies consciously weighed this nonreason against their own needs, one would expect them to refuse in the same proportion as in the case in which no reason was offered—about 40 percent. But if the very act of giving a reason was important enough to trigger the "yes" aspect of the script, regardless of the fact that the excuse itself had no validity, only about 6 percent should refuse, as occurred in the case in which the reason provided—"I'm in a rush"—was compelling. And that's exactly what the researchers found. When the experimenter said, "Excuse me, I have five pages. May I use the Xerox machine, because I have to make some copies?" only 7 percent refused, virtually the same number as when a valid and compelling reason was given. The lame reason swayed as many people as the legitimate one.

In their research report, those who conducted this experiment wrote that to unconsciously follow preset scripts "may indeed be the most common mode of social interaction. While such mindlessness may at times be troublesome, this degree of selective attention, of tuning the external world out, may be an achievement." Indeed, in evolutionary terms, here is the unconscious performing its usual duty, automating tasks so as to free us to respond to other demands of the environment. In modern society, that is the essence of multitasking—the ability to focus on one task while, with the aid of automatic scripts, performing others.

Throughout the 1980s, study after study seemed to show that, because of the influence of the unconscious, people did not realize the reasons for their feelings, behavior, and judgments of other people, or how they communicated nonverbally with others. Eventually psychologists had to rethink the role of conscious thought in social interactions. And so the term "unconscious" was resurrected, though also sometimes replaced by the untainted "nonconscious," or more specific terms like "automatic," "implicit," or "uncontrolled." But these experiments were mainly clever behavioral studies, and psychologists could still only guess at the mental processes that caused the participants' reactions. You can tell a lot about a restaurant's recipes by sitting at a table and sampling the food, but to really know what is going on, you have to look in the kitchen, and the human brain remained hidden behind the closed doors of the skull, its inner workings virtually as inaccessible as they had been a century earlier.

THE FIRST SIGN that the brain *could* be observed in action came in the nineteenth century when scientists noted that nerve activity causes changes in blood flow and oxygen levels. By monitoring those levels, one could, in theory, watch a reflection of the brain at work. In his 1890 book *The Principles of Psychology*, William James references the work of the Italian physiologist Angelo Mosso, who recorded the pulsation of the brain in patients who had gaps in their skull following brain surgery.[33] Mosso observed that the pulsation in certain regions increased during mental activity, and he speculated, correctly, that the changes were due to neuronal activity in those regions. Unfortunately, with the technology of that day, one could make such observations and measurements only if the skull was physically cut away, making the brain accessible.[34] That's not a viable strategy for studying the human brain, but that is exactly what scientists at Cambridge University did in 1899—to dogs, cats, and rabbits. The Cambridge scientists employed electric currents to stimulate various nerve pathways in each animal, then measured the brain's response with tools applied directly to the living tissue. They showed a link between brain circulation and metabolism, but the method was both crude and cruel, and it didn't catch on. Nor did the invention of X-rays provide an alternative, for X-rays can detect only the physical structures of the brain, not its dynamic, ever-changing electrical and chemical processes. And so for another century the working brain remained off-limits. Then, in the late 1990s, about a hundred years after Freud's book *The Interpretation of Dreams*, fMRI suddenly became widely available.

As I mentioned in the Prologue, fMRI, or functional magnetic resonance imaging, is a twist on the ordinary MRI machine your doctor uses. The nineteenth-century scientists had concluded correctly that the key to identifying what part of the brain is at work at any given time is that when nerve cells are active, circulation increases, because the cells increase their consumption of oxygen. With fMRI, scientists can map oxygen consumption from outside the skull, through the quantum electromagnetic interactions of atoms within the brain. Thus fMRI allows the noninvasive three-dimensional exploration of the normal human brain in operation. It not only provides a map of the structures in the brain but indicates which among them are active at any given moment, and allows scientists to follow how the areas that are active change over time. In that way, mental processes can now be associated with specific neural pathways and brain structures.

On many occasions in the past pages I've said that an experimental subject's brain had been imaged, or remarked that a particular part of the brain was or was not active in some circumstance. For example, I said that patient TN's occipital lobe was not functioning, explained that it is the orbitofrontal cortex that is associated with the experience of pleasure, and reported that brain-imaging studies show the existence of two centers of physical pain. All these statements were made possible by the technology of fMRI. There have been other new and exciting technologies developed in recent years, but the advent of fMRI changed the way scientists study the mind, and this advance continues to play a role of unparalleled importance in basic research.

Were we sitting in front of a computer housing your fMRI data, scientists would be able to make a slice of any section of your brain, and in any orientation, and view it almost as if they had dissected the brain itself. The

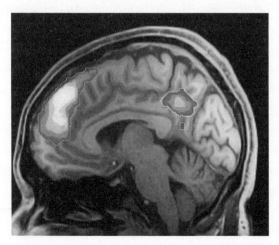

Courtesy of Mike Tyszka

image above, for example, displays a slice along the brain's central plane, as the subject engages in daydreaming. The shaded areas on the left and right indicate activity in the medial prefrontal cortex and the posterior cingulate cortex, respectively.

Neuroscientists today commonly divide the brain into three crude regions, based on their function, physiology, and evolutionary development.[35] In that categorization, the most primitive region is the "reptilian brain," responsible for basic survival functions such as eating, breathing, and heart rate, and also for primitive versions of the emotions of fear and aggression that drive our fight-or-flight instincts. All vertebrate creatures—birds, reptiles, amphibians, fish, and mammals—have the reptilian brain structures.

The second region, the limbic system, is more sophisticated, the source of our unconscious social perception. It is a complex system whose definition can vary a bit from researcher to researcher, because although the original designation was anatomical, the limbic system has come to be defined instead by its function as the system in the brain instrumental in the formation of social emotions. In humans, the limbic system is often defined as a ring of structures, some of which we have already run into, including the ventromedial prefrontal cortex, dorsal anterior cingulate cortex, amygdala, hippocampus, hypothalamus, components of the basal ganglia, and, sometimes, the orbitofrontal cortex.[36] The limbic system augments the reflexive reptilian emotions and is important in the genesis of social behaviors.[37] Many of the structures in this second region are sometimes grouped together into what is called the "old mammalian brain," which all mammals have, as opposed to the third region—the neocortex, or "new" mammalian brain—whose structures the more primitive mammals generally lack.

The neocortex lies above most of the limbic system.[38] You may recall from Chapter 2 that it is divided into lobes and is oversized in humans. It is this gray matter that people usually think of when they talk about the brain. In Chapter 2, I talked about the occipital lobe, which is located at the back of your head and contains your visual primary processing centers. In this chapter, I've talked about the frontal lobe, which is, as the name indicates, located at the front.

The genus *Homo*, of which humans, *Homo sapiens*, are the only surviving species, first evolved about two million years ago. Anatomically, *Homo sapiens* reached its present form about two hundred thousand years ago, but as I've said, behaviorally, we humans did not take on our present characteristics, such as culture, until about fifty thousand years ago. In the time between the original *Homo* species and ourselves, the brain doubled in size. A disproportionate share of that growth occurred in the frontal lobe, and so it stands to reason that the frontal lobe is the location of some of the specific qualities that make humans human. What does this expanded structure do to enhance our survival ability to a degree that might have justified nature's favoring it?

The frontal lobe contains regions governing the selection and execution of fine motor movements—especially of the fingers, hands, toes, feet, and tongue—that are clearly important for survival in the wild. It is interesting to note that control of the motor movements of the face is based in the frontal lobe, too. As we'll see in Chapter 5, the fine nuances of facial expression are also crucial to survival because of the role they play in social communication. In addition to regions associated with motor movements, as I mentioned earlier, the frontal lobe contains a structure called the prefrontal cortex. "Prefrontal" means, literally, "in front of the front," and that's where the prefrontal cortex sits, just behind the forehead. It is in this structure that we most clearly see our humanity. The prefrontal cortex is responsible for planning and orchestrating our thoughts and actions in accordance with our goals, and integrating conscious thought, perception, and emotion; it is thought to be the seat of our consciousness.[39] The ventromedial prefrontal cortex and the orbitofrontal cortex, parts of the limbic system, are subsystems within the prefrontal cortex.

Though this anatomical division of the brain into reptilian; limbic, or old mammalian; and neocortex, or new mammalian, is useful—and I'll occasionally refer to it—it's important to realize that it is a simplified picture. The full story is more complex. For example, the neat evolutionary steps it implies are not quite the way things happened; some so-called primitive creatures have neocortical-like tissue.[40] As a result, the behavior of those animals may not be as completely instinct-driven as once thought. Also, the three discrete areas are described as almost independent, but in reality they are integrated and work in concert, with numerous neural interconnections among them. The complexity of the brain is reflected by the fact that the hippocampus alone, a tiny structure deep in the brain, is the subject of a textbook several inches thick. Another recent work, an academic article that described research on a single type of nerve cell in the hypothalamus, was over one hundred pages long and cited seven hundred intricate experiments. That's why, despite all the research, the human mind, both conscious and unconscious, still holds enormous mystery, and why tens of thousands of scientists worldwide are still working to elucidate the function of these regions, on the molecular, cellular, neural, and psychological levels, providing ever deeper insights into how the pathways interact to produce our thoughts, feelings, and behavior.

With the advent of fMRI and the growing ability of scientists to study how different brain structures contribute to thoughts, feelings, and behavior, the two movements that followed behaviorism began to join forces. Social psychologists realized they could untangle and validate their theories of psychological processes by connecting them to their sources in the brain. Cognitive psychologists realized they could trace the origins of mental states. Also, the neuroscientists who focused on the physical brain realized they could better understand its functioning if they learned about the mental states and psychological processes the different structures produce. And so the new field of social cognitive neuroscience, or, simply, social neuroscience, emerged. It is a ménage à trois, a "household of three": social psychology, cognitive psychology, and neuroscience. I said earlier that the first ever social neuroscience meeting took place in April 2001. To get an idea of how fast the field exploded, consider this: The first ever academic publication employing fMRI came in 1991.[41] In 1992, there were only four such publications in the entire year. Even as late as 2001, an Internet search using the words "social cognitive neuroscience" yielded just 53 hits. But an identical search performed in 2007 yielded more than 30,000.[42] By then, neuroscientists were turning out fMRI studies every three hours.

Today, with researchers' new ability to watch the brain at work and to understand the origins and depth of the unconscious, the dreams of Wundt, James, and the others in the New Psychology who wanted to make that field into a rigorous experimental science are finally being realized. And though Freud's concept of the unconscious was flawed, his stress on the importance of unconscious thought is appearing ever more valid. Vague concepts like the id and the ego have now given way to maps of brain structure, connectivity, and function. What we've learned is that much of our social perception—like our vision, hearing, and memory—appears to proceed along pathways that are not associated with awareness, intention, or conscious effort. How this subliminal programming affects our lives, the way we present ourselves, the way we communicate with and judge people, the way we react to social situations, and the way we think of ourselves, is the territory we are about to explore.

PART II

The Social Unconscious

CHAPTER 5

Reading People

Your amicable words mean nothing if your body seems to be saying something different. —JAMES BORG

I N THE LATE summer of 1904, just a few months before the start of Einstein's "miracle year," the *New York Times* reported on another German scientific miracle, a horse that "can do almost everything but talk."[1] The story, the reporter assured us, was not drawn from the imagination but was based on the observations of a commission appointed by the Prussian minister of education, as well as the observations of the reporter himself. The subject of the article was described as a stallion, later dubbed Clever Hans, who could perform arithmetic and intellectual tasks on the level of those performed in one of today's third-grade classrooms. Since Hans was nine that would have been appropriate for his age, if not his species. In fact, rather like the average human nine-year-old, Hans had by then received four years of formal instruction, homeschooled by his owner, a Herr Wilhelm von Osten. Von Osten, who taught math at a local gymnasium—something like a high school—had a reputation for being an old crank, and also for not caring if he was viewed that way. Every day at a certain hour von Osten stood before Hans—in full view of his neighbors—and instructed the horse by employing various props and a blackboard, then rewarded him with a carrot or a piece of sugar.

Hans learned to respond to his master's questions by stamping his right hoof. The *New York Times* reporter described how, on one occasion, Hans was told to stamp once for gold, twice for silver, and three times for copper, and then correctly identified coins made from those metals. He identified colored hats in an analogous manner. Using the sign language of hoof taps, he could also tell time; identify the month and the day of the week; indicate the number of 4's in 8, 16, and 32; add 5 and 9; and even indicate the remainder when 7 was divided by 3. By the time the reporter witnessed this display, Hans had become something of a celebrity. Von Osten had been exhibiting him at gatherings throughout Germany—even at a command performance before the kaiser himself—and he never charged admission, because he was trying to convince the public of the potential for humanlike intelligence in animals. So much interest was there in the phenomenon of the high-IQ horse that a commission had been convened to assess von Osten's claims, and it concluded that no trickery was involved in Hans's feats. According to the statement issued by the commission, the explanation for the horse's ability lay in the superior teaching methods employed by von Osten—methods that corresponded to those employed in Prussia's own elementary schools. It's not clear if the "superior teaching methods" referred to the sugar or the carrots, but according to one commission member, the director of the Prussian Natural History Museum, "Herr von Osten has succeeded in training Hans by cultivating in him a desire for delicacies." He added, "I doubt whether the horse really takes pleasure in his studies." Even more evidence, I suppose, of Hans's startling humanity.

But not everyone was convinced by the commission's conclusions. One telling indication that there might be more to Hans's feats than an advance in equine teaching methodology was that Hans could sometimes answer von Osten's questions even if von Osten didn't verbalize them. That is, von Osten's horse seemed to be able to read his mind. A psychologist named Oskar Pfungst decided to investigate. With von Osten's encouragement, Pfungst conducted a series of experiments. He discovered that the horse could answer questions posed by people other than von Osten, but only if the questioners knew the answer, and only if they were visible to Hans during the hoof tapping.

It required a series of additional careful experiments, but Pfungst eventually found that the key to the horse's intellectual feats lay in involuntary and unconscious cues displayed by the questioner. As soon as a problem was posed, Pfungst discovered, the questioner would involuntarily and almost imperceptibly bend forward, which prompted Hans to begin tapping. Then, as the correct answer was reached, another slight bit of body language would signal Hans to stop. It was a "tell," as the poker crowd calls it, an unconscious change of demeanor that broadcasts a clue to a person's state of mind. Every one of the horse's questioners, Pfungst noted, made similar "minimal muscular movements" without being aware of doing so. Hans might not have been a racehorse, but he had the heart of a poker player.

In the end Pfungst demonstrated his theory with a flourish by playing the role of Hans and enlisting twenty-five experimental subjects to question *him*. None were aware of the precise purpose of the experiment, but all were aware they were being observed for clues that might give the answer away. Twenty-three of the twenty-five made such movements anyway, though all denied having done so. Von Osten, for the record, refused to accept Pfungst's conclusions and continued to tour Germany with Hans, drawing large and enthusiastic crowds.

As anyone who has ever been on the receiving end of a fellow driver's display of the middle finger knows, nonverbal communication is sometimes quite obvious and conscious. But then there are those times when a significant other says, "Don't look at me like that," and you respond, "Don't look at you like what?," knowing full well the nature of the feelings you were so sure you had hidden. Or you might smack your lips and proclaim that your spouse's scallop-and-cheddar casserole is yummy but somehow still elicit the response "What, you don't like it?" Don't fret; if a horse can read you, why not your spouse?

Scientists attach great importance to the human capacity for spoken language. But we also have a parallel track of nonverbal communication, and those messages may reveal more than our carefully chosen words and sometimes be at odds with them. Since much, if not most, of the nonverbal signaling and reading of signals is automatic and performed outside our conscious awareness and control, through our nonverbal cues we unwittingly communicate a great deal of information about ourselves and our state of mind. The gestures we make, the position in which we hold our bodies, the expressions we wear on our faces, and the nonverbal qualities of our speech—all contribute to how others view us.

THE POWER OF nonverbal cues is particularly evident in our relationship with animals because, unless you live in a Pixar movie, nonhuman species have a limited understanding of human speech. Like Hans, though, many animals *are* sensitive to human gestures and body language.[2] One recent study, for example, found that when trained properly, a wolf can be a decent acquaintance and respond to a human's nonverbal signals.[3] Though you wouldn't want to name a wolf Fido and leave it to play with your one-year-old, wolves are actually very social animals, and one reason they can respond to nonverbal cues from humans is that they have a rich repertoire of such signals within their own community. Wolves engage in a number of cooperative behaviors that require skill in predicting and interpreting the body language of their peers. So if you're a wolf, you know that when a fellow wolf holds its ears erect and forward and its tail vertical, it is signaling dominance. If it pulls its ears back and narrows its eyes, it is suspicious. If it flattens its ears against its head and tucks its tail between its legs, it is fearful. Wolves haven't been explicitly tested, but their behavior seems to imply that they are capable of at least some degree of ToM. Still, wolves are not man's best friend. Instead it is the dog, which originated from wolves, that is best at reading human social signals. At that task, dogs appear even more skilled than our primate relatives. That finding surprised a lot of people because primates are far superior at other typical human endeavors, like problem solving and cheating.[4] This suggests that during the process of domestication, evolution favored those dogs who developed mental adaptations allowing them to be better companions to our species[5]—and hence to avail themselves of the benefits of home and hearth.

One of the most revealing studies of human nonverbal communication was performed using an animal with which humans rarely share their homes, at least not intentionally: the rat. In that study, students in an experimental psychology class were each given five of those creatures, a T-shaped maze, and a seemingly simple assignment.[6] One arm of the T was colored white, the other gray. Each rat's job was to learn to run to the gray side, at which time it would be rewarded with food. The students' job was to give each rat ten chances each day to learn that the gray side of the maze was the one that led to food and to objectively record each rat's learning progress, if any. But it was actually the students, not the rats, who were the guinea pigs in this experiment. The students were informed that through careful breeding it was possible to create strains of maze-genius and maze-dummy rats. Half the students were told that their rats were the Vasco da Gamas of maze explorers, while the other half were told that theirs had been bred to have no sense of direction at all. In reality, no such selective breeding had been performed, and the animals were effectively interchangeable, except perhaps to their mothers. The real point of the experiment was to compare the results obtained by the two distinct groups of *humans*, to see if their expectations would bias the results achieved by their rats.

The researchers found that the rats the students thought were brilliant performed significantly better than the rats believed to be on the dumb side. The researchers then asked each student to describe his or her behavior toward the rats, and an analysis showed differences in the manner in which students in each group related to the animals. For example, judging from their reports, those who believed their rats to be high achievers handled them more and were gentler, thereby communicating their attitude. Of course, that might have been intentional, and the cues we are interested in are those that are unintentional and difficult to control. Luckily, another pair of researchers shared that curiosity.[7] They essentially repeated the experiment but added an admonishment to the students that a key part of their task was to treat each rat as they would if they had no prior knowledge about its breeding. Differences in handling, they were warned, could skew the results and, by implication, their grade. Despite these caveats, the researchers also found superior performance among the rats whose handlers expected it. The students attempted to act impartially, but they couldn't. They unconsciously delivered cues, based on their expectations, and the rats responded.

It's easy to draw analogies with how unconsciously communicated expectations might also affect human performance, but are they accurate? One of the researchers in the rat study, Robert Rosenthal, decided to find out.[8] His plan was to again have his students conduct an experiment, but this time they would experiment on people, not rats. That, of course, involved altering the experiment to be better suited to human subjects. Rosenthal came up with this: he asked the student experimenters—who were themselves the true subjects of the experiment—to show their subjects photographs of people's faces and request that they rate each face on the degree of success or failure they felt it reflected. Rosenthal had pretested a large set of photos, and he gave his students only those photos that had been judged as neutral. But that's not what he told them. He said he was trying to duplicate an experiment that had already been performed, and he told half the experimenters that their stack of photos depicted faces that had been rated as successful, and the other half that theirs were rated as failures.

In order to make sure the student experimenters did not use any verbal language to communicate their expectations, Rosenthal gave them all a written script to follow and warned them not to deviate from it in any way or speak any other words. Their job was merely to present the photos to their subjects, read the instructions, and record their subjects' responses. One could hardly take stronger precautions to discourage experimenter bias. But would their nonverbal communication nevertheless flag their expectations? Would the human subjects respond to these cues just as the rats had done?

Not only, on average, did the students who expected their subjects to accord high success ratings to the photos obtain such ratings but, in addition, *every single student* who had been led to expect high ratings obtained higher ratings from their subjects than did *any* of those expecting low ratings. Somehow they were subliminally communicating their expectations. But how?

A year later, another set of researchers repeated Rosenthal's study, with a twist.[9] During the course of that study, they recorded the experimenters' instructions to their subjects. Then they conducted *another* experiment, in which they eliminated the human experimenters and instead communicated the instructions to the subjects using the tape recordings, thus getting rid of all cues other than those that could be transmitted through the sound of the voice. Again the results were biased, but only about half as much. So one important way the experimenters' expectations were communicated was through the inflection and tonal quality of their voices. But if that is just half the story, what's the other half? No one knows for sure. Over the years, many scientists have tried to find out by doing variants of the experiment, but though they confirmed the effect, none was ever able to specify any more precisely just what the other nonverbal signals were. Whatever they were, they were subtle and unconscious and probably varied considerably among the individuals.

The lesson learned has obvious applications in our personal and professional lives, with regard to our family, our friends, our employees, our employers and even the subjects being interviewed in a marketing focus group: whether or not we wish to, we communicate our expectations to others, and they often respond by fulfilling those expectations. You can probably think of expectations, whether stated or not, that you have regarding most people you interact with. And they have expectations of you. That's one of the gifts I received from my parents: to be treated like the Vasco da Gama rats, to be made to feel as if I could navigate my way to success in whatever I set out to do. It's not that my parents talked to me about their belief in me, but I somehow felt it, and it has always been a source of strength.

Rosenthal went on to study precisely that—what expectations mean for our children.[10] In one line of research he showed that teachers' expectations greatly affect their students' academic performance, even when the teachers try to treat them impartially. For example, he and a colleague asked schoolkids in eighteen classrooms to complete an IQ test. The teachers, but not the students, were given the results. The researchers told the teachers that the test would indicate which children had unusually high intellectual potential.[11] What the teachers didn't know was that the kids named as gifted did not really score higher than average on the IQ test—they actually had average scores. Shortly afterward, the teachers rated those not labeled gifted as less curious and less interested than the gifted students—and the students' subsequent grades reflected that.

But what is really shocking—and sobering—is the result of another IQ test, given eight months later. When you administer an IQ test a second time, you expect that each child's score will vary some. In general, about half of the children's scores should go up and half down, as a result of changes in the individual's intellectual development in relation to his peers or simply of random variation. When Rosenthal administered the second test, he indeed found that about half the kids labeled "normal" showed a gain in IQ. But among those who'd been singled out as brilliant, he obtained a different result: about 80 percent had an increase of at least 10 points. What's more, about 20 percent of the "gifted" group gained 30 *or more* IQ points, while only 5 percent of the other children gained that many. Labeling children as gifted had proved to be a powerful self-fulfilling prophecy. Wisely, Rosenthal hadn't falsely labeled any kids as being below average. The sad thing is that such labeling does happen, and it is reasonable to assume that the self-fulfilling prophecy also works the other way: that branding a child a poor learner will contribute to making the child exactly that.

HUMANS COMMUNICATE VIA a rich linguistic system whose development was a defining moment in the evolution of our species, an innovation that remade the character of human society. It's an ability that seems to be unique.[12] In other animals, communication is limited to simple messages, such as identifying themselves or issuing warnings; there is little complex structure. Had Hans, for example, been required to answer in complete sentences, the gig would have been up. Even among primates, no species naturally acquires more than a few signals or combines them in anything but a rudimentary manner. The average human, on the other hand, is familiar with tens of thousands of words and can string them together according to complex rules, with hardly any conscious effort, and without formal instruction.

Scientists don't understand yet how language evolved. Many believe that earlier human species, such as *Homo habilis* and *Homo erectus*, possessed primitive language-like or symbolic communication systems. But the development of language as we know it probably didn't occur until modern humans came into the picture. Some say language originated one hundred thousand years ago, some later; but the need for sophisticated communication certainly became more urgent once "behaviorally modern" social humans developed, fifty thousand years ago. We've seen how important social interactions are to our species, and social interactions go hand in hand with the need to communicate. That need is so powerful that even deaf babies develop language-like gesture systems and, if taught sign language, will babble using their hands.[13]

Why did humans develop *nonverbal* communication? One of the first to seriously study the issue was an English fellow, spurred by his interest in the theory of evolution. By his own assessment, he was no genius. He had "no great quickness of apprehension or wit" or "power to follow a long and purely abstract train of thought."[14] On the many occasions when I share those feelings, I find it encouraging to review those words because that Englishman did okay for himself—his name was Charles Darwin. Thirteen years after publishing *The Origin of Species*, Darwin published another radical book, this one called *The Expression of the Emotions in Man and Animals*. In it, Darwin argued that emotions—and the ways they are expressed—provide a survival advantage and that they are not unique to humans but occur in many species. Clues to the role of emotions therefore can be found by examining the similarities and differences of nonverbal emotional expression across various species.

If Darwin didn't consider himself brilliant, he did believe he possessed one great intellectual strength: his powers of careful and detailed observation. And, indeed, though he was not the first to suggest the universality of emotion and its expression,[15] he spent several decades meticulously studying the physical manifestations of mental states. He watched his countrymen, and he observed foreigners, too, looking for cultural similarities and differences. He even studied domestic animals and those in the London Zoo. In his book, Darwin categorized numerous human expressions and gestures of emotion and offered hypotheses about their origin. He noted how lower animals, too, display intent and emotion through facial expression, posture, and gesture. Darwin speculated that much of our nonverbal communication might be an innate and automatic holdover from earlier phases of our evolution. For example, we can bite affectionately, as do other animals. We also sneer like other primates by flaring our nostrils and baring our teeth.

The smile is another expression we share with lower primates. Suppose you're sitting in some public place and notice someone looking at you. If you return the gaze and the other person smiles, you'll probably feel good about the exchange. But if the other person continues to stare without any hint of a smile, you'll probably feel uncomfortable. Where do these instinctual responses come from? In trading the currency of smiles, we are sharing a feeling experienced by many of our primate cousins. In the societies of nonhuman primates, a direct stare is an aggressive signal. It often precedes an attack—and, therefore, can precipitate one. As a result, if, say, a submissive monkey wants to check out a dominant one, it will bare its teeth as a peace signal. In monkey talk, bared teeth means *Pardon my stare. True, I'm looking, but I don't plan to attack, so PLEASE don't attack me first.* In chimpanzees, the smile can also go the other way—a dominant individual may smile at a submissive one, saying, analogously, *Don't worry, I'm not going to attack you.* So when you pass a stranger in the corridor and that person flashes a brief smile, you're experiencing an exchange with roots deep in our primate heritage. There is even evidence that with chimps, as with humans, when a smile is exchanged, it can be a sign of friendship.[16]

You might think a smile is a rather shoddy barometer of true feelings because, after all, anyone can fake one. It's true that we can consciously decide to exhibit a smile, or any other expression, by using the muscles in our faces in ways we are practiced at doing. Think about what you do when trying to make a good impression at a cocktail party, even though you are miserable about being there. But our facial expressions are also governed subliminally, by muscles over which we have no conscious control. So our real expressions cannot be faked. Sure, anyone can create a posed smile by contracting the zygomatic major muscles, which pull the corners of the mouth up toward the cheekbones. But a genuine smile involves contraction of an additional pair of actors, the orbicularis oculi muscles, which pull the skin surrounding the eye toward the eyeball, causing an effect that looks like crow's-feet but can be very subtle. That was first pointed out by the nineteenth-century French neurologist Duchenne de Boulogne, who was an influence on Darwin and collected a large number of photographs of people smiling. There are two distinct neural pathways for these smile muscles: a voluntary one for the zygomatic major, and an involuntary one for the orbicularis oculi.[17] So a smile-seeking photographer might implore us to say "cheese," which nudges our mouths into the smile position, but unless you're the kind who actually rejoices when asked to speak the word "cheese," the smile won't look genuine.

In viewing photographs of the two types of smiles given to him by Duchenne de Boulogne, Darwin remarked that though people could sense the difference, he found it very difficult to consciously pinpoint what that difference was, remarking, "It has often struck me as a curious fact that so many shades of expression are instantly recognized without any conscious process of analysis on our part."[18] No one paid much attention to such issues until recently, but modern studies have shown that, as Darwin observed, even people untrained in smile analysis have a good enough gut feeling to distinguish real smiles from phony ones when they can observe the same individual creating both.[19] Smiles we intuitively recognize as fake are one reason used-car salesmen, politicians, and others who smile when they don't mean it are often described as looking sleazy. Actors in the Method dramatic tradition try to get around this by training themselves to actually *feel* the emotion they are supposed to manifest, and many successful politicians are said to be talented at conjuring up genuine feelings of friendliness and empathy when talking to a roomful of strangers.

Darwin realized that if our expressions evolved along with our species, then many of the ways we express the basic emotions—happiness, fear, anger, disgust, sadness, and surprise—should be shared by humans from different cultures. And so in 1867 he arranged for a questionnaire to be circulated on five continents among indigenous people, some of whom had had little contact with Europeans.[20] The survey asked questions like "Is astonishment expressed by the eyes and mouth being opened wide and by the eyebrows being raised?" On the basis of the answers he received, Darwin concluded that "the same state of mind is expressed throughout the world with remarkable uniformity." Darwin's study was biased in that his questionnaire asked such leading questions, and like so many other early contributions to psychology, his were overridden—in this case, by the idea that facial expressions are learned behavior, acquired during infancy, as a baby mimics its caretakers and others in the immediate environment. However, in recent years a substantial body of cross-cultural research has offered evidence that Darwin was right after all.[21]

In the first of a series of famous studies, the psychologist Paul Ekman showed photos of people's expressions to subjects in Chile, Argentina, Brazil, the United States, and Japan.[22] Within a few years, he and a colleague had shown such pictures to people in twenty-one countries. Their findings were the same as Darwin's, demonstrating that people across a diversity of cultures had a similar understanding of the emotional meaning of a range of facial expressions. Still, such studies alone don't necessarily mean that those expressions are innate, or even truly universal. Adherents of the "learned expressions" theory argued that Ekman's results conveyed no deeper truth than the fact that people in the societies studied had all watched *Gilligan's Island*, or other movies and television shows. So Ekman traveled to New Guinea, where an isolated Neolithic culture had recently been discovered.[23] The natives there had no written language and were still using stone implements. Very few had seen a photograph, much less film or television. Ekman recruited hundreds of these subjects, who had never been previously exposed to outside cultures, and, through a translator, presented them with photographs of American faces illustrating the basic emotions.

The primitive foragers proved to be as nimble as those in the twenty-one literate countries at recognizing happiness, fear, anger, disgust, sadness, and surprise in the face of an emoting American. The scientists also reversed the research design. They photographed the New Guineans as they acted out how they would respond if they saw that their child had died, or found a dead pig that had been lying there for a long time, and so on. The expressions Ekman recorded were unequivocally recognizable.[24]

This universal capability to create and recognize facial expressions starts at or near birth. Young infants have been observed making nearly all the same facial muscle movements used by adults to signify emotion. Infants can also discriminate among the facial expressions of others and, like adults, modify their behavior based on what they see.[25] It is doubtful that these are learned behaviors. In fact, congenitally blind young children, who have never seen a frown or a smile, express a range of spontaneous facial emotions that are almost identical to those of the sighted.[26] Our catalog of facial expressions seems to be standard equipment—it comes with the basic model. And because it is a largely innate, unconscious part of our being, communicating our feelings comes naturally, while hiding them requires great effort.

In humans, body language and nonverbal communication are not limited to simple gestures and expressions. We have a highly complex system of nonverbal language, and we routinely participate in elaborate nonverbal exchanges, even when we are not consciously aware of doing so. For example, in the case of casual contact with the opposite sex, I'd have been willing to bet a year's pass to a Manhattan cinema that if a male pollster type approached a guy's date while they were standing in line to buy a ticket at said theater, few of the fellows approached would be so insecure that they'd consciously feel threatened by the pollster. And yet, consider this experiment, conducted over two mild autumn weekend evenings in an "upper-middle-class" neighborhood in Manhattan.[27] The subjects approached were all couples, yes, waiting in line to buy tickets to a movie.

The experimenters worked in teams of two. One team member discreetly observed from a short distance while the other approached the female of the couple and asked if she would be willing to answer a few survey questions. Some of the women were asked neutral questions, such as "What is your favorite city and why?" Others were asked personal questions, such as "What is your most embarrassing childhood memory?" The researchers expected these more personal questions to be more threatening to the boyfriend, more invasive to his sense of intimate space. How did the boyfriends respond?

Unlike the male hamadryas baboon, who starts a fight when he sees another male sitting too close to a female in his group,[28] the boyfriends didn't do anything overtly aggressive; but they did display certain nonverbal cues. The scientists found that when the interviewer was nonthreatening—either a male who asked impersonal questions or a female—the man in the couple tended to just hang out. But when the interviewer was a male asking personal questions, the boyfriend would subtly inject himself into the powwow, flashing what are called "tie-signs," nonverbal cues meant to convey a connection with the woman. These male smoke signals included orienting himself toward his partner and looking into her eyes as she interacted with the other man. It is doubtful that the men consciously felt the need to defend their relationship from the polite interviewer, but even though the tie-signs fell short of a baboon-like fist in the face, they *were* an indication of the men's inner primate pushing its way to the fore.

Another, more complex mode of nonverbal "conversation" has to do with dominance. Nonhuman primates actually maintain fine distinctions along that dimension; they have precise dominance hierarchies, something like the ranks in the army. Without the pretty insignias, though, one might wonder how a chimp knows whom to salute. Dominant primates pound their chests and use voice and other signals to indicate their high rank. One way a chimp can signal its acknowledgment that it is lower in rank, as I said, is to smile. Another is to turn around, bend over, and moon its superior. Yes, that particular behavior, though still practiced by humans, seems to have changed its meaning somewhere along the road of evolution.

In modern human society, there are two kinds of dominance.[29] One is physical dominance, based on aggression or the threat of aggression. Physical dominance in humans is similar to dominance in nonhuman primates, though we signal it differently: it is the rare chimpanzee who announces his dominance, as some humans do, by carrying around a switchblade or a .357 Magnum, or by wearing a tight muscle shirt. Humans, however, can also achieve another kind of dominance: social dominance.

Social dominance is based on admiration rather than fear and is acquired through social accomplishment rather than physical prowess. Signals of social dominance—like wearing a Rolex or driving a Lamborghini— can be just as clear and overt as the chest-pounding a male baboon might display. But they can also be subtle, such as declining any conspicuous display of affluence by showing up unexpectedly in torn, faded nondesigner jeans and an old Gap T-shirt, or by refusing to wear anything with a logo on it. (Take that, you silly Prada and Louis Vuitton bag toters!)

Humans have many ways indeed of signaling "I'm the general and you're not" without mooning or wearing a shoulder patch with stars on it. As in other primate societies, gaze direction and stare are important signals of dominance in human society.[30] For example, if a child looks away while the parent is scolding, the adult might say, "Look at me while I'm talking to you!" I've said that myself on occasion, though since you don't hear with your eyes, the demand seems to serve no functional purpose. The interaction is really about the parent's demand for respect—or in primate language, dominance. What the adult is really saying is *Stand at attention. Salute. I am dominant, so when I speak, you must look at me!*

We may not realize it, but we don't just play the gaze game with our children; we play it with our friends and acquaintances, our superiors and subordinates, when we speak to a queen or a president, to a gardener or a store clerk, or to strangers we meet at a party. We automatically adjust the amount of time we spend looking into another's eyes as a function of our relative social position, and we typically do it without being aware that we are doing it.[31] That might sound counterintuitive, because some people like to look everyone in the eye, while others tend to always look elsewhere, whether they are speaking to a CEO or the guy dropping a pack of chicken thighs into their bag at the local grocery store. So how can gazing behavior be related to social dominance?

It is not your overall tendency to look at someone that is telling but the way in which you adjust your behavior when you switch between the roles of listener and speaker. Psychologists have been able to characterize that behavior with a single quantitative measure, and the data they produce using that measure is striking.

Here is how it works: take the percentage of time you spend looking into someone's eyes while you are speaking and divide it by the percentage spent looking at that same person's eyes while you are listening. For example, if, no matter which of you is talking, you spend the same amount of time looking away, your ratio would be 1.0. But if you tend to look away more often while you are speaking than when you are listening, your ratio will be less than 1.0. If you tend to look away less often when you are speaking than when you are listening, you have a ratio higher than 1.0. That quotient, psychologists discovered, is a revealing statistic. It is called the "visual dominance ratio," and it reflects your position on the social dominance hierarchy relative to your conversational partner. A visual dominance ratio near 1.0, or larger, is characteristic of people with relatively high social dominance. A visual dominance ratio less than 1.0 is indicative of being lower on the dominance hierarchy. In other words, if your visual dominance ratio is around 1.0 or higher, you are probably the boss; if it is around 0.6, you are probably the bossed.

The unconscious mind provides us with many wonderful services and performs many awesome feats, but I can't help being impressed by this one. What is so striking about the data is not just that we subliminally adjust our gazing behavior to match our place on the hierarchy but that we do it so consistently, and with numerical precision. Here is a sample of the data: when speaking to each other, ROTC officers exhibited ratios of 1.06, while ROTC cadets speaking to officers had ratios of 0.61;[32] undergraduates in an introductory psychology course scored 0.92 when talking to a person they believed to be a high school senior who did not plan to go to college but 0.59 when talking to a person they believed to be a college chemistry honor student accepted into a prestigious medical school;[33] expert men speaking to women about a subject in their own field scored 0.98, while men talking to expert women about *the women's* field, 0.61; expert women speaking to nonexpert men scored 1.04, and nonexpert women speaking to expert men scored 0.54.[34] These studies were all performed on Americans. The numbers probably vary among cultures, but the phenomenon probably doesn't.

Whatever your culture, since people unconsciously detect these signals, it stands to reason that one can also adjust the impression one makes by *consciously* looking at or away from a conversational partner. For example, when applying for a job, talking to your boss, or negotiating a business deal, it might be advantageous to signal a certain level of submission—but how much would depend on the circumstances. In a job interview, if the job requires great leadership ability, a display of too much submissiveness would be a bad strategy. But if the interviewer seemed very insecure, a pleasing display of just the right amount of submissiveness could be reassuring and incline that person in the applicant's favor. A highly successful Hollywood agent once mentioned to me that he made a point to negotiate only over the telephone so as to avoid being influenced—or inadvertently revealing anything—through eye contact with the opposite party.

My father learned both the power and the danger of a simple look when he was imprisoned in the Buchenwald concentration camp. Weighing under a hundred pounds, he was then little more than a walking corpse. In the camp, if you were not being spoken to, locking eyes with one of your captors could spur rage. Lower forms were not supposed to make uninvited eye contact with the master race. Sometimes when I think in terms of the dichotomy between humans and "lower primates," I remember my father's experience, and the thin margin of extra frontal lobe that distinguishes civilized human from brute animal. If the purpose of that extra brain matter is to elevate us, it sometimes fails. But my father also told me that with certain guards, the right kind of eye contact could bring a word, a conversation, even a minor kindness. He said that when that happened it was because the eye contact raised him to the status of being human. But I think that by eliciting a human response from a guard, what his eye contact really did was raise the level of humanity of his *captor*.

TODAY MOST HUMANS live in large, crowded cities. In many cities, a single neighborhood could encompass the entire world population at the time of the great human social transformation. We walk down sidewalks and through crowded malls and buildings with hardly a word, and no traffic signs, and yet we don't bump into others or get into fights about who is going to step through the swinging door first. We hold conversations with people we don't know or hardly know or wouldn't want to know and automatically stand at a distance that is acceptable to both of us. That distance varies from culture to culture and from individual to individual, and yet, without a word, and usually without giving it any thought, we adjust to a distance of mutual comfort. (Or most of us do, anyway. We can all think of exceptions!) When we talk, we automatically sense when it is time to leave a pause for others to jump in. As we're about to yield the floor, we typically lower our volume, stretch out our last word, cease gesturing, and look at the other person.[35] Along with ToM, these skills aided our survival as a species, and it is still these skills that allow us to maneuver through the complex social world of the human.

Nonverbal communication forms a social language that is in many ways richer and more fundamental than our words. Our nonverbal sensors are so powerful that just the *movements* associated with body language—that is, minus the actual bodies—are enough to engender within us the ability to accurately perceive emotion. For example, researchers made video clips of participants who had about a dozen small lights or illuminated patches attached at certain key positions on their bodies, as in the picture on page 124.[36] The videos were shot in light so dim that only the patches were visible. In these studies, when the participants stood still, the patches gave the impression of a meaningless collection of points. But when the partici-

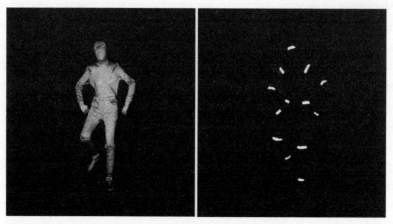

Courtesy of A. P. Atkinson. From A. P. Atkinson et al., "Emotion Perception from Dynamic and Static Body Expressions in Point-Light and Full-Light Displays," Perception 33, 724. Copyright 2004.

pants stirred, observers were able to decode a surprising amount of information from the moving lights. They were able to judge the participants' sex, and even the identity of people with whom they were familiar, from their gait alone. And when the participants were actors, mimes, or dancers asked to move in a way that expressed the basic emotions, the observers had no trouble detecting the emotion portrayed.

By the time children reach school age, there are some with full social calendars, while others spend their days shooting spitballs at the ceiling. One of the major factors in social success, even at an early age, is a child's sense of nonverbal cues. For example, in a study of sixty kindergartners, the children were asked to identify which of their classmates they'd prefer to sit with at storytime, play a game with, or work with on a painting. The same children were judged on their ability to name the emotions exhibited in twelve photographs of adults and children with differing facial expressions. The two measures proved to be related. That is, the researchers found a strong correlation between a child's popularity and his or her ability to read others.[37]

In adults, nonverbal ability bestows advantages in both personal and business life and plays a significant role in the perception of a person's warmth,[38] credibility,[39] and persuasive power.[40] Your uncle Stu might be the kindest man in the world, but if he tends to speak at length on subjects

like the moss he observed in Costa Rica and never notices the moss beginning to grow on his listeners' faces, he's probably not the most popular guy
to hang out with. Our sensitivity to other people's signals regarding their
thoughts and moods helps make social situations proceed smoothly, with
a minimum of conflict. From early childhood on, those who are good at
giving and receiving signals have an easier time forming social structures
and achieving their goals in social situations.

In the early 1950s, many linguists, anthropologists, and psychiatrists
attempted to classify nonverbal cues in much the same way we classify
verbal language. One anthropologist even developed a transcription system, providing a symbol for virtually every possible human movement
so that gestures could be written down like speech.[41] Today social psychologists sometimes categorize our nonverbal communication into three
basic types. One category concerns body movements: facial expression,
gestures, posture, eye movements. Another is called paralanguage, which
includes the quality and pitch of your voice, the number and duration of
pauses, and nonverbal sounds such as clearing one's throat or saying "uh."
And finally, there is proxemics, the use of personal space.

Many popular books claim to provide guides to the interpretation of
these factors and advise how you can employ them to your benefit. They
tell you that tensely folded arms mean you are closed to what someone is
telling you, while if you like what you hear, you'll probably adopt an open
posture, maybe even lean forward a little. They'll say that moving your
shoulders forward signifies disgust, despair, or fear, and that maintaining
a large interpersonal distance while you speak signals low social stature.[42]
There haven't been a lot of studies on the efficacy of the hundred and one
ways these books tell you to act, but it's probably true that assuming those
different postures can have at least a subtle effect on how people perceive
you, and that understanding what nonverbal cues mean can bring to your
consciousness clues about people that otherwise only your unconscious
might pick up. Yet even without a conscious understanding, you are a
storehouse of information about nonverbal cues. The next time you view a
film in a language you don't know, try blocking out the subtitles. You'll be
surprised by how much of the story you can comprehend without a single
word to communicate what is happening.

CHAPTER 6

Judging People by Their Covers

There is a road from the eye to the heart that does not go through the intellect. —G. K. CHESTERTON

I F YOU ARE a man, being compared to a cowbird probably doesn't sound like a compliment, and it probably isn't. The male cowbird, you see, is a real slacker: he doesn't stake out a territory, take care of the baby cowbirds, or bring home a paycheck (which scientists call "resources"). In cowbird society, as one research paper asserted, "females gain few direct benefits from males."[1] Apparently all a male cowbird is good for—or after—is one thing. But the one thing a male cowbird does have to offer is very desirable, so female cowbirds seek out male cowbirds, at least in mating season.

To an amorous female cowbird, the equivalent of a chiseled face or great pecs is the male cowbird's song. Since it is hard to smile when you have a beak, when she hears a song she finds attractive, a female will often signal interest with her own seductive vocalization, called "chatter." And, like an eager teenage girl of our own species, if a female cowbird is led to believe that other females find a certain male attractive, she will find that male attractive, too. In fact, suppose that prior to mating season a girl cowbird repeatedly hears recordings of a boy's voice followed by the admiring chatter of other nubile females. Will that girl cowbird exercise the independent judgment our sober parents all urge? No. When mating season comes, upon hearing that male's song, she will automatically respond with displays inviting him to mate with her. Why do I say her response is *automatic*, and not part of some thoughtful strategy aimed at wooing the fellow with whom she'd like to share birdseed in her golden years? Because upon hearing the male's song, the female will commence her come-on behavior even if that song is coming not from a live bird but from a stereo speaker.[2]

We humans may share many behaviors with lower animals, but flirting with a stereo speaker is surely not one of them. Or is it? We've seen that people unintentionally *express* their thoughts and feelings even when they might prefer to keep them secret, but do we also *react* automatically to nonverbal social cues? Do we respond, like the smitten cowbird, even in situations in which our logical and conscious minds would deem the reaction inappropriate or undesirable?

A few years ago, a Stanford communications professor named Clifford Nass sat a couple hundred computer-savvy students in front of computers that spoke to them in prerecorded voices.[3] The purpose of the exercise, the students were told, was to prepare for a test with the assistance of a computerized tutoring session. The topics taught ranged from "mass media" to "love and relationships." After completing the tutoring and the test, the students received an evaluation of their performance, delivered either by the same computer that taught them or by another computer. Finally, the students themselves completed the equivalent of a course evaluation form, in which they rated both the course and their computer tutor.

Nass was not really interested in conducting a computer course on mass media or love and relationships. These earnest students were Nass's cowbirds, and in a series of experiments he and some colleagues studied them carefully, gathering data on the way they responded to the lifeless electronic computer, gauging whether they would react to a machine's voice as if the machine had human feelings, motivations, or even a human gender. It would be absurd, of course, to expect the students to say "Excuse me" if they bumped into the monitor. That would be a conscious reaction, and in their conscious ruminations, these students certainly realized that the machine was not a person. But Nass was interested in another level of their behavior, behavior the students did not purposely engage in, social behavior he describes as "automatic and unconscious."

In one of the experiments, the researchers arranged for half their subjects to be tutored and evaluated by computers with male voices, and half by computers with female voices. Other than that, there was no difference in the sessions—the male computers presented the same information in the same sequence as the females, and the male and female computers delivered identical assessments of the students' performance. As we'll see in Chapter 7, if the tutors had been real people, the students' evaluations of their teachers would probably reflect certain gender stereotypes. For example, consider the stereotype that women know more about relationship issues than men. Ask a woman what bonds couples together, and you might expect her to respond, "Open communication and shared intimacy." Ask a guy, and you might expect him to say, "Huh?" Studies show that as a result of this stereotype, even when a woman and a man have equal ability in that area, the woman is often perceived as more competent. Nash sought to discover whether the students would apply those same gender stereotypes to the computers.

They did. Those who had female-voiced tutors for the love-and-relationships material rated their teachers as having more sophisticated knowledge of the subject than did those who had male-voiced tutors, even though the two computers had given identical lessons. But the "male" and "female" computers got equal ratings when the topic was a gender-neutral one, like mass media. Another unfortunate gender stereotype suggests that forcefulness is desirable in men, but unseemly in women. And sure enough, students who heard a forceful male-voiced computer tutor rated it as being significantly more likable than those who heard a forceful female-voiced tutor, even though, again, both the male and the female voices had uttered the same words. Apparently, even when coming from a computer, an assertive personality in a female is more likely to come off as overbearing or bossy than the same personality in a male.

The researchers also investigated whether people will apply the social norms of politeness to computers. For example, when put in a position where they have to criticize someone face-to-face, people often hesitate or sugarcoat their true opinion. Suppose I ask my students, "Did you like my discussion of the stochastic nature of the foraging habits of wildebeests?" Judging from my experience, I'll get a bunch of nods and a few audible murmurs. But no one will be honest enough to say, "Wildebeests? I didn't hear a word of your boring lecture. But the monotonic drone of your voice did provide a soothing background as I surfed the web on my laptop." Not even those who sat in the front row and clearly *were* surfing the web on their laptops would be that blunt. Instead, students save that kind of critique for their anonymous course-evaluation forms. But what if the one asking for the input was a talking computer? Would the students have the same inhibition against delivering a harsh judgment "face-to-face" to a machine? Nass and his colleagues asked half the students to enter their course evaluation on the same computer that had tutored them, and the other half to enter it on a different machine, a machine that had a different voice. Certainly the students would not *consciously* sugarcoat their words to avoid hurting the machine's feelings—but as you probably guessed, they did indeed hesitate to criticize the computer to its "face." That is, they rated the computer teacher as far more likable and competent when offering their judgment directly to that computer than when a different computer was gathering the input.[4]

Having social relations with a prerecorded voice is not a trait you'd want to mention in a job application. But, like the cowbirds, these students did treat it as if it were a member of their species, even though there was no actual person attached. Hard to believe? It was for the actual subjects. When, after some of the studies had been concluded, the researchers informed the students of the experiment's true purpose, they all insisted with great confidence that they would never apply social norms to a computer.[5] The research shows they were wrong. While our conscious minds are busy thinking about the meaning of the words people utter, our unconscious is busy judging the speaker by other criteria, and the human voice connects with a receiver deep within the human brain, whether that voice emanates from a human being or not.

PEOPLE SPEND A lot of time talking and thinking about how members of the opposite sex look but very little time paying attention to how they sound. To our unconscious minds, however, voice is very important. Our genus, *Homo*, has been evolving for a couple million years. Brain evolution happens over many thousands or millions of years, but we've lived in civilized society for less than 1 percent of that time. That means that though we may pack our heads full of twenty-first-century knowledge, the organ inside our skull is still a Stone Age brain. We think of ourselves as a civilized species, but our brains are designed to meet the challenges of an earlier era. Among birds and many other animals, voice seems to play a great role in meeting one of those demands—reproduction—and it seems to be similarly important in humans. As we'll see, we pick up a great many sophisticated signals from the tone and quality of a person's voice and from the cadence, but perhaps the most important way we relate to voice is directly analogous to the reaction of the cowbirds, for in humans, too, females are attracted to males by certain aspects of their "call."

Women may disagree on whether they prefer dark-skinned men with beards, clean-shaven blonds, or men of any appearance sitting in the driver's seat of a Ferrari—but when asked to rate men they can hear but not see, women miraculously tend to agree: men with deeper voices are rated as more attractive.[6] Asked to guess the physical characteristics of the men whose voices they hear in such experiments, women tend to associate low voices with men who are tall, muscular, and hairy-chested—traits commonly considered sexy.

As for men, a group of scientists recently discovered that men unconsciously adjust the pitch of their voices higher or lower in accordance with their assessment of where they stand on the dominance hierarchy with respect to possible competitors. In that experiment, which involved a couple hundred men in their twenties, each man was told he'd be competing with another man for a lunch date with an attractive woman in a nearby room.[7] The competitor, it was explained, was a man in a third room.

Each contestant communicated with the woman via a digital video feed, but when he communicated with the other man, he could only hear him, and not see him. In reality, both the competitor and the woman were confederates of the researchers, and they followed a fixed script. Each man was asked to discuss—with both the woman and his competitor—the reasons he might be respected or admired by other men. Then, after pouring his heart out about his prowess on the basketball court, his potential for winning the Nobel Prize, or his recipe for asparagus quiche, the session was ended, and he was asked to answer some questions assessing himself, his competitor, and the woman. The subjects were then dismissed. There would, alas, be no winners anointed.

The researchers analyzed a tape recording of the male contestants' voices and scrutinized each man's answers to the questionnaire. One issue the questionnaires probed was the contestant's appraisal of his level of physical dominance as compared to that of his competitor. And the researchers found that when the participants believed they were physically dominant—that is, more powerful and aggressive—they lowered the pitch of their voices, and when they believed they were less dominant, they raised the pitch, all apparently without realizing what they were doing.

From the point of view of evolution, what's interesting about all this is that a woman's attraction to men with low voices is most pronounced when she is in the fertile phase of her ovulatory cycle.[8] What's more, not only do women's voice preferences vary with the phases of their reproductive cycle, so do their own voices—in their pitch and smoothness—and research indicates that the greater a woman's risk of conception, the sexier men find her voice.[9] As a result, both women and men are especially attracted to each other's voices during a woman's fertile period. The obvious conclusion is that our voices act as subliminal advertisements for our sexuality. During a woman's fertile phase, those ads flash brightly on both sides, tempting us to click the "Buy" button when we are most likely to obtain not only a mate but, for no extra (upfront) cost, also a child.

But there is still something to be explained. Why is it a deep voice, in particular, that attracts women? Why not a high, squeaky voice or one in mid-range? Was it just nature's random choice, or does a deep voice correlate with male virility? We've seen that—in a woman's eyes—a deep voice is considered indicative of men who are taller, hairier, and more muscular. The truth is, there is little or no correlation between a deep voice and any of those traits.[10] However, studies show that what *does* correlate with a low-pitched voice is testosterone level. Men with lower voices tend to have higher levels of that male hormone.[11]

It is difficult to test whether nature's plan works—whether men with more testosterone really produce more children—because modern birth control methods prevent us from judging a man's reproductive potential by the number of children he fathers. Still, a Harvard anthropologist and some colleagues found a way. In 2007 they traveled to Africa to study the voices and family size of the Hadza people, a monogamous hunter-gatherer population of about one thousand in the savannah woodlands of Tanzania, where men are still men, tubers are plentiful, and no one uses birth control. In those savannahs, the baritones indeed beat the tenors. The researchers found that while the pitch of *women's* voices was not a predictor of their reproductive success, *men* with lower-pitched voices on average fathered more children.[12] A woman's sexual attraction to a deep male voice does seem to have a neat evolutionary explanation. So if you're a woman and you want a large family, follow your instincts and go for the Morgan Freeman type.

YOU'RE CERTAINLY MORE likely to satisfy an employee by saying, "I value you and will do everything I can to increase your salary" than by explaining, "I have to keep my budget down, and one of the easiest ways is to pay you as little as possible." But you can also communicate either sentiment, though not the precise meaning, simply by the *way* you say it. That's why some people can recount things like "He enjoyed chewing on plump grapes while speeding down a mountain in a monogrammed bobsled" and still give the impression of being profound, while others can say, "The large-scale geometry of the universe is determined by the density of the matter within it" and sound like they are whining. The pitch, timbre, volume, and cadence of your voice, the speed with which you speak, and even the way you *modulate* pitch and volume, are all hugely influential factors in how convincing you are, and how people judge your state of mind and your character.

Scientists have developed fascinating computer tools that allow them to determine the influence of voice alone, devoid of content. In one method they electronically scramble just enough syllables that the words cannot be deciphered. In another, they excise just the highest frequencies, which wreaks havoc with our ability to accurately identify consonants. Either way, the meaning is unintelligible while the feel of speech remains. Studies show that when people listen to such "content-free" speech, they still perceive the same impressions of the speaker and the same emotional content as do subjects who hear the unaltered speech.[13] Why? Because as we are decoding the meaning of the utterances we call language, our minds are, in parallel, analyzing, judging, and being affected by qualities of voice that have nothing to do with words.

In one experiment scientists created recordings of a couple dozen speakers answering the same two questions, one political, one personal: "What is your opinion of college admissions designed to favor minority groups?" and "What would you do if you suddenly won or inherited a great sum of money?"[14] Then they created four additional versions of each answer by electronically raising and lowering the speakers' pitch by 20 percent, and by quickening and slowing their speech rate by 30 percent. The resulting speech still sounded natural, and its acoustic properties remained within the normal range. But would the alterations affect listeners' perceptions?

The researchers recruited dozens of volunteers to judge the speech samples. The judges each heard and rated just one version of each speaker's voice, randomly chosen from among the original and the altered recordings. Since the content of the speakers' answers didn't vary among the different versions but the vocal qualities did, differences in the listeners' assessments would be due to the influence of those vocal qualities and not the content of the speech. The result: speakers with higher-pitched voices were judged to be less truthful, less emphatic, less potent, and more nervous than speakers with lower-pitched voices. Also, slower-talking speakers were judged to be less truthful, less persuasive, and more passive than people who spoke more quickly. "Fast-talking" may be a cliché description of a sleazy salesman, but chances are, a little speedup will make you sound smarter and more convincing. And if two speakers utter exactly the same words but one speaks a little faster and louder and with fewer pauses and greater variation in volume, that speaker will be judged to be more energetic, knowledgeable, and intelligent. Expressive speech, with modulation in pitch and volume and with a minimum of noticeable pauses, boosts credibility and enhances the impression of intelligence. Other studies show that, just as people signal the basic emotions through facial expressions, we also do it through voice. For example listeners instinctively detect that when we lower the usual pitch of our voice, we are sad and that when we raise it, we are angry or fearful.[15]

If voice makes such a huge impression, the key question becomes, To what extent can someone consciously alter their voice? Consider the case of Margaret Hilda Roberts, who in 1959 was elected as a Conservative member of British Parliament for North London. She had higher ambitions, but to those in her inner circle, her voice was an issue.[16] "She had a schoolmarmish, very slightly bossy, slightly hectoring voice," recalled Tim Bell, the mastermind of her party's publicity campaigns. Her own publicity adviser, Gordon Reese, was more graphic. Her high notes, he said, were "dangerous to passing sparrows." Proving that though her politics were fixed, her voice was pliable, Margaret Hilda Roberts took her confidants' advice, lowered the pitch, and increased her social dominance. There is no way to measure exactly how much difference the change made, but she did pretty well for herself. After the Conservatives were defeated in 1974, Margaret Thatcher—she had married the wealthy businessman Denis Thatcher in 1951—became the party's leader and, eventually, prime minister.

WHEN I WAS in high school, the few times I gathered the courage to approach a girl, the experience felt like I was administering a multiple-choice test and she kept answering, "None of the above." I had more or less resigned myself to the fact that a boy who spent his free time reading books on non-Euclidean geometry was not likely to be voted "big man on campus." Then one day when I was in the library looking for a math book, I took a wrong turn and stumbled upon a work whose title went something like *How to Get a Date*. I hadn't realized people wrote instructional books on subjects like *that*. Questions raced through my mind: Didn't the mere fact that I was interested in such a book mean it would never fulfill the promise of its title? Could a boy who'd rather talk about curved space-time than touchdown passes ever score himself? Was there really a bag of tricks?

The book emphasized that if a girl doesn't know you very well—and that applied to every girl in my high school—you should not expect her to agree to a date, and you shouldn't take the rejection personally. Instead, you should ignore the possibly enormous number of girls who turn you down and keep asking, because, even if the odds are low, the laws of mathematics say eventually your number will come up. Since mathematical laws are my kinds of laws, and I've always believed that persistence is a good life philosophy, I took the advice. I can't say the results were statistically significant, but decades later, I was shocked to find that a group of French researchers essentially repeated the exercise the book had suggested. And they did it in a controlled scientific manner, achieving results that *were* statistically significant. Furthermore, to my surprise, they revealed a way I could have improved my chance of success.[17]

French culture is known for many great attributes, some of which probably have nothing to do with food, wine, and romance. But regarding the latter, the French are thought to especially excel, and in the experiment in question, they literally made a science of it. The scene was a particularly sunny June day in a pedestrian zone in the city of Vannes, a medium-sized town on the Atlantic coast of Brittany, in the west of France. Over the course of that day, three young and handsome French men randomly approached 240 young women they spotted walking alone and propositioned each and every one of them. To each, they would utter exactly the same words: "Hello. My name's Antoine. I just want to say that I think you're really pretty. I have to go to work this afternoon but I wonder if you would give me your phone number. I'll phone you later and we can have a drink together someplace." If the woman refused, they'd say, "Too bad. It's not my day. Have a nice afternoon." And then they'd look for another young woman to approach. If the woman handed over her number, they'd tell her the proposition was all in the name of science, at which time, according to the scientists, most of the women laughed. The key to the experiment was this: with half the women they propositioned, the young men added a light one-second touch to the woman's forearm. The other half received no touch.

The researchers were interested in whether the men would be more successful when they touched the women than when they didn't. How important is touch as a social cue? Over the course of the day, the young men collected three dozen phone numbers. When they didn't touch the women, they had a success rate of 10 percent; when they touched them, their success rate was 20 percent. That light one-second touch doubled their popularity. Why were the touched women twice as likely to agree to a date? Were they thinking, *This Antoine is a good toucher—it'd prob-*

ably be fun to knock down a bottle of Bordeaux with him some night at Bar de l'Océan? Probably not. But on the unconscious level, touch seems to impart a subliminal sense of caring and connection.

Unlike non-Euclidean geometry, touch research has many obvious applications.[18] For example, in an experiment involving eight servers and several hundred restaurant diners, the servers were trained to touch randomly selected customers briefly on the arm toward the end of the meal while asking if "everything was all right." The servers received an average tip of about 14.5 percent from those they didn't touch, but 17.5 percent from those they did. Another study found the same effect on tipping at a bar. And in another restaurant study, about 60 percent of diners took the server's suggestion to order the special after being touched lightly on the forearm, compared with only about 40 percent of those who were not touched. Touching has been found to increase the fraction of single women in a nightclub who will accept an invitation to dance, the number of people agreeing to sign a petition, the chances that a college student will risk embarrassment by volunteering to go to the blackboard in a statistics class, the proportion of busy passersby in a mall willing to take ten minutes to fill out a survey form, the percentage of shoppers in a supermarket who purchase food they had sampled, and the odds that a bystander who had just provided someone with directions will help him pick up a bunch of computer disks he drops.

You might be skeptical of this. After all, some people recoil when a stranger touches them. And it is possible that some of the subjects in the studies I quoted did recoil but that their reactions were outweighed by the reactions of those who reacted positively. Remember, though, these were all very subtle touches, not gropes. In fact, in studies in which the touched person was later debriefed about the experience, typically less than one-third of the subjects were even aware that they had been touched.[19]

So are touchy-feely people more successful at getting things done? There is no data on whether bosses who dole out the occasional pat on the head run a smoother operation, but a 2010 study by a group of researchers in Berkeley found a case in which a habit of congratulatory slaps to the skull really is associated with successful group interactions.[20] The Berkeley researchers studied the sport of basketball, which both requires extensive second-by-second teamwork and is known for its elaborate language of touching. They found that the number of "fist bumps, high fives, chest bumps, leaping shoulder bumps, chest punches, head slaps, head grabs, low fives, high tens, half hugs, and team huddles" correlated significantly with the degree of cooperation among teammates, such as passing to those who are less closely defended, helping others escape defensive pressure by setting what are called "screens," and otherwise displaying a reliance on a teammate at the expense of one's own individual performance. The teams that touched the most cooperated the most, and won the most.

Touch seems to be such an important tool for enhancing social cooperation and affiliation that we have evolved a special physical route along which those subliminal feelings of social connection travel from skin to brain. That is, scientists have discovered a particular kind of nerve fiber in people's skin—especially in the face and arms—that appears to have developed specifically to transmit the pleasantness of social touch. Those nerve fibers transmit their signal too slowly to be of much use in helping you do the things you normally associate with the sense of touch: determining *what* is touching you and telling you, with some precision, *where* you were touched.[21] "They won't help you distinguish a pear from pumice or your cheek from your chin," says the social neuroscientist pioneer Ralph Adolphs. "But they *are* connected directly to areas of the brain such as the insular cortex, which is associated with emotion."[22]

To primatologists, the importance of touch is no surprise. Nonhuman primates touch each other extensively during grooming. And while grooming is ostensibly about hygiene, it would take only about ten minutes of grooming a day for an animal to stay clean. Instead, some species spend hours on it.[23] Why? Remember those grooming cliques? In nonhuman primates, social grooming is important for maintaining social relationships.[24] Touch is our most highly developed sense when we are born, and it remains a fundamental mode of communication throughout a baby's first year and an important influence throughout a person's life.[25]

AT A QUARTER to eight on the evening of September 26, 1960, Democratic presidential candidate John F. Kennedy strode into the studio of the CBS affiliate WBBM in downtown Chicago.[26] He appeared rested, bronzed, and fit. The journalist Howard K. Smith would later compare

Kennedy to an "athlete come to receive his wreath of laurel." Ted Rogers, the TV consultant to Kennedy's Republican opponent, Richard Nixon, remarked, "When he came into the studio I thought he was Cochise, he was so tan."

Nixon, on the other hand, looked haggard and pale. He had arrived fifteen minutes before Kennedy's grand entrance. The two candidates were in Chicago for the first presidential debate in U.S. history. But Nixon had recently been hospitalized for a knee infection, which still plagued him. Then, ignoring advice to continue resting, he'd resumed a grueling cross-country campaign schedule and had lost considerable weight. As he climbed out of his Oldsmobile, he suffered from a 102 degree fever, yet he insisted he was well enough to go through with the debate. When judged by the candidates' words, Nixon was indeed destined to hold his own that night. But the debate would proceed on two levels, the verbal and the nonverbal.

The issues of the day included the conflict with communism, agriculture and labor problems, and the candidates' experience. Since elections are high-stakes affairs and debates are about important philosophical and practical issues, the candidates' words are all that should matter, right? Would you be swayed to vote against a candidate because a knee infection had made him look tired? Like voice and touch, posture, facial appearance, and expression exert a powerful influence on how we judge people. But would we elect a president based on demeanor?

CBS's debate producer, Don Hewitt, took one look at Nixon's gaunt face and immediately heard alarm bells. He offered both candidates the services of a makeup artist, but after Kennedy declined, so did Nixon. Then, while an aide rubbed an over-the-counter cosmetic called Lazy Shave over Nixon's famously heavy five o'clock shadow, out of their view Kennedy's people proceeded to give Kennedy a full cosmetic touch-up. Hewitt pressed Rogers, Nixon's TV consultant, about his candidate's appearance, but Rogers said he was satisfied. Hewitt then elevated his concern to his boss at CBS. He, too, approached Rogers but received the same response.

Some seventy million people watched the debate. When it was over, one prominent Republican in Texas was heard to say, "That son of a bitch just cost us the election." That prominent Republican was in a good position to know. He was Henry Cabot Lodge Jr., Richard Nixon's running mate. When the election was held, some six weeks later, Nixon and Lodge lost the popular vote by a hair, just 113,000 out of the 67,000,000 votes cast. That's less than 1 vote in 500, so even if the debate had convinced just a small percentage of viewers that Nixon wasn't up to the job, it would have been enough to swing the election.

What's really interesting here is that, while viewers like Lodge were thinking that Nixon did horribly, a slew of other prominent Republicans had a completely different experience. For example, Earl Mazo, the national political correspondent for the *New York Herald Tribune*—and a Nixon supporter—attended a kind of debate party with eleven governors and members of their staffs, all in town for the Southern Governors Conference in Hot Springs, Arkansas.[27] They thought Nixon did splendidly. Why was their experience so different from Lodge's? They had listened to the debate over the radio, because the television broadcast was delayed by one hour in Arkansas.

Of the radio broadcast, Mazo said, "[Nixon's] deep, resonant voice conveyed more conviction, command, and determination than Kennedy's higher-pitched voice and his Boston-Harvard accent." But when the television feed came, Mazo and the governors switched to it and watched the first hour again. Mazo then changed his mind about the winner, saying, "On television, Kennedy looked sharper, more in control, more firm." A Philadelphia commercial research firm, Sindlinger & Co., later confirmed that analysis. According to an article in the trade journal *Broadcasting*, their research showed that among radio listeners, Nixon won by more than a two-to-one margin, but among the far greater number of television viewers, Kennedy beat him.

The Sindlinger study was never published in a scientific journal, and little niceties like sample size—and the methodology for accounting for demographic differences between radio and TV users—were not revealed. That's how the issue stood for some forty years. Then, in 2003, a researcher enlisted 171 summer school students at the University of Minnesota to assess the debate, half after watching a video of it, half after listening to the audio only.[28] As scientific subjects, these students had an advantage over any group that might have been assembled at the time of the actual debate: they had no vested interest in either candidate and little or no knowledge of the issues. To the voters in 1960, the name Nikita Khru-shchev carried great emotional significance. To these students, he sounded like just another hockey player. But their impression of the debate was no different from that of the voters four decades earlier: those students who watched the debate were significantly more likely to think Kennedy won than those who only listened to it.

IT'S LIKELY THAT, like the voters in the 1960 U.S. presidential election, we have all at some time chosen one individual over another based on looks. We vote for political candidates, but we also select from among candidates for spouse, friend, auto mechanic, attorney, doctor, dentist, vendor, employee, boss. How strong an influence does a person's appearance have on us? I don't mean beauty—I mean something more subtle, a look of intelligence, or sophistication, or competence. Voting is a good stand-in for probing the effect of appearance in many realms because there is not only plenty of data available but plenty of money to study it.

In one pair of experiments, a group of researchers in California created campaign flyers for several fictional congressional elections.[29] Each supposedly pitted a Republican against a Democrat. In reality, the "candidates" were models hired by the researchers to pose for the black-and-white photographs that would appear in the flyers. Half the models looked able and competent. The other half did not look very able. The researchers didn't rely on their own judgment to determine that: they conducted a preliminary rating session in which volunteers rated each model's visual appeal. Then, when the researchers made up the campaign flyers, in each case they pitted one of the more able-looking individuals against one of the less able-looking ones to see if the candidate with the better demeanor would get more votes.

In addition to each candidate's (fake) name and picture, the flyers included substantive information such as party affiliation, education, occupation, political experience, and a three-line position statement on each of three campaign issues. To eliminate the effects of party preference, half the voters saw flyers in which the more able-looking candidate was a Republican, and half saw flyers in which he was a Democrat. In principle, it should have been only the substantive information that would be relevant to a voter's choice.

The scientists recruited about two hundred volunteers to play the role of voters. The researchers told the volunteers that the campaign flyers were based on *real* information concerning *real* candidates. They also misled the volunteers about the purpose of the experiment, saying that they sought to examine how people vote when they have equal information—such as that on the flyers—on all of the candidates. The volunteers' job, the scientists explained to them, was merely to look over the flyers and vote for the candidate of their choice in each of the elections presented. The "face effect" proved to be large: the candidate with the better demeanor, on average, won 59 percent of the vote. That's a landslide in modern politics. In fact the only American president since the Great Depression to have won by that big a margin was Lyndon Johnson, when he beat Goldwater with 61 percent of the vote in 1964. And *that* was an election in which Goldwater was widely portrayed as a man itching to start a nuclear war.

In the second study, the researchers' methodology was similar, except this time the pool of people whose photos were used to portray the candidates was chosen differently. In the first study, the candidates were all men who'd been judged by a voting committee as looking either more or less competent. In this study, the candidates were all women whose appearance had been assessed by a committee as being neutral. The scientists then employed a Hollywood-style makeup specialist and a photographer to create two photographic versions of each candidate: one in which she appeared more competent, and another in which she appeared less competent. In this mock election, a competent version of one woman was always pitted against an incompetent version of another. The result: on average, looking more like a leader equated to a vote swing of 15 percent at the polls. To get an idea of the magnitude of that effect, consider that in one recent California congressional election, a swing of that size would have changed the outcome in fifteen of the fifty-three districts.

I found these studies astounding and alarming. They imply that before anyone even discusses the issues, the race may be over, since looks alone can give a candidate a huge head start. With all the important issues of the day, it's hard to accept that a person's face would really sway our vote. One obvious criticism of this research is that these were mock elections. The studies might show that a competent appearance can give a candidate a boost, but they don't address the issue of how "soft" that preference may be. Certainly one would expect that voters with strong ideological preferences would not be easily swayed by appearance. Swing voters ought to be more easily affected but is the phenomenon strong enough to affect elections in the real world?

In 2005, researchers at Princeton gathered black-and-white head shots of all the winners and runners-up in ninety-five races for the U.S. Senate and six hundred races for the House of Representatives from 2000, 2002, and 2004.[30] Then they assembled a group of volunteers to evaluate the candidates' competence based on just a quick look at the photographs, discarding the data on any of the faces a volunteer recognized. The results were astonishing: the candidate the volunteers perceived as more competent had won in 72 percent of the Senate races and 67 percent of the House races, even higher success rates than in the California laboratory experiment. Then, in 2006, the scientists performed an experiment with even more astonishing—and, when you think about it, depressing—results. They conducted the face evaluations *before* the elections in question and predicted the winners based solely on the candidates' appearance. They were strikingly accurate: the candidate voted as more competent-looking went on to win in 69 percent of the gubernatorial races and 72 percent of the Senate races.

I've gone into detail regarding these political studies not just because they are important in themselves but because, as I said earlier, they shed light on our broader social interactions. In high school, our vote for class president might be based on looks. It would be nice to think that we outgrow those primitive ways, but it's not easy to graduate from our unconscious influences.

In his autobiography, Charles Darwin reported that he was almost denied the chance to make his historic voyage on the *Beagle* on account of his looks, in particular, because of his nose, which was large and somewhat bulbous.[31] Darwin himself later used his nose, facetiously, as an argument against intelligent design, writing, "Will you honestly tell me . . . whether you believe that the shape of my nose was ordained and 'guided by an intelligent cause'?"[32] The *Beagle*'s captain wanted to keep Darwin off the ship because he had a personal belief that you could judge character by the shape of the nose, and a man with Darwin's, he felt, could not possibly "possess sufficient energy and determination for the voyage." In the end, of course, Darwin got the job. Of the captain, Darwin later wrote, "I think he was afterwards well-satisfied that my nose had spoken falsely."[33]

TOWARD THE END of *The Wizard of Oz*, Dorothy and company approach the great Wizard, offering him the broomstick of the Wicked Witch of the West. They can see only fire, smoke, and a floating image of the Wizard's face as he responds in booming, authoritative tones that have Dorothy and her cohorts trembling with fear. Then Dorothy's dog, Toto, tugs aside a curtain, revealing that the ominous Wizard is just an ordinary-looking man speaking into a microphone and pulling levers and twisting dials to orchestrate the fireworks. He yanks the curtain closed and admonishes, "Pay no attention to that man behind the curtain," but the jig is up, and Dorothy discovers that the Wizard is just a genial old man.

There is a man or woman behind the curtain of everybody's persona. Through our social relationships we get to know a small number of beings with the level of intimacy that allows us to peel back the curtain—our friends, close neighbors, family members, and perhaps the family dog (though certainly not the cat). But we don't get to pull the curtain very far back on most of the people we meet, and it is usually drawn fully closed when we encounter someone for the first time. As a result, certain superficial qualities, such as voice, face and expression, posture, and the other nonverbal characteristics I've been talking about, mold many of the judgments we make about people—the nice or nasty people we work with, our neighbors, our doctors, our kids' teachers, the politicians we vote for or against or simply try to ignore. Every day we meet people and form judgments like *I trust that babysitter, This lawyer knows what she is doing,* or *That guy seems like the type who would gently stroke my back while reciting Shakespeare sonnets by candlelight.* If you are a job applicant, the quality of your handshake can affect the outcome of your employment interview. If you are a salesperson, your degree of eye contact can influence your rating of customer satisfaction. If you are a doctor, the tone of your voice can have an impact on not only your patients' assessment of their visit but their propensity to sue if something goes wrong. We humans are superior to cowbirds in our conscious understanding. But we also have a deep inner cowbird mind that reacts to nonverbal cues, uncensored by those logical judgments of consciousness. The expression "to be a real human being" means to act with compassion. Other languages have similar expressions, such as the German *"ein Mensch sein."* A human being, by nature, cannot help but pick up on the emotions and intentions of others. That ability is built into our brains, and there is no off switch.

CHAPTER 7

Sorting People and Things

We would be dazzled if we had to treat everything we saw, every visual input, as a separate element, and had to figure out the connections anew each time we opened our eyes.   —GARY KLEIN

I F YOU READ someone a list of ten or twenty items that could be bought at a supermarket, that person will remember only a few. If you recite the list repeatedly, the person's recall will improve. But what really helps is if the items are mentioned within the categories they fall into—for example, vegetables, fruits, and cereals. Research suggests that we have neurons in our prefrontal cortex that respond to categories, and the list exercise illustrates the reason: categorization is a strategy our brains use to more efficiently process information.[1] Remember Shereshevsky, the man with the flawless memory who had great trouble recognizing faces? In his memory, each person had many faces: faces as viewed from different angles, faces in varying lighting, faces for each emotion and for each nuance of emotional intensity. As a result, the encyclopedia of faces on the bookshelf of Shereshevsky's brain was exceptionally thick and difficult to search, and the process of identifying a new face by matching it to one previously seen—which is the essence of what categorization is—was correspondingly cumbersome.

Every object and person we encounter in the world is unique, but we wouldn't function very well if we perceived them that way. We don't have the time or the mental bandwidth to observe and consider each detail of every item in our environment. Instead, we employ a few salient traits that we do observe to assign the object to a category, and then we base our assessment of the object on the category rather than the object itself. By maintaining a set of categories, we thus expedite our reactions. If we hadn't evolved to operate that way, if our brains treated everything we encountered as an individual, we might be eaten by a bear while still deciding whether this particular furry creature is as dangerous as the one that ate Uncle Bob. Instead, once we see a couple bears eat our relatives, the whole species gets a bad reputation. Then, thanks to categorical thinking, when we spot a huge, shaggy animal with large, sharp incisors, we don't hang around gathering more data; we act on our automatic hunch that it is dangerous and move away from it. Similarly, once we see a few chairs, we assume that if an object has four legs and a back, it was made to sit on; or if the driver in front of us is weaving erratically, we judge that it is best to keep our distance.

Thinking in terms of generic categories such as "bears," "chairs," and "erratic drivers" helps us to navigate our environment with great speed and efficiency; we understand an object's gross significance first and worry about its individuality later. Categorization is one of the most important mental acts we perform, and we do it all the time. Even your ability to read this book depends on your ability to categorize: mastering reading requires grouping similar symbols, like *b* and *d*, in *different* letter categories, while recognizing that symbols as disparate as b, **b**, ℓ, and *b* all represent the same letter.

Classifying objects isn't easy, *which is* wh**ɣ** th**e**ᵉe **words aᶉe** *anno*ɣ-**ıng** to r**e**ad. Mixed fonts aside, it is easy to underestimate the complexity of what is involved in categorization because we usually do it quickly and without conscious effort. When we think of food types, for example, we automatically consider an apple and a banana to be in the same category—fruit—though they appear quite different, but we consider an apple and a red billiard ball to be in different categories, even though they appear quite similar. An alley cat and a dachshund might both be brown and of roughly similar size and shape, while an Old English sheepdog is far different—large, white, and shaggy—but even a child knows that the alley cat is in the category feline and the dachshund and sheepdog are canines. To get an idea of just how sophisticated that categorization is, consider this: it was just a few years ago that computer scientists finally learned how to design a computer vision system that could accomplish the task of distinguishing cats from dogs.

As the above examples illustrate, one of the principal ways we categorize is by maximizing the importance of certain differences (the orientation of *d* versus *b* or the presence of whiskers) while minimizing the relevance of others (the curviness of ɓ versus *b* or the color of the animal). But the arrow of our reasoning can also point the other way. If we conclude that a certain set of objects belongs to one group and a second set of objects to another, we may then perceive those within the same group as more similar than they really are—and those in different groups as less similar than they really are. Merely placing objects in groups can affect our judgment of those objects. So while categorization is a natural and crucial shortcut, like our brain's other survival-oriented tricks, it has its drawbacks.

One of the earliest experiments investigating the distortions caused by categorization was a simple study in which subjects were asked to estimate the lengths of a set of eight line segments. The longest of those lines was 5 percent longer than the next in the bunch, which, in turn, was 5 percent longer than the third longest, and so on. The researchers asked half their subjects to estimate the lengths of each of the lines, in centimeters. But before asking the other subjects to do the same, they artificially grouped the lines into two sets—the longer four lines were labeled "Group A," the shorter four labeled "Group B." The experimenters found that once the lines were thought of as belonging to a group, the subjects perceived them differently. They judged the lines within each group as being closer in length to one another than they really were, and the length difference between the two groups as being greater than it actually was.[2]

Analogous experiments have since shown the same effect in many other contexts. In one experiment, the judgment of length was replaced by a judgment of color: volunteers were presented with letters and numbers that varied in hue and asked to judge their "degree of redness." Those who were given the color samples with the reddest characters grouped together judged those to be more alike in color and more different from the other group than did volunteers who appraised the same samples presented without being grouped.[3] In another study, researchers found that if you ask people in a given city to estimate the difference in temperature between June 1 and June 30, they will tend to underestimate it; but if you ask them to estimate the difference in temperature between June 15 and July 15, they will overestimate it.[4] The artificial grouping of days into months skews our perception: we see two days within a month as being more similar to each other than equally distant days that occur in two different months, even though the time interval between them is identical.

In all these examples, when we categorize, we polarize. Things that for one arbitrary reason or another are identified as belonging to the same category seem more similar to each other than they really are, while those in different categories seem more different than they really are. The unconscious mind transforms fuzzy differences and subtle nuances into clear-cut distinctions. Its goal is to erase irrelevant detail while maintaining information on what is important. When that's done successfully, we simplify our environment and make it easier and faster to navigate. When it's done inappropriately, we distort our perceptions, sometimes with results harmful to others, and even ourselves. That's especially true when our tendency to categorize affects our view of other humans—when we view the doctors in a given practice, the attorneys in a given law firm, the fans of a certain sports team, or the people in a given race or ethnic group as more alike than they really are.

A CALIFORNIA ATTORNEY wrote about the case of a young Salvadoran man who had been the only nonwhite employee at a box-manufacturing plant in a rural area. He had been denied a promotion, then fired for habitual tardiness and for being "too easy-going." The man claimed that the same could be said of others but that their tardiness went unnoticed. With them, he said, the employer seemed to understand that sometimes a sickness in the family, a problem with a child, or trouble with the car can lead to being late. But with him, lateness was automatically attributed to laziness. His shortcomings were amplified, he said, and his achievements went unrecognized. We'll never know whether his employer really overlooked the Salvadoran man's individual traits, whether his employer lumped him in the general category "Hispanic" and then interpreted his behavior in terms of a stereotype. The employer certainly disputed that accusation. And then he added, "Mateo's being a Mexican didn't make any difference to me. It's like I didn't even notice."[5]

The term "stereotype" was coined in 1794 by the French printer Firmin Didot.[6] It referred to a type of printing process by which cookie-cutter-like molds could be used to produce duplicate metal plates of hand-set type. With these duplicate plates, newspapers and books could be printed on several presses at once, enabling mass production. The term was first used in its current sense by the American journalist and intellectual Walter Lippmann in his 1922 book *Public Opinion*, a critical analysis of modern democracy and the role of the public in determining its course. Lippmann was concerned with the ever-growing complexity of the issues facing the voters and the manner in which they developed their views on those issues. He was particularly worried about the role of the mass media. Employing language that sounds as if it was pulled from a recent scholarly article on the psychology of categories, Lippmann wrote, "The real environment is altogether too big, too complex, and too fleeting for direct acquaintance. . . . And although we have to act in that environment, we have to reconstruct it on a simpler model before we can manage with it."[7] That simpler model was what he called the stereotype.

Lippmann recognized that the stereotypes people use come from cultural exposure. His was an era in which mass-circulation newspapers and magazines, as well as the new medium of film, were distributing ideas and information to audiences larger and more far-flung than had ever before been possible. They made available to the public an unprecedentedly wide array of experiences of the world, yet without necessarily providing an accurate picture. The movies, in particular, conveyed a vivid, real-looking portrait of life, but one often peopled by stock caricatures. In fact, in the early days of film, filmmakers combed the streets looking for "character actors," easily identifiable social types, to play in their movies.

As Lippmann's contemporary Hugo Münsterberg wrote, "If the [producer] needs the fat bartender with his smug smile, or the humble Jewish peddler, or the Italian organ grinder, he does not rely on wigs and paint; he finds them all ready-made on the East Side [of New York]." Stock character types were (and still are) a convenient shorthand—we recognize them at once—but their use amplifies and exaggerates the character traits associated with the categories they represent. According to the historians Elizabeth Ewen and Stuart Ewen, by noting the analogy between social perception and a printing process capable of generating an unlimited number of identical impressions, "Lippmann had identified and named one of the most potent features of modernity."[8]

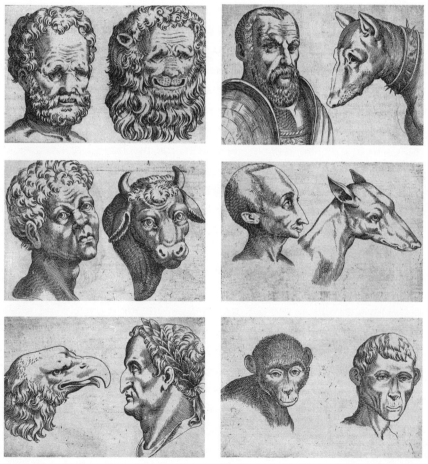

People, categorized according to the animal they resemble. Courtesy of the National Library of Medicine.

Though categorizations due to race, religion, gender, and nationality get the most press, we categorize people in many other ways as well. We can probably all think of cases in which we lumped athletes with athletes, or bankers with bankers, in which we and others have categorized people we've met according to their profession, appearance, ethnicity, education, age, or hair color or even by the cars they drive. Some scholars in the sixteenth and seventeenth centuries even categorized people according to the animal they best resembled, as pictured on the facing page, in images from *De Humana Physiognomonia*, a kind of field guide to human character written in 1586 by the Italian Giambattista della Porta.[9]

A more modern illustration of categorization by appearance played out early one afternoon in an aisle of a large discount department store in Iowa City. There, an unshaven man in soiled, patched blue jeans and a blue workman's shirt shoved a small article of clothing into the pocket of his jacket. A customer down the aisle looked on. A little later, a well-groomed man in pressed dress slacks, a sports jacket, and a tie did the same, observed by a different customer who happened to be shopping nearby. Similar incidents occurred again and again that day, well into the evening, over fifty more times, and there were a hundred more such episodes at other nearby stores. It was as if a brigade of shoplifters had been dispatched to rid the town of cheap socks and tacky ties. But the occasion wasn't National Kleptomaniacs' Day; it was an experiment by two social psychologists.[10] With the full cooperation of the stores involved, the researchers' aim was to study how the reactions of bystanders would be affected by the social category of the offender.

The shoplifters were all accomplices of the researchers. Immediately after each shoplifting episode, the thief walked out of hearing distance of the customer but remained within eyesight. Then another research accomplice, dressed as a store employee, stepped to the vicinity of the customer and began rearranging merchandise on the shelves. This gave the customer an easy opportunity to report the crime. The customers all observed the identical behavior, but they did not all react to it in the same way. Significantly fewer of the customers who saw the well-dressed man commit the crime reported it, as compared to those who had watched the scruffy individual. Even more interesting were the differences in attitude the customers had when they did alert the employee to the crime.

Their analysis of events went beyond the acts they had observed—they seemed to form a mental picture of the thief based as much on his social category as on his actions. They were often hesitant when reporting the well-dressed criminal but enthusiastic when informing on the unkempt perpetrator, spicing up their accounts with utterances along the lines of "that son of a bitch just stuffed something down his coat." It was as if the unkempt man's appearance was a signal to the customers that shoplifting must be the least of his sins, an indicator of an inner nature as soiled as his clothes.

We like to think we judge people as individuals, and at times we consciously try very hard to evaluate others on the basis of their unique characteristics. We often succeed. But if we don't know a person well, our minds can turn to his or her social category for the answers. Earlier we saw how the brain fills in gaps in visual data—for instance, compensating for the blind spot where the optic nerve attaches to the retina. We also saw how our hearing fills gaps, such as when a cough obliterated a syllable or two in the sentence "The state governors met with their respective legislatures convening in the capital city." And we saw how our memory will add the details of a scene we remember only in broad strokes and provide a vivid and complete picture of a face even though our brains retained only its general features. In each of these cases our subliminal minds take incomplete data, use context or other cues to complete the picture, make educated guesses, and produce a result that is sometimes accurate, sometimes not, but always convincing. Our minds also fill in the blanks when we judge people, and a person's category membership is part of the data we use to do that.

The realization that perceptual biases of categorization lie at the root of prejudice is due largely to the psychologist Henri Tajfel, the brain behind the line-length study. The son of a Polish businessman, Tajfel would likely have become a forgotten chemist rather than a pioneering social psychologist were it not for the particular social category to which he himself was assigned. Tajfel was a Jew, a category identification that meant he was banned from enrolling in college, at least in Poland. So he moved to France. There he studied chemistry, but he had no passion for it. He preferred partying—or, as one colleague put it, "savoring French culture and Parisian life."[11] His savoring ended when World War II began, and in November 1939, he joined the French army. Even less savory was where he ended up: in a German POW camp. There Tajfel was introduced to the extremes of social categorization that he would later say led him to his career in social psychology.

The Germans demanded to know the social group to which Tajfel belonged. Was he French? A French Jew? A Jew from elsewhere? If the Nazis thought of Jews as less than human, they nevertheless distinguished between pedigrees of Jew, like vintners distinguishing between the châteaus of origin of soured wine. To be French meant to be treated as an enemy. To be a French Jew meant to be treated as an animal. To admit being a Polish Jew meant swift and certain death. No matter what his personal characteristics or the quality of his relationship with his German captors, as he would later point out, if his identity were discovered, it would be his classification as a Polish Jew that would determine his fate.[12] But there was also danger in lying. So, from the menu of stigmatization, Tajfel chose the middle dish: he spent the next four years pretending to be a French Jew.[13] He was liberated in 1945 and in May of that year, as he put it, was "disgorged with hundreds of others from a special train arriving at the Gare d'Orsay in Paris . . . [soon to discover] that hardly anyone I knew in 1939—including my family—was left alive."[14] Tajfel spent the next six years working with war refugees, especially children and adolescents, and mulling over the relationships between categorical thinking, stereotyping, and prejudice. According to the psychologist William Peter Robinson, today's theoretical understanding of those subjects "can almost without exception be traced back to Tajfel's theorizing and direct research intervention."[15]

Unfortunately, as was the case with other pioneers, it took the field many years to catch up with Tajfel's insights. Even well into the 1980s, many psychologists viewed discrimination as a conscious and intentional behavior, rather than one commonly arising from normal and unavoidable cognitive processes related to the brain's vital propensity to categorize.[16] In 1998, however, a trio of researchers at the University of Washington published a paper that many see as providing smoking-gun evidence that unconscious, or "implicit," stereotyping is the rule rather than the exception.[17] Their paper presented a computerized tool called the "Implicit

Association Test," or IAT, which has become one of social psychology's standard tools for measuring the degree to which an individual unconsciously associates traits with social categories. The IAT has helped revolutionize the way social scientists look at stereotyping.

IN THEIR ARTICLE, the IAT pioneers asked their readers to "consider a thought experiment." Suppose you are shown a series of words naming male and female relatives, such as "brother" or "aunt." You are asked to say "hello" when presented with a male relative and "good-bye" when shown a female. (In the computerized version you see the words on a screen and respond by pressing letters on the keyboard.) The idea is to respond as quickly as possible while not making too many errors. Most people who try this find that it is easy and proceed rapidly. Next, the researchers ask that you repeat the game, only this time with male and female names, like "Dick" or "Jane" instead of relatives. The names are of unambiguous gender, and again, you can fly through them. But this is just an appetizer.

The real experiment starts now: in phase 1, you are shown a series of words that can be *either* a name *or* a relative. You are asked to say "hello" for the male names and relatives and "good-bye" for the female names and relatives. It's a slightly more complex task than before, but still not taxing. What's important is the time it takes you to make each selection. Try it with the following word list; you can say "hello" or "good-bye" to yourself if you are afraid of scaring away your own relatives who may be within earshot (hello = male name or relative; good-bye = female name or relative):

John, Joan, brother, granddaughter, Beth, daughter, Mike, niece, Richard, Leonard, son, aunt, grandfather, Brian, Donna, father, mother, grandson, Gary, Kathy.

Now for phase 2. In phase 2 you see a list of the names and relatives again, but this time you are asked to say "hello" when seeing a male name or *female* relative and "good-bye" when you see a female name or *male* relative. Again, what's important is the time it takes to make your selections. Try it (hello = male name or female relative; good-bye = female name or male relative):

John, Joan, brother, granddaughter, Beth, daughter, Mike, niece, Richard, Leonard, son, aunt, grandfather, Brian, Donna, father, mother, grandson, Gary, Kathy.

The phase 2 response times are typically far greater than those for phase 1: perhaps three-fourths of a second per word, as opposed to just half a second. To understand why, let's look at this as a task in sorting. You are being asked to consider four categories of objects: male names, male relatives, female names, and female relatives. But these are not independent categories. The categories male names and male relatives are associated—they both refer to males. Likewise, the categories female names and female relatives are associated. In phase 1 you are asked to label the four categories in a manner consistent with that association—to label all males in the same manner, and all females in the same manner. In phase 2, however, you are asked to ignore your association, to label males one way if you see a name but the other way if you see a relative, and to also label female terms differently depending upon whether the term is a name or a relative. That is complicated, and the complexity eats up mental resources, slowing you down.

That is the crux of the IAT: *when the labeling you are asked to do follows your mental associations, it speeds you up, but when it mixes across associations, it slows you down.* As a result, by examining the difference in speed between the two ways you are asked to label, researchers can probe how strongly a person associates traits with a social category.

For example, suppose that instead of words denoting male and female relatives, I showed you terms related to either science or the arts. If you had no mental association linking men and science or women and the arts, it wouldn't matter if you had to say "hello" for men's names and science terms and "good-bye" for women's names and arts terms, or "hello" for men's names and arts terms and "good-bye" for women's names and science terms. Hence there would be no difference between phase 1 and phase 2. But if you had strong associations linking women and the arts and linking men and science—as most people do—the exercise would be very similar to the original task, with male and female relatives and male and female names, and there would be a considerable difference in your response times in phase 1 and phase 2.

When researchers administer tests analogous to this, the results are stunning. For example, they find that about half the public shows a strong or moderate bias toward associating men with science and women with the arts, whether they are aware of such links or not. In fact, there is little correlation between the IAT results and measures of "explicit," or conscious, gender bias, such as self-reports or attitude questionnaires. Similarly, researchers have shown subjects images of white faces, black faces, hostile words (awful, failure, evil, nasty, and so on), and positive words (peace, joy, love, happy, and so on). If you have pro-white and anti-black associations, it will take you longer to sort words and images when you have to connect positive words to the black category and hostile words to the white category than when black faces and hostile words go in the same bin. About 70 percent of those who have taken the test exhibit this pro-white association, including many who are (consciously) appalled at learning that they hold such attitudes. Even many black people, it turns out, exhibit an unconscious pro-white bias on the IAT. It is difficult not to when you live in a culture that embodies negative stereotypes about African Americans.

Though your evaluation of another person may feel rational and deliberate, it is heavily informed by automatic, unconscious processes—the kind of emotion-regulating processes carried out within the ventromedial prefrontal cortex. In fact, damage to the VMPC has been shown to eliminate unconscious gender stereotyping.[18] As Walter Lippmann recognized, we can't avoid mentally absorbing the categories defined by the society in which we live. They permeate the news, television programming, films, all aspects of our culture. And because our brains naturally categorize, we are vulnerable to acting on the attitudes those categories represent. But before you recommend incorporating VMPC obliteration into your company's management training course, remember that the propensity to categorize, even to categorize people, is for the most part a blessing. It allows us to understand the difference between a bus driver and a bus passenger, a store clerk and a customer, a receptionist and a physician, a maître d' and a waiter, and all the other strangers we interact with, without our having to pause and consciously puzzle out everyone's role anew during each encounter. The challenge is not how to stop categorizing but how to become aware of when we do it in ways that prevent us from being able to see individual people for who they really are.

THE PSYCHOLOGY PIONEER Gordon Allport wrote that categories saturate all that they contain with the same "ideational and emotional flavor."[19] As evidence of that, he cited a 1948 experiment in which a Canadian social scientist wrote to 100 different resorts that had advertised in newspapers around the holidays.[20] The scientist drafted two letters to each resort, requesting accommodations on the same date. He signed one letter with the name "Mr. Lockwood" and the other with the name "Mr. Greenberg." Mr. Lockwood received a reply with an offer of accommodations from 95 of the resorts. Mr. Greenberg received such a reply from just 36. The decisions to spurn Mr. Greenberg were obviously not made on Mr. Greenberg's own merits but on the religious category to which he presumably belonged.

Prejudging people according to a social category is a time-honored tradition, even among those who champion the underprivileged. Consider this quote by a famed advocate for equality:

Ours is one continued struggle against degradation sought to be inflicted upon us by the European, who desire to degrade us to the level of the raw Kaffir [black African] . . . whose sole ambition is to collect a certain number of cattle to buy a wife with, and then pass his life in indolence and nakedness.[21]

That was Mahatma Gandhi. Or consider the words of Che Guevara, a revolutionary who, according to *Time* magazine, left his native land "to pursue the emancipation of the poor of the earth" and helped overthrow the Cuban dictator Fulgencio Batista.[22] What did this Marxist champion of poor oppressed Cubans think of the poor blacks in the United States? He said, "The Negro is indolent and lazy, and spends his money on frivolities, whereas the European is forward-looking, organized and intelligent."[23] And how about this famous advocate for civil rights:

I will say then that I am not, nor ever have been in favor of bringing about in any way the social and political equality of the white and black races . . . there is a physical difference between the white and black races which I believe will forever forbid the two races living together on terms of social and political equality . . . and I as much as any other man am in favor of having the superior position assigned to the white race.

That was Abraham Lincoln in a debate at Charlestown, Illinois, in 1858. He was incredibly progressive for his time but still believed that social, if not legal, categorization would forever endure. We've made progress. Today in many countries it is difficult to imagine a serious candidate for national political office voicing views such as Lincoln's—or if he did, at least he wouldn't be considered the *pro*–civil rights candidate. Today culture has evolved to the point where most people feel it is wrong to willfully cheat someone out of an opportunity because of character traits we infer from their category identity. But we are only beginning to come to grips with *unconscious* bias.

Unfortunately, if science has recognized unconscious stereotyping, the law has not. In the United States, for example, individuals claiming discrimination based on race, color, religion, sex, or national origin must prove not only that they were treated differently but that the discrimination was purposeful. No doubt discrimination often *is* purposeful. There will always be people like the Utah employer who consciously discriminated against women and was quoted in court as having said, "Fucking women, I hate having fucking women in the office."[24] It is relatively easy to address discrimination by people who preach what they practice. The challenge science presents to the legal community is to move beyond that, to address the more difficult issue of unconscious discrimination, of bias that is subtle and hidden even from those who exercise it.

We can all personally fight unconscious bias, for research has shown that our tendency to categorize people can be influenced by our conscious goals. If we are aware of our bias and motivated to overcome it, we can. For example, studies of criminal trials reveal one set of circumstances in which people's bias regarding appearance is routinely overcome. In particular, it has long been known that people's attributions of guilt and recommendations of punishment are subliminally influenced by the looks of the defendant.[25] But: typically, more attractive defendants receive more lenient treatment *only* when accused of minor crimes such as traffic infractions or swindles, and *not* with regard to more serious crimes like murder. Our unconscious judgment, which relies heavily on the categories to which we assign people, is always competing with our more deliberative and analytical conscious thought, which may see them as individuals. As these two sides of our minds battle it out, the degree to which we view a person as an individual versus a generic group member can vary on a sliding scale. That's what seems to be happening in criminal trials. Serious crimes usually involve longer, more detailed examination of the defendant, with more at stake, and the added conscious focus seems to outweigh the attractiveness bias.

The moral of the story is that if we wish to overcome unconscious bias, it requires effort. A good way to start is by taking a closer look at those we are judging, even if they are not on trial for murder but, instead, are simply asking for a job or a loan—or our vote. Our personal knowledge of a specific member of a category can easily override our category bias, but more important, over time repeated contact with category members can act as an antidote to the negative traits society assigns to people in that category.

I recently had my eyes opened to the way experience can trump bias. It happened after my mother moved into an assisted living center. Her cohorts there are mainly around ninety. Since I have had little exposure to large numbers of people that age, I initially viewed all of them as alike: white hair, slouched posture, tethered to their walkers. I figured that if they'd ever held a job, it must have been building the pyramids. I saw them not as individuals but, rather, as exemplars of their social stereotype, assuming they were all (except my mother, of course) rather dim and feebleminded and forgetful.

My thinking changed abruptly one day in the dining room, when my mother remarked that on the afternoons when the hairdresser visited the assisted living center, she felt pain and dizziness as she leaned her head back to have her hair washed. One of my mother's friends said that this was a very bad sign. My initial thoughts were dismissive: *What does she mean by a bad sign? Is that an astrological prediction?* But the friend went on to explain that my mother's complaints were the classic symptoms of an occluded carotid artery, which could lead to a stroke, and urged that she see her physician about it. My mother's friend wasn't just a ninety-year-old; she was a doctor. And as I got to know others in the home, over time, I started to see ninety-year-olds as varied and unique characters, with many different talents, none of which related to the pyramids.

The more we interact with individuals and are exposed to their particular qualities, the more ammunition our minds have to counteract our tendency to stereotype, for the traits we assign to categories are products not just of society's assumptions but of our own experience. I didn't take the IAT before and after, but my guess is that my implicit prejudice concerning the very old has been considerably reduced.

IN THE 1980s, scientists in London studied a seventy-seven-year-old shopkeeper who had had a stroke in the lower part of his occipital lobe.[26] His motor system and memory were unaffected, and he retained good speaking and visual skills. For the most part he seemed cognitively normal, but he did have one problem. If shown two objects that had the same function but were not identical—say, two different trains, two brushes, or two jugs—he could not recognize the connection between them. He could not tell, even, that the letters *a* and A meant the same thing. As a result, the patient reported great difficulty in everyday life, even when attempting simple tasks such as setting the table. Scientists say that without our ability to categorize we would not have survived as a species, but I'll go further: without that ability, one could hardly survive even as an *individual*. In the previous pages, we've seen that categorization, like many of our unconscious mental processes, has both up- and downsides. In the next chapter, we'll find out what happens when we categorize *ourselves*, when we define ourselves as being connected, by some trait, to certain other individuals. How does that affect the way we view and treat those within our group and those on the outside?

CHAPTER 8

In-Groups and Out-Groups

All groups . . . develop a way of living with characteristic codes and beliefs. —GORDON ALLPORT

THE CAMP WAS in a densely wooded area in southeastern Oklahoma, about seven miles from the nearest town. Hidden from view by heavy foliage and ringed by a fence, it was situated in the midst of a state park called Robbers Cave. The park got its name because Jesse James had once used it as a hideout, and it was still an ideal place to hole up if being left undisturbed was a priority. There were two large cabins inside the perimeter, separated by rough terrain and out of sight and hearing both from any road and from each other. In the 1950s, before cell phones and before the Internet, this was enough to ensure their occupants' isolation. At ten-thirty on the night of the raid, the inhabitants of one of those cabins darkened their faces and arms with dirt, then quietly made their way through the forest to the other cabin and, while its occupants slept, entered through the unlocked door. The intruders were angry and out for revenge. They were eleven years old.

For these kids, revenge meant ripping the mosquito netting off the beds, yelling insults, and grabbing a prized pair of blue jeans. Then, as their victims awoke, the invaders ran back to their own cabin as suddenly as they had arrived. They'd intended to inflict insult, not injury. Sounds like nothing more than a typical story of summer camp gone awry, but this camp was different. As these boys played and fought, ate and talked, planned and plotted, a corps of adults was secretly watching and listening, studying their every move with neither their knowledge nor their consent.

The boys at Robbers Cave that summer had been enrolled in a pioneering and ambitious—and, by today's standards, unethical—field experiment in social psychology.[1] According to a later report on the study, the experimental subjects had been carefully chosen for uniformity. A researcher laboriously screened each child before recruiting him, surreptitiously observing him on the playground and perusing his school records. The subjects were all middle-class, Protestant, Caucasian, and of average intelligence. All were well-adjusted boys who had just completed the fifth grade. None knew any of the others. After targeting two hundred prospects, the researchers had approached their parents offering a good deal. They could enroll their son in a three-week summer camp for a nominal fee, provided they agreed to have no contact with their child throughout that period. During that time, the parents were told, the researchers would study the boys and their "interactions in group activities."

Twenty-two sets of parents took the bait. The researchers divided the boys into two groups of eleven, balanced for height, weight, athletic ability, popularity, and certain skills related to the activities they would be engaging in at camp. The groups were assembled separately, not told of each other's existence, and kept isolated during their first week. In that week, there were really two boys' camps at Robbers Cave, and the boys in each were kept unaware of the other.

As the campers engaged in baseball games, singing, and other normal camp activities, they were watched closely by their counselors, who in reality were all researchers studying them and secretly taking notes. One point of interest to the researchers was whether, how, and why each collection of boys would coalesce into a cohesive group. And coalesce they did, each group forming its own identity, choosing a name (the Rattlers and the Eagles), creating a flag, and coming to share "preferred songs, practices and peculiar norms" that were different from those of the other group. But the real point of the study was to investigate how and why, once the groups *had* coalesced, they would react to the presence of a new group. And so, after the first week, the Rattlers and the Eagles were introduced to each other.

Films and novels depicting either the distant past or the postapocalyptic future warn that isolated groups of *Homo sapiens* should always be approached with care, their members more likely to cut off your nose than offer you free incense. The physicist Stephen Hawking once famously endorsed that view, arguing that it would be better to beware of aliens than to invite them in for tea. Human colonial history seems to confirm this. When people from one nation land on the shores of another with a far different culture, they may say they come in peace, but they soon start shooting. In this case, the Rattlers and Eagles had their Christopher Columbus moment at the start of the second week. That's when an observer-counselor separately told each group of the other's existence. The groups had a similar reaction: let's challenge the other to a sports tournament. After some negotiations, a series of events was arranged to take place over the following week, including baseball games, tug-of-war matches, tent-pitching contests, and a treasure hunt. Camp counselors agreed to provide trophies, medals, and prizes for the winners.

It didn't take long for the Rattlers and the Eagles to settle into the dynamics of the countless other warring factions that had preceded them. On the first day of competition, after losing at tug-of-war, the Eagles, on their way back to their cabin, happened by the ball field where the Rattlers had hung their flag high up on the backstop. A couple of Eagles, agitated about getting beaten, climbed up and took it down. They set it on fire, and when the fire went out, one of them climbed back up and rehung it. The counselors had no response to the flag burning, except to dutifully and surreptitiously take their notes. And then they arranged the next meeting of the members of the two groups, who were told that they would now compete at baseball and other activities.

After breakfast the following morning, the Rattlers were taken to the ball field, where, while they waited for the Eagles to arrive, they discovered their burnt flag. The researchers watched as the Rattlers plotted their retaliation, which resulted in a mass brawl when the Eagles did show up. The staff observed for a while, then intervened to stop the fighting. But the feud continued, with the Rattlers' raid on the Eagles' cabin the next night, and other events in the days that followed. The researchers had hoped that by setting up groups with competitive goals but no inherent differences, they could observe the generation and evolution of derogatory social stereotypes, genuine intergroup hostility, and all the other symptoms of intergroup conflict we humans are known for. They were not disappointed. Today, the boys of Robbers Cave are past retirement age, but the tale of their summer, and the researchers' analysis of it, is still being cited in the psychological literature.

Humans have always lived in bands. If competing in a tug-of-war contest generated intergroup hostility, imagine the hostility between bands of humans with too many mouths to feed and too few elephant carcasses to dine on. Today we think of war as being at least in part based on ideology, but the desire for food and water is the strongest ideology. Long before communism, democracy, or theories of racial superiority were invented, neighboring groups of people regularly fought with and even massacred each other, inspired by the competition for resources.[2] In such an environment, a highly evolved sense of "us versus them" would have been crucial to survival.

There was also a sense of "us versus them" *within* bands, for, as in other hominid species, prehistoric humans formed alliances and coalitions inside their own groups.[3] While a talent for office politics is useful in the workplace today, twenty thousand years ago group dynamics might determine who got fed, and the human resources department might have disciplined slackers with a spear through the back. So if the ability to pick up cues that signal political allegiances is important in contemporary work, in prehistoric times it was vital, for the equivalent of being fired was being dead.

Scientists call any group that people feel part of an "in-group," and any group that excludes them an "out-group." As opposed to the colloquial usage, the terms "in-group" and "out-group" in this technical sense refer not to the popularity of those in the groups but simply to the us-them distinction. It is an important distinction because we think differently about members of groups we are part of and those in groups we are not part of, and, as we shall see, we also behave differently toward them. And we do this automatically, regardless of whether or not we consciously intend to discriminate between the groups. In the last chapter I talked about how putting other people into categories affects our assessment of them. Putting ourselves into in- and out-group categories also has an effect—on the way we see our own place in the world and on how we view others. In what follows we'll learn what happens when we use categorization to define ourselves, to differentiate "us" from others.

WE ALL BELONG to many in-groups. As a result, our self-identification shifts from situation to situation. At different times the same person might think of herself as a woman, an executive, a Disney employee, a Brazilian, or a mother, depending on which is relevant—or which makes her feel good at the time. Switching the in-group affiliation we're adopting for the moment is a trick we all use, and it's helpful in maintaining a cheery outlook, for the in-groups we identify with are an important component of our self-image. Both experimental and field studies have found, in fact, that people will make large financial sacrifices to help establish a feeling of belonging to an in-group they aspire to feel part of.[4] That's one reason, for example, that people pay so much to be members of exclusive country clubs, even if they don't utilize the facilities. A computer games executive once shared with me a great example of the willingness to give up money for the prestige of a coveted in-group identity. One of his senior producers marched into his office after finding out that he had given another producer a promotion and raise. He told her he couldn't promote *her* for a while yet, because of financial constraints. But she was insistent on being given a raise, now that she knew her colleague had gotten one. It was tough for this executive because his business was ultracompetitive, and other companies were always hovering in the background looking to steal good producers, yet he didn't have the funds to hand out raises to all who deserved them. After discussing the matter for a while, he noticed that what really bothered his employee was not the lack of a raise but that the other producer, who was junior to her, now had the same title. And so they agreed on a compromise: he would promote her and give her a new title now, but the raise would come later. Like the country club sales office, this executive had awarded her a high-status in-group membership in exchange for money. Advertisers are very much attuned to that dynamic. That's why, for example, Apple spends hundreds of millions of dollars on marketing campaigns in an attempt to associate the Mac in-group with smarts, elegance, and hipness, and the PC in-group with loser qualities, the opposites of those.

Once we think of ourselves as belonging to an exclusive country club, executive rank, or class of computer users, the views of others in the group seep into our thinking, and color the way we perceive the world. Psychologists call those views "group norms." Perhaps the purest illustration of their influence came from the man who engineered the Robbers Cave study. His name was Muzafer Sherif. A Turk who immigrated to America for graduate school, Sherif earned his PhD from Columbia University in 1935. His dissertation focused on the influence of group norms on vision. You'd think vision would arise through an objective process, but Sherif's work showed that a group norm can affect something as basic as the way you perceive a point of light.

In his work, decades ahead of its time, Sherif brought subjects into a dark room and displayed a small illuminated dot on a wall. After a few moments, the dot would appear to move. But that was just an illusion. That appearance of motion was the result of tiny eye movements that caused the image on the retina to jiggle. As I mentioned in Chapter 2, under normal conditions the brain, detecting the simultaneous jiggling of all the objects in a scene, corrects for this jiggling, and you perceive the scene as motionless. But when a dot of light is viewed without context the brain is fooled and perceives the dot as moving in space. Moreover, since there are no other objects for reference, the magnitude of the motion is open to a wide degree of interpretation. Ask different people how far the dot has moved and you get widely different answers.

Sherif showed the dot to three people at a time and instructed them that whenever they saw the dot move, they should call out how far it had moved. An interesting phenomenon occurred: people in a given group would call out different numbers, some high and some low, but eventually their estimates would converge to within a narrow range, the "norm" for that group of three. Although the norm varied widely from group to group, *within* each group the members came to agree upon a norm, which they arrived at without discussion or prompting. Moreover, when individual group members were invited back a week later to repeat the experiment, this time on their own, they replicated the estimates arrived at by their group. The perception of the subjects' in-group had become their perception.

———

SEEING OURSELVES AS a member of a group automatically marks everyone as either an "us" or a "them." Some of our in-groups, like our family, our work colleagues, or our bicycling buddies, include only people we know. Others, like females, Hispanics, or senior citizens, are broader groups that society defines and assigns traits to. But whatever in-groups we belong to, they consist by definition of people we perceive as having some kind of commonality with us. This shared experience or identity causes us to see our fate as being intertwined with the fate of the group, and thus the group's successes and failures as our own. It is natural, then, that we have a special place in our hearts for our in-group members.

We may not like people in general, but however little or much we like our fellow human beings, our subliminal selves tend to like our fellow in-group members more. Consider the in-group that is your profession. In one study, researchers asked subjects to rate the likability of doctors, lawyers, waiters, and hairdressers, on a scale from 1 to 100.[5] The twist was, every subject in this experiment was him- or herself either a doctor, a lawyer, a waiter, or a hairdresser. The results were very consistent: those in three of the four professions rated the members of the *other* professions as average, with a likability around 50. But they rated those in their own profession significantly higher, around 70. There was only one exception: the lawyers, who rated both those in the other professions *and* other lawyers at around 50. That probably brings to mind several lawyer jokes, so there is no need for me to make any. However, the fact that lawyers do not favor fellow lawyers is not necessarily due to the circumstance that the only difference between a lawyer and a catfish is that one is a bottom-feeding scavenger and the other is a fish. Of the four groups assessed by the researchers, lawyers, you see, form the only one whose members regularly *oppose* others in their own group. So while other lawyers may be in a given lawyer's in-group, they are also potentially in his or her out-group. Despite that anomaly, research suggests that, whether with regard to religion, race, nationality, computer use, or our operating unit at work, we generally have a built-in tendency to prefer those in our in-group. Studies show that common group membership can even trump negative personal attributes.[6] As one researcher put it, "One may like people as group members even as one dislikes them as individual persons."

This finding—that we find people more likable merely because we are associated with them in some way—has a natural corollary: we also tend to favor in-group members in our social and business dealings, and we evaluate their work and products more favorably than we might otherwise, even if we think we are treating everyone equally.[7] For example, in one study researchers divided people into groups of three. Each group was paired with another, and then each of the paired groups was asked to perform three varied tasks: to use a children's toy set to make a work of art, to sketch a plan for a senior housing project, and to write a symbolic fable that imparts a moral to the reader. For each task, one member of each group in the pair (the "nonparticipant") was separated from his or her cohorts, and did not take part in the tasks. After each pair of groups had completed a task, the two nonparticipants were asked to rate the results of the efforts of both groups.

The nonparticipants had no vested interest in the products their in-group had turned out; nor had the groups been formed with regard to any distinctive shared qualities. If the nonparticipants had been objective, therefore, you'd think that on average they would have preferred the products of their out-group just as often as they preferred those of their in-group. But they didn't. In two cases out of three, when they had a preference, it was for what their in-group had produced.

Another way the in- and out-group distinction affects us is that we tend to think of our in-group members as more variegated and complex than those in the out-group. For example, the researcher conducting the study involving doctors, lawyers, waiters, and hairdressers asked all of his subjects to estimate how much those in each profession vary with regard to creativity, flexibility, and several other qualities. They all rated those in the other professions as significantly more homogeneous than those in their own group. Other studies have come to the same conclusion with regard to groups that differ by age, nationality, gender, race, and even the college people attended and the sorority women belonged to.[8] That's why, as one set of researchers pointed out, newspapers run by the predominantly white establishment print headlines such as "Blacks Seriously Split on Middle East," as if it is news when all African Americans don't think alike, but they don't run headlines like "White People Seriously Split on Stock Market Reform."[9]

It might seem natural to perceive more variability in our in-groups because we often know their members better, as individuals. For instance, I know a great many theoretical physicists personally, and to me they seem to be quite a varied bunch. Some like piano music; others prefer the violin. Some read Nabokov; others, Nietzsche. Okay, maybe they're not *that* varied. But now suppose I think of investment bankers. I know very few of those, but in my mind I see them as even less varied than theoretical physicists: I imagine they *all* read only the *Wall Street Journal,* drive fancy cars, and don't listen to music at all, preferring to watch the financial news on television (unless the news is bad, in which case they just skip it and pop open a $500 bottle of wine). The surprise is that the feeling that our in-group is more varied than our out-group *does not depend* on having more knowledge of our in-group. Instead, the categorization of people into in-groups and out-groups alone is enough to trigger that judgment. In fact, as we'll see in just a bit, our special feelings toward our in-group persist even when researchers artificially sort strangers into random in-groups and out-groups. When Mark Antony addressed the throngs after Caesar's assassination, saying, in Shakespeare's version of the events, "Friends, Romans, countrymen, lend me your ears," he was really saying, "In-group members, in-group members, in-group members . . ." A wise appeal.

A FEW YEARS ago, three Harvard researchers gave dozens of Asian American women at Harvard a difficult math test.[10] But before getting them started, the researchers asked them to fill out a questionnaire about themselves. These Asian American women were members of two in-groups with conflicting norms: they were Asians, a group identified with being good at math, and they were women, a group identified as being poor at it. One set of participants received a questionnaire asking about what languages they, their parents, and grandparents spoke and how many generations of their family had lived in America. These questions were designed to trigger the women's identity as Asian Americans. Other subjects answered queries about coed dormitory policy, designed to trigger their identity as women. A third group, the control group, was quizzed about their phone and cable

TV service. After the test, the researchers gave the participants an exit survey. Measured by the subjects' self-reports in that exit questionnaire, the initial questionnaire had had no impact on their conscious assessment of either their ability or the test. Yet something had clearly affected them subliminally, because the women who had been manipulated to think of themselves as Asian Americans had done better on the test than did the control group, who, in turn, had done better than the women reminded of their female in-group. Your in-group identity influences the way you judge people, but it also influences the way you feel about yourself, the way you behave, and sometimes even your performance.

We all belong to multiple in-groups, and, like the groups Asian Americans and women, they can have conflicting norms. I've found that once we are conscious of this, we can use it to our advantage. For example, I occasionally smoke a cigar, and when I do I feel a certain in-group kinship with my best friend in college, my PhD adviser, and Albert Einstein, all fellow physicists who liked their cigars. But when I think my smoking is getting dangerously out of hand, I find I can kill the urge quickly by coaxing myself to focus instead on another in-group of smokers, one that includes my father, who suffered from lung problems, and my cousin, who had debilitating mouth cancer.

The conflicting norms of our in-groups can at times lead to rather curious contradictions in our behavior. For example, from time to time, the media will broadcast public service announcements aimed at reducing petty crimes like littering and pilfering relics from national parks. These ads often also decry the alarming frequency with which these crimes occur. In one such ad, a Native American dressed in traditional garb canoes across a debris-ridden river. After the Native American reaches the heavily littered opposite shore, a driver—John Q. Public—zooms down an adjacent road and tosses trash out of his car, strewing garbage at the Native American's feet. The ad cuts to a close-up, showing a lone teardrop running down the man's face. That ad explicitly preaches an anti-litter message to our conscious minds. But it also conveys a message to our unconscious: those in our in-group, our fellow parkgoers, *do* litter. So which message wins out, the ethical appeal or the group norm reminder? No one studied the effects of that particular ad, but in a controlled study done on public service announcements, another ad that simply denounced littering was successful in inhibiting the practice, while a similar ad that included the phrase "Americans will produce more litter than ever!" led to *increased* littering.[11] It's doubtful that anyone consciously interpreted "Americans will produce more litter than ever!" as an order rather than a criticism, but by identifying littering as a group norm, it had that result.

In a related study, researchers created a sign condemning the fact that many visitors steal the wood from Petrified Forest National Park.[12] They placed the sign on a well-used pathway, along with some secretly marked pieces of wood. Then they watched to see what effect the sign would have. They found that in the absence of a sign, souvenir hunters stole about 3 percent of the wood pieces in just a ten-hour period. But with the warning sign in place, that number almost tripled, to 8 percent. Again, it is doubtful that many of the pilferers literally said to themselves, *Everyone does it, so why not me?* But that seems to be the message received by their unconscious. The researchers pointed out that messages that condemn yet highlight undesired social norms are common, and that they invite counterproductive results. So while a college administration may think it is *warning* students when it says, "Remember! You must cut down on binge drinking, which is prevalent on campus!" what sinks in may instead be a call to action: *Remember! Binge drinking is prevalent on campus!* When, as a child, I tried to use my friend's habits to justify, say, playing baseball on Saturday instead of going to the synagogue, my mother would say something like "So, if Joey jumped into a volcano, would you do it, too?" Now, decades later, I realize I should have said, "Yeah, Mom. Studies show that I would."

I'VE SAID THAT we treat our in-groups and out-groups differently in our thinking, whether or not we consciously intend to make the distinction. Over the years, curious psychologists have tried to determine the minimal requirements necessary for a person to feel a kinship with an in-group. They have found that there is no minimal requirement. It is not necessary for you to share any attitudes or traits with your fellow group members, or even for you to have met the other group members. It is the simple act of knowing that you belong to a group that triggers your in-group affinity.

In one study, researchers had subjects look at images of paintings by the

Swiss artist Paul Klee and the Russian painter Wassily Kandinsky and then indicate which they preferred.[13] The researchers labeled each subject as either a Kandinsky fan or a Klee fan. The two painters had distinctive styles, but unless the subjects happened to be fanatic art historians specializing in early-twentieth-century avant-garde European painters, they probably had no reason to feel any particular warmth for those who shared their opinion. For the vast majority of people, on the passion scale, Klee versus Kandinsky was not exactly Brazil versus Argentina or fur coat versus cloth coat.

After labeling their subjects, the researchers did something that may appear odd. They, in essence, gave each subject a bucket of money and told them to divide it among the other subjects in any way they saw fit. The division was carried out in private. None of the subjects knew any of the other subjects, or could even see them during the course of the experiment. Still, when passing out the money, they favored their in-group, those who shared their group label.

A large body of research replicates the finding that our group-based social identity is so strong that we will discriminate against *them* and favor *us* even if the rule that distinguishes *them* from *us* is akin to flipping a coin. That's right: not only do we identify with a group based on the flimsiest of distinctions, we also look at group members differently—even if group membership is unrelated to any relevant or meaningful personal qualities. That's not just important in our personal lives; it also affects organizations. For example, companies can gain by fostering their employees' in-group identification, something that can be accomplished by creating and making salient a distinctive corporate culture, as was done very successfully by companies such as Disney, Apple, and Google. On the other hand, it can be dicey when a company's *internal* departments or divisions develop a strong group identity, for that can lead to both in-group favoritism and out-group discrimination, and research suggests that hostility erupts more readily between groups than between individuals.[14] But regardless of what kind of shared identity does or doesn't exist within a company, many companies find it effective to use marketing to foster a group identity among their *customers*. That's why in-groups based on Mac versus PC ownership, or Mercedes versus BMW versus Cadillac, are more than just computer clubs or car clubs: we treat such categorizations as meaningful in a far broader realm than they have any right to be.

Dog person versus cat person. Rare meat versus medium. Powdered detergent versus liquid. Do we really draw broad inferences from such narrow distinctions as these? The Klee/Kandinsky study, and literally dozens more like it, followed a classic experimental paradigm invented by Henri Tajfel, who conducted the line-length experiment.[15] In this paradigm, subjects were assigned to one of two groups. They were told that their group assignments had been made on the basis of something they shared with other members of the group but which, objectively speaking, was really quite meaningless as a way of affiliating with a group—either the Klee/Kandinsky preference or whether they had overestimated or underestimated the number of dots that were quickly flashed on a screen.

As in the study I quoted earlier, Tajfel allowed his subjects to dole out awards to their fellow subjects. To be precise, he had them give out points that could later be cashed in for money. The subjects did not know the identities of the people they were giving points to. But in all cases they knew the group to which the person belonged. In Tajfel's original study, the handing out of points was a bit complicated, but the crux of the experiment lies in just the way it was done, so it is worth describing.

The experiment consisted of over a dozen stages. At each stage, a subject ("awarder") had to make a choice regarding how to dole out points to two other subjects ("recipients"), who, as I said, were anonymous. Sometimes the two recipients were both members of the subject's own group or both members of the other group; sometimes one was a member of the subject's own group and the other was a member of the other group.

The catch was that the choices offered to awarders did not represent a zero-sum game. That is, they did not entail simply deciding how to divide a fixed number of points. Rather, the options offered added up to varying point totals, as well as differing ways of splitting those points among the two recipients. At each stage, the awarder had to choose from among over a dozen alternative ways to award points. If the awarders felt no in-group favoritism, the logical action would be to choose whichever alternative bestows upon the two recipients the greatest total number of points. But the awarders did that in only one circumstance: when they were dividing points among two members of their in-group. When awarding points to two members of the out-group, they chose options that resulted in awarding far fewer points. And what is really extraordinary is that when the options required awarders to divide points between one in-group member and one out-group member, they tended to make choices that maximized the *difference* between the rewards they gave to the two group members, *even if that action resulted in a lesser reward for their own group member!*

That's right: as a trend, over dozens of individual reward decisions, subjects sought not to maximize their own group's reward but the difference between the reward their group would receive and that which the other group would be awarded. Remember, this experiment has been replicated many times, with subject pools of all ages and many different nationalities, and all have reached the same conclusion: we are highly invested in feeling different from one another—and superior—no matter how flimsy the grounds for our sense of superiority, and no matter how self-sabotaging that may end up being.

You may find it discouraging to hear that, even when group divisions are anonymous and meaningless, and even at their group's own personal cost, people unambiguously choose to discriminate in favor of their in-group, rather than acting for the greatest good. But this does not doom us to a world of never-ending social discrimination. Like unconscious stereotyping, unconscious discrimination can be overcome. In fact, though it doesn't take much to establish grounds for group discrimination, it takes less than we think to erase those grounds. In the Robbers Cave experiment, Sherif noted that mere contact between the Eagles and the Rattlers did not reduce the negative attitude each group had for the other. But another tactic did: he set up a series of difficulties that the groups had to work *together* to overcome.

In one of those scenarios, Sherif arranged for the camp water supply to be cut off. He announced the problem, said its cause was a mystery, and asked twenty-five volunteers to help check the water system. In reality, the researchers had turned off a key valve and shoved two boulders over it and had also clogged a faucet. The kids worked together for about an hour, found the problems, and fixed them. In another scenario, Sherif arranged for a truck that was supposed to get food for the boys not to start. The staff member who drove the truck "struggled and perspired" and got the truck to make all sorts of noises, as more and more of the boys gathered around to watch. Finally the boys figured out that the driver might be able to start the truck if they could just get it moving. But the truck was on an uphill slope. So twenty of the boys, from both groups, tied a tug-of-war rope to the truck and pulled it until it started.

These and several other scenarios that gave the groups common goals and required cooperative intergroup actions, the researchers noted, sharply reduced the intergroup conflict. Sherif wrote, "The change in behavior patterns of interaction between the groups was striking."[16] The more that people in different traditionally defined in-groups, such as race, ethnicity, class, gender, or religion, find it advantageous to work together, the less they discriminate against one another.[17]

As one who lived near the World Trade Center in New York City, I experienced that personally on September 11, 2001, and in the months that followed. New York is called a melting pot, but the different elements tossed into the pot often don't melt, or even blend very well with one another. The city is perhaps more like a stew made of diverse ingredients—bankers and bakers, young and old, black and white, rich and poor—that may not mingle and sometimes distinctly clash. As I stood beneath the north tower of the World Trade Center at 8:45 a.m. on that September 11, among the bustling crowd of immigrant street vendors, suited Wall Street types, and Orthodox Jews in their traditional garb, the city's class and ethnic divisions were amply apparent. But at 8:46 a.m., as that first plane hit the north tower and chaos erupted, as the fiery debris fell toward us and a horrific sight of death unfolded above us, something subtle and magical also transpired. All those divisions seemed to evaporate, and people began to help other people, regardless of who they were. For a few months, at least, we were all first and foremost New Yorkers. With thousands dead, and tens of thousands of all professions, races, and economic status suddenly homeless, or jobless because their place of work had been shut down, and with millions of us in shock over what those in our midst had suffered, we New Yorkers of all kinds pulled together as I had never before experienced. As entire blocks continued to smolder, as the corrosive smell of the destruction filled the air we breathed, and as the photos of the missing looked down on us from buildings and lampposts, subway stations and cyclone fences, we showed a kindness to one another, in acts large and small, that was probably unprecedented. It was the best of our human social nature at work, a vivid exhibition of the positive healing power of our human group instinct.

CHAPTER 9

Feelings

Each of us *is* a singular narrative, which is constructed, continually, unconsciously, by, through, and in us. — OLIVER SACKS

I N THE EARLY 1950s, a twenty-five-year-old woman named Chris Costner Sizemore walked into a young psychiatrist's office complaining of severe and blinding headaches.[1] These, she said, were sometimes followed by blackouts. Sizemore appeared to be a normal young mother, in a bad marriage but with no major psychological problems. Her doctor would later describe her as demure and constrained, circumspect, and meticulously truthful. He and she discussed various emotional issues, but nothing that occurred over the next few months of treatment indicated that Sizemore had actually lost consciousness or that she suffered from any serious mental condition. Nor was her family aware of any unusual episodes. Then one day during therapy she mentioned that she had apparently gone on a recent trip but had no memory of it. Her doctor hypnotized her, and the amnesia cleared. Several days later, the doctor received an unsigned letter. From the postmark and the familiar penmanship, he knew it had come from Sizemore. In the letter, Sizemore said she was disturbed by the recovered memory—how could she be sure she remembered everything, and how could she know the memory loss wouldn't happen again? There was also another sentence scrawled at the bottom of the letter, in a different handwriting that was difficult to decipher.

On her next visit Sizemore denied having sent the letter, though she recalled having begun one that, she said, she had never completed. Then she began to exhibit signs of stress and agitation. Suddenly she asked—with obvious embarrassment—if hearing an imaginary voice meant she was insane. As the therapist thought about it, Sizemore altered her posture, crossed her legs, and took on a "childishly daredevil air" he had never before seen in her. As he later described it, "A thousand minute alterations of manner, gesture, expression, posture, of nuances in reflex or instinctive reaction, of glance, of eyebrow tilting and eye movement, all argued that this could only be another woman." Then that "other woman" began to speak of Chris Sizemore and her problems in the third person, using "she" or "her" in every reference.

When asked her identity, Sizemore now replied with a different name. It was she, this person who suddenly had a new name, she said, who had found the unfinished letter, added a sentence, and mailed it. In the coming months Sizemore's doctor administered psychological personality tests while Sizemore took on each of her two identities. He submitted the tests to independent researchers, who were not told that they'd come from the same woman.[2] The analysts concluded that the two personalities had markedly different self-images. The woman who'd originally entered therapy saw herself as passive, weak, and bad. She knew nothing of her other half, a woman who saw herself as active, strong, and good. Sizemore was eventually cured. It took eighteen years.[3]

Chris Sizemore's was an extreme case, but we all have many identities. Not only are we different people at fifty than we are at thirty, we also change throughout the day, depending on circumstances and our social environment, as well as on our hormonal levels. We behave differently when we are in a good mood than when we are in a bad one. We behave differently having lunch with our boss than when having lunch with our subordinates. Studies show that people make different moral decisions after seeing a happy film,[4] and that women, when ovulating, wear more revealing clothing, become more sexually competitive, and increase their preference for sexually competitive men.[5] Our character is not indelibly stamped on us but is dynamic and changing. And as the studies of implicit prejudice revealed, we can even be two different people at the same time, an unconscious "I" who holds negative feelings about blacks—or the elderly, or fat people, or gays, or Muslims—and a conscious "I" who abhors prejudice.

Despite this, psychologists have traditionally assumed that the way a person feels and behaves reflects fixed traits that form the core of that individual's personality. They've assumed that people know who they are and that they act consistently, as a result of conscious deliberation.[6] So compelling was this model that in the 1960s one researcher suggested that, rather than performing costly and time-consuming experiments, psychologists might collect reliable information by simply asking people to predict how they would feel and behave in certain circumstances of interest.[7] Why not? Much of clinical psychotherapy is based on what is essentially the same idea: that through intense, therapeutically guided reflection we can learn our true feelings, attitudes, and motives.

But remember the statistics on Browns marrying Browns, and investors undervaluing the IPOs of companies with tongue-twister names? None of the Browns had consciously set out to choose a spouse who shared their name; nor did professional investors think their impressions of a new company had been influenced by the ease of pronouncing that company's name. Because of the role of subliminal processes, the source of our feelings is often a mystery to us, and so are the feelings themselves. We feel many things we are not aware of feeling. To ask us to talk about our feelings may be valuable, but some of our innermost feelings will not yield their secrets to even the most profound introspection. As a result, many of psychology's traditional assumptions about our feelings simply do not hold.

"I'VE GONE THROUGH years of psychotherapy," a well-known neuroscientist told me, "to try to find out why I behave in certain ways. I think about my feelings, my motivations. I talk to my therapist about them, I finally come up with a story that seems to make sense, and it satisfies me. I need a story I can believe, but is it true? Probably not. The real truth lies in structures like my thalamus and hypothalamus, and my amygdala, and I have no conscious access to those no matter how much I introspect." If we are to have a valid understanding of who we are and, therefore, of how we would react in various situations, we have to understand the reasons for our decisions and behavior, and—even more fundamentally—we have to understand our feelings and their origins. Where *do* they come from?

Let's start with something simple: the feeling of pain. The sensory and emotional feeling of pain arises from distinct neural signals and has a well-defined and obvious role in our lives. Pain encourages you to put down that red-hot frying pan, punishes you for pounding your thumb with that hammer, and reminds you that when sampling six brands of single-malt Scotch, you should not make them doubles. A friend may have to draw you out before you understand your feelings toward that financial analyst who took you to the wine bar last night, but a pounding headache is a feeling you'd think you could get in touch with without anyone's help. And yet it is not that simple, as evidenced by the famous placebo effect.

When we think of the placebo effect, we may imagine an inert sugar pill that relieves a mild headache as well as a Tylenol, as long as we believe we've taken the real thing. But the effect can be dramatically more powerful than that. For example, angina pectoris, a chronic malady caused by inadequate blood supply in the muscle of the heart wall, often causes very severe pain. If you have angina and attempt to exercise—which can mean simply walking to answer the door—nerves in your heart muscle act like a "check engine" sensor: they carry signals via your spinal cord to your brain to alert you that improper demands are being placed on your circulatory system. The result can be excruciating pain, a warning light that is hard to ignore. In the 1950s, it was common practice for surgeons to tie off certain arteries in the chest cavity as a treatment for patients with severe angina pain. They believed new channels would sprout in nearby heart muscle, improving circulation. The surgery was performed on a large number of patients with apparent success. Yet something was amiss: pathologists who later examined these patients' cadavers never saw any of the expected new blood vessels.

Apparently the surgery was a success at relieving the patients' symptoms but a failure at addressing their cause. In 1958, curious cardiac surgeons conducted an experiment that, for ethical reasons, would not be permitted today: they carried out sham operations. For five patients, surgeons cut through the skin to expose the arteries in question but then stitched each patient back together without actually tying off the arteries. They also performed the true operation on another group of thirteen patients. The surgeons told neither the patients nor their cardiologists which subjects had had the real operation. Among the patients who did receive the real operation, 76 percent saw an improvement in their angina pain. But so did *all five* in the sham group. Both groups, believing that a relevant surgical procedure had been performed, reported far milder pain than they had had before surgery. Since the surgery produced no physical changes in either group (in terms of the growth of new blood vessels to improve circulation to the heart), both groups would have continued to experience the same level of sensory input to the pain centers of their brains. Yet both groups had a greatly reduced *conscious* experience of pain. It seems our knowledge of our feelings—even physical ones—is so tenuous that we can't even reliably know when we are experiencing excruciating pain.[8]

The view of emotion that is dominant today can be traced not to Freud—who believed that unconscious content was blocked from awareness via the mechanism of repression—but to William James, whose name has already come up in several other contexts. James was an enigmatic character. Born in New York City in 1842 to an extremely wealthy man who used some of his vast fortune to finance extensive travels for himself and his family, James had attended at least fifteen different schools in Europe and America by the time he was eighteen—in New York; Newport, Rhode Island; London; Paris; Boulogne-sur-Mer, in northern France; Geneva; and Bonn. His interests flitted similarly, from subject to subject, landing for a while on art, chemistry, the military, anatomy, and medicine. The flitting consumed fifteen years. At one point during those years he accepted an invitation from the famous Harvard biologist Louis Agassiz to go on an expedition to the Amazon River basin in Brazil, during which James was seasick most of the time and, in addition, contracted smallpox. In the end, medicine was the only course of study James completed, receiving an MD from Harvard in 1869, at the age of twenty-seven. But he never practiced or taught medicine.

It was an 1867 visit to mineral springs in Germany—where he traveled to recuperate from the health problems resulting from the Amazon trip—that led James to psychology. Like Münsterberg sixteen years later, James attended some of Wilhelm Wundt's lectures and got hooked on

*William James self-portrait. By permission of the
Houghton Library, Harvard University.*

the subject, in particular the challenge of turning psychology into a science. He began to read works of German psychology and philosophy, but
he returned to Harvard to complete his medical degree. After his gradua-
tion from Harvard, he became deeply depressed. His diary from that time
reveals little but misery and self-loathing. His suffering was so severe that
he had himself committed to an asylum in Somerville, Massachusetts,
for treatment; however, he credited his recovery not to the treatment he
received but to his discovery of an essay on free will by the French philosopher Charles Renouvier. After reading it, he resolved to use his own
free will to break his depression. In truth, it doesn't seem to have been that
simple, for he remained incapacitated for another eighteen months and
suffered from chronic depression for the rest of his life.

Still, by 1872 James was well enough to accept a teaching post in physiology at Harvard, and by 1875 he was teaching The Relations Between
Physiology and Psychology, making Harvard the first university in the
United States to offer instruction in experimental psychology. It was
another decade before James put forth to the public his theory of emotions, providing the outline of that theory in an article he published in

1884 called "What Is an Emotion?" The article appeared in a philosophy journal called *Mind*, rather than in a psychology journal, because the first English-language journal of research psychology wouldn't be established until 1887.

In his article, James addressed emotions such as "surprise, curiosity, rapture, fear, anger, lust, greed and the like," which are accompanied by bodily changes such as quickened breath or pulse or movements of the body or the face.[9] It may seem obvious that these bodily changes are caused by the emotion in question, but James argued that such an interpretation is precisely backward. "My thesis on the contrary," James wrote, "is that the bodily changes follow directly the PERCEPTION of [an] exciting fact, and that our feeling of the same changes as they occur IS the emotion. . . . Without the bodily state following on the perception, the latter would be purely cognitive in form, pale, colorless, destitute of emotional warmth." In other words, we don't tremble because we're angry or cry because we feel sad; rather, we are aware of feeling angry because we tremble, and we feel sad because we cry. James was proposing a physiological basis for emotion, an idea that has gained currency today—thanks in part to the brain-imaging technology that allows us to watch the physical processes involved in emotion as they are actually occurring in the brain.

Emotions, in today's neo-Jamesian view, are like perceptions and memories—they are reconstructed from the data at hand. Much of that data comes from your unconscious mind, as it processes environmental stimuli picked up by your senses and creates a physiological response. The brain also employs other data, such as your preexisting beliefs and expectations, and information about the current circumstances. All of that information is processed, and a conscious feeling of emotion is produced. That mechanism can explain the angina studies—and, more generally, the effect of placebos on pain. If the subjective experience of pain is constructed from both our physiological state and contextual data, it's no surprise that our minds can interpret the same physiological data—the nerve impulses signifying pain—in different ways. As a result, when nerve cells send a signal to the pain centers of your brain, your experience of pain can vary even if those signals don't.[10]

James elaborated on his theory of emotion, among many other things, in his book *The Principles of Psychology*, which I mentioned in Chapter 4 regarding Angelo Mosso's experiments on the brains of patients who had gaps in their skulls following surgery. James had been given a contract to write the book in 1878. He began it, with a flurry of work, on his honeymoon. But once the honeymoon was over, it took him twelve years to finish it. It became a classic, so revolutionary and influential that, in a 1991 survey of historians of psychology, James ranked second among psychology's most important figures, behind only his early inspiration, Wundt.[11]

Ironically, neither Wundt nor James was pleased with the book. Wundt was dissatisfied because James's revolution had by then strayed from Wundt's brand of experimental psychology, in which everything must be measured. How, for instance, do you quantify and measure emotions? By 1890, James had decided that since one couldn't, psychology must move beyond pure experiment, and he derided Wundt's work as "brass instrument psychology."[12] Wundt, on the other hand, wrote of James's book that "It is literature, it is beautiful, but it is not psychology."[13]

James had much more stinging criticism for himself. He wrote, "No one could be more disgusted than I at the sight of the book. No subject is worth being treated of in 1000 pages. Had I ten years more, I could rewrite it in 500; but as it stands it is this or nothing—a loathsome, distended, tumefied, bloated, dropsical mass, testifying to nothing but two facts: 1st, that there is no such thing as a *science* of psychology, and 2nd, that W. J. is an incapable."[14] After publication of the book, James decided to abandon psychology in favor of philosophy, leading him to lure Münsterberg from Germany to take over the lab. James was then forty-eight.

JAMES'S THEORY OF emotion dominated psychology for a while, but then gave way to other approaches. In the 1960s, as psychology took its cognitive turn, his ideas—now called the James-Lange theory—experienced a new popularity, for the notion that different sorts of data are processed in your brain to create emotions fit nicely into James's framework. But a nice theory does not necessarily equate to a correct theory, so scientists sought additional evidence. The most famous of the early studies was an experiment performed by Stanley Schachter, the famed Dr. Zilstein in the University of Minnesota experiment, but then at Columbia. He partnered in the research with Jerome Singer, who would later be called the "best second author in psychology" because he held that position on a number of famous research studies.[15] If emotions are constructed from limited data rather than direct perception, similar to the way vision and memory are constructed, then, as with perception and memory, there must be circumstances when the way the mind fills in the gaps in the data results in your "getting it wrong." The result would be "emotional illusions" that are analogous to optical and memory illusions.

For example, suppose you experience the physiological symptoms of emotional arousal for no apparent reason. The logical response would be to think, *Wow, my body is experiencing unexplained physiological changes for no apparent reason! What's going on?* But suppose further that when you experience those sensations they occur in a context that encourages you to interpret your reaction as due to some emotion—say, fear, anger, happiness, or sexual attraction—even though there is no actual cause for that emotion. In that sense your experience would be an emotional illusion. To demonstrate this phenomenon, Schachter and Singer created two different artificial emotional contexts—one "happy," one "angry"—and studied physiologically aroused volunteers who were placed in those situations. The researchers' goal was to see whether those scenarios could be used to "trick" the volunteers into having an emotion that the psychologists themselves had chosen.

Here is how it worked. Schachter and Singer told all their experimental subjects that the purpose of the experiment they were participating in was to determine how the injection of a vitamin called "Suproxin" would affect their visual skills. Actually, the drug was adrenaline, which causes increased heart rate and blood pressure, a feeling of flushing, and accelerated breathing—all symptoms of emotional arousal. The subjects were divided into three groups. One group (the "informed") was accurately told about the effects of the injection, explained as the "side effects" of the Suproxin. Another group (the "ignorant") was told nothing. Its members would feel the same physiological changes but have no explanation for them. The third group, which acted as a control group, was injected with an inert saline solution. This group would feel no physiological effects and was not told that there would be any.

After administering the injection, the researcher excused himself and left each subject alone for twenty minutes with another supposed subject, who was actually a confederate of the scientists. In what was called the "happiness" scenario, this person acted strangely euphoric about the privilege of participating in the experiment, providing the artificial social context. Schachter and Singer also designed an "anger" scenario, in which the person the subjects were left alone with complained incessantly about the experiment and how it was being conducted. The experimenters hypothesized that, depending on which social context they'd been placed in, the "ignorant" subjects would interpret their physiological state as arising from either happiness or anger, while the "informed" subjects would not have any subjective experience of emotion because, even though they had been exposed to the same social context, they already had a good explanation for their physiological changes and would therefore have no need to attribute them to any kind of emotion. Schachter and Singer also expected that those in the control group, who did not experience any physiological arousal, would not experience any emotion, either.

The subjects' reactions were judged in two ways. First, they were surreptitiously watched from behind a two-way mirror by impartial observers, who coded their behavior according to a prearranged rubric. Second, the subjects were later given a written questionnaire, in which they reported their level of happiness on a scale from 0 to 4. By both measures, all three groups reacted exactly as Schachter and Singer had expected.

Both the informed and the control subjects observed the apparent emotions—euphoria or anger—of the confederate who had been planted in their midst but felt no such emotion in themselves. The ignorant subjects, however, observed the fellow and, depending on whether he seemed to be expressing euphoria or anger about the experiment, drew the conclusion that the physical sensations they themselves were experiencing constituted either happiness or anger. In other words, they fell victim to an "emotional illusion," mistakenly believing that they were reacting to the situation with the same "emotions" the fake subject was experiencing.

The Schachter and Singer paradigm has been repeated over the years in many other forms, employing means gentler than adrenaline to stimulate the physiological reaction and examining a number of different emotional contexts, one of which—the feeling of sexual arousal—has been particularly popular. Like pain, sex is an area in which we assume we know what we are feeling, and why. But sexual feelings turn out not to be so straightforward after all. In one study, researchers recruited male college students to participate in two back-to-back experiments, one ostensibly having to do with the effects of exercise, and a second in which they would rate a series of "short clips from a film."[16] In reality, both phases were part of the same experiment. (Psychologists never tell their subjects the truth about the point of their experiments, because if they did so the experiments would be compromised.) In the first phase, exercise played the role of the adrenaline injection to provide an unrecognized source of physiological arousal. It would be reasonable to wonder what kind of burnouts wouldn't realize that their quickened pulse and breathing were due to their just having run a mile on the treadmill, but it turns out that there is a window of several minutes after exercise during which you feel that your body has calmed but it is actually still in an aroused state. It was during that window that the experimenters showed the "uninformed" group the film clips. The "informed" group, on the other hand, saw the clips immediately after exercising, and thus knew the source of their heightened physiological state. As in the Schachter-Singer experiment, there was also a control group, which did no exercise and, hence, experienced no arousal.

Now for the sex. As you may have guessed, in the second phase the "short clips from a film" weren't taken from a Disney movie. The film was an erotic French movie, *The Girl on a Motorcycle*, renamed, in America, *Naked Under Leather*. Both titles are descriptive. The French title relates to the plot: the film is a road movie about a newlywed who deserts her husband and takes off on her motorcycle to visit her lover in Heidelberg.[17] That may sound like a compelling plot line to the French, but the American distributor apparently had a different idea about how to telegraph to an audience the nature of the film's appeal. And it is indeed the "naked under leather" aspect of the movie that inspired the researchers' choice of clips. On that score, however, the film did not seem to succeed. When asked to rate their degree of sexual arousal, the students in the control group gave the film a 31 on a scale of 100. The informed group agreed; its members rated their sexual stimulation at just 28. But the subjects in the ignorant group—who were aroused by their recent exercise but didn't know it—apparently mistook their arousal as being of a sexual nature. They gave the film a 52.

An analogous result was obtained by another group of researchers, who arranged for an attractive female interviewer to ask male passersby to fill out a questionnaire for a school project. Some of the subjects were intercepted on a solid wood bridge only ten feet above a small rivulet. Others were queried on a wobbly five-foot-wide, 450-foot-long bridge of wooden boards with a 230-foot drop to rocks below. After the interaction, the interviewer gave out her contact information in case the subject "had any questions." The subjects interviewed on the scary bridge presumably felt a quickened pulse and other effects of adrenaline. They must have been aware, to some extent, of their bodily reaction to the dangerous bridge. But would they mistake their reaction for sexual chemistry? Of those interviewed on the low, safe bridge, the woman's appeal was apparently limited: only 2 of the 16 later called her. But of those on the high-anxiety bridge, 9 of the 18 phoned her.[18] To a significant number of the male subjects, the prospect of falling hundreds of feet onto an assemblage of large boulders apparently had the same effect as a flirtatious smile and a black silk nightgown.

These experiments illustrate how our subliminal brain combines information about our physical state with other data arising from social and emotional contexts to determine what we are feeling. I think there's a lesson here for everyday life. There is, of course, a direct analogue, the interesting corollary that walking up a few flights of stairs before evaluating a new business proposal may cause you to say, "Wow" when you would have normally said, "Hmm." But think, too, about stress. We all know that mental stress leads to unwanted physical effects, but what is less discussed is the other half of the feedback loop: physical tension causing or perpetuating mental stress. Say you have a conflict with a friend or colleague that results in an agitated physical state. Your shoulders and your neck feel tight, you have a headache, your pulse is elevated. If that state persists, and you find yourself having a conversation with someone who had nothing to do with the conflict that precipitated those sensations, it could cause you to misjudge your feelings about that person. For example, a book editor friend of mine told me of an instance in which she had an unexpectedly acrimonious exchange with an agent and concluded that the agent was a particularly belligerent sort, someone she'd try to avoid working with in the future. But in the course of our discussion it became clear that the anger she felt toward the agent had not arisen from the issue at hand but had been baggage she had unconsciously carried over from an unrelated but upsetting incident that had immediately preceded her conflict with the agent.

For ages, yoga teachers have been saying, "Calm your body, calm your mind." Social neuroscience now provides evidence to support that prescription. In fact, some studies go further and suggest that actively taking on the physical state of a happy person by, say, forcing a smile can cause you to actually feel happier.[19] My young son Nicolai seemed to understand this intuitively: after breaking his hand in a freak accident while playing basketball, he suddenly stopped crying and started to laugh—and then explained that when he has pain laughing seems to make it feel better. The old "Fake it till you make it" idea, which Nicolai had rediscovered, is now also the subject of serious scientific research.

THE EXAMPLES I'VE talked about so far imply that we often don't understand our feelings. Despite that, we usually think that we do. Moreover, when asked to explain why we feel a certain way, most of us, after giving it some thought, have no trouble supplying reasons. Where do we find those reasons, for feelings that may not even be what we think they are? We make them up.

In one interesting demonstration of that phenomenon, a researcher held out snapshots of two women's faces, each about the size of a playing card, one in each hand. He asked his subject to choose the more attractive one.[20] He then flipped both photos facedown, and slid the selected picture over to the participant. He asked the participant to pick up the card and explain the choice he or she had made. Then the researcher went on to another pair of photos, for about a dozen pairs in all. The catch is that in a few cases the experimenter made a switch: through a sleight of hand, he actually slid to his subjects the photograph of the woman they had found *less* attractive. Only about one-quarter of the time did the subjects see through the ruse. But what is really interesting is what happened the 75 percent of the time they did not see through it: when asked why they preferred the face they really hadn't preferred, they said things like "She's radiant. I would rather have approached her in a bar than the other one" or "I like her earrings" or "She looks like an aunt of mine" or "I think she seems nicer than the other one." Time after time, they confidently described their reasons for preferring the face that, in reality, they had not preferred.

The research was no fluke—the scientists pulled a similar trick in a supermarket, with regard to shoppers' preferences in taste tests of jam and tea.[21] In the jam test, shoppers were asked which of two jams they preferred and were then supposedly given a second spoonful of the one they said they liked better so that they could analyze the reasons for their preference. But the jam jars had a hidden internal divider and a lid on both ends, allowing the deft researchers to dip the spoon into the non-preferred jam for the second taste. Again, only about a third of the participants noticed the switch, while two-thirds had no difficulty explaining the reasons for their "preference." A similar ruse, with a similar outcome, occurred in an experiment involving tea.

Sounds like a market researcher's nightmare: ask people their opinion about a product or packaging to pick up insights about their appeal, and you get wonderful explanations that are sincere, detailed, and emphatic but happen to bear little relation to the truth. That's also a problem for political pollsters who routinely ask people why they voted the way they did or why they will vote the way they plan to. It's one thing when people claim to have no opinion, but quite another when you can't even trust them to know what they think. Research, however, suggests that you can't.[22]

The best hints as to what is going on come from research on people with brain abnormalities—for example, a series of famous studies on split-brain patients.[23] Recall that information presented to one side of such a patient's brain is not available to the other hemisphere. When the patient sees something on the left side of his visual field, only the right hemisphere of his brain is aware of it, and vice versa. Similarly, it is the right hemisphere alone that controls the movement of the left hand, and the left hemisphere alone that controls the right hand. One exception to this symmetry is that (in most people) the speech centers are located in the left hemisphere, and so if the patient speaks, it is usually the left hemisphere talking.

Taking advantage of this lack of communication between brain hemispheres, researchers instructed split-brain patients, via their right hemisphere, to perform a task and then asked their left hemisphere to explain why they'd done it. For example, the researchers instructed a patient, via his right hemisphere, to wave. Then they asked the patient why he'd waved. The left hemisphere had observed the waving but was unaware of the instruction to wave. Nevertheless, the left hemisphere did not allow the patient to admit ignorance. Instead, the patient said he'd waved because he'd thought he'd seen someone he knew. Similarly, when researchers instructed the patient, through the right hemisphere, to laugh and then asked him why he was laughing, the patient said he'd laughed because the researchers were funny. Again and again, the left hemisphere responded as if it knew the answer. In these and similar studies, the left brain generated many false reports, but the right brain did not, leading the researchers to speculate that the left hemisphere of the brain has a role that goes beyond simply registering and identifying our emotional feelings, to trying to understand them. It's as though the left hemisphere has mounted a search for a sense of order and reason in the world in general.

Oliver Sacks wrote about a patient with Korsakoff's syndrome, a type of amnesia in which victims can lose the ability to form new memories.[24] Such patients may forget what is said within seconds, or what they see within minutes. Still, they often delude themselves into thinking that they know what is going on. When Sacks walked in to examine the patient, a Mr. Thompson, Thompson would not remember him from his previous encounters. But Thompson wouldn't realize he didn't know. He would always latch onto some available hint and convince himself that he did remember Sacks. On one occasion, since Sacks was wearing a white coat and Thompson had been a grocer, Thompson remembered him as the butcher from down the street. Moments later he forgot that "realization" and altered his story, remembering Sacks as a particular customer. Thompson's understanding of his world, his situation, his self, was in a constant state of change, but he believed in each of the rapidly changing explanations he evolved in order to make sense of what he was seeing. As Sacks put it, Thompson "must seek meaning, *make* meaning, in a desperate way, continually inventing, throwing bridges of meaning over abysses of meaninglessness."

The term "confabulation" often signifies the replacement of a gap in one's memory by a falsification that one believes to be true. But we also confabulate to fill in gaps in our knowledge about our feelings. We all have those tendencies. We ask ourselves or our friends questions like "Why do you drive that car?" or "Why do you like that guy?" or "Why did you laugh at that joke?" Research suggests that we think we know the answers to such questions, but really we often don't. When asked to explain ourselves, we engage in a search for truth that may feel like a kind of introspection. But though we think we know what we are feeling, we often know neither the content nor the unconscious origins of that content. And so we come up with plausible explanations that are untrue or only partly accurate, and we believe them.[25] Scientists who study such errors have noticed that they are not haphazard.[26] They are regular and systematic. And they have their basis in a repository of social, emotional, and cultural information we all share.

IMAGINE YOU'RE BEING driven home from a cocktail party that was in the penthouse of a posh hotel. You remark that you had a lovely time, and your designated driver asks you what you liked about it. "The people," you say. But did your joy really stem from the fascinating repartee with that woman who wrote the best seller about the virtues of a vegan diet? Or was it something far subtler, like the quality of the harp music? Or the scent of roses that filled the room? Or the expensive champagne you quaffed all night? If your response was not the result of true and accurate introspection, on what basis did you make it?

When you come up with an explanation for your feelings and behavior, your brain performs an action that would probably surprise you: it searches your mental database of cultural norms and picks something plausible. For example, in this case it might have looked up the entry "Why People Enjoy Parties" and chosen "the people" as the most likely hypothesis. That might sound like the lazy way, but studies suggest we take it: when asked how we felt, or will feel, we tend to reply with descriptions or predictions that conform to a set of standard reasons, expectations, and cultural and societal explanations for a given feeling.

If the picture I just painted is correct, there is an obvious consequence that can be tested by experiment. Accurate introspection makes use of our private knowledge of ourselves. Identifying a generic, social-and-cultural-norms explanation as the source of our feelings doesn't. As a result, if we are truly in touch with our feelings, we should be able to make predictions about ourselves that are more accurate than predictions that others make about us; but if we merely rely on social norms to explain our feelings, outside observers should be just as accurate in predicting our feelings as we are, and ought to make precisely the same mistakes.

One context scientists used to examine this question is familiar to anyone involved in hiring.[27] Hiring is difficult because it is an important decision, and it is hard to know someone from the limited exposure afforded by an interview and a résumé. If you've ever had to hire people, you might have asked yourself why you thought a particular individual was the right pick. No doubt you could always find justification, but in hindsight, are you sure you chose that person for the reasons you thought you did? Perhaps your reasoning went the other way—you got a feeling about someone, formed a preference, and then, retroactively, your unconscious employed social norms to explain your feelings about that person.

One doctor friend told me that he was certain he had gotten into the top-rated medical school he'd attended for only one reason: he had clicked with one of the professors who'd interviewed him; the man's parents, like his, had immigrated from a certain town in Greece. After matriculating at the school he got to know that professor, who maintained that my friend's scores, grades, and character—the criteria demanded by social norms—were the reasons their interview had gone so well. But my friend's scores and grades were below that school's average, and he still believes it was their shared family origin that really influenced the professor.

To explore why some people get the job and others don't, and whether those doing the hiring are aware of what drove their choices, researchers recruited 128 volunteers. Each subject—all of them female—was asked to study and assess an in-depth portfolio describing a woman applying for a job as a counselor in a crisis intervention center. The documents included a letter of recommendation and a detailed report of an interview the applicant had had with the center's director. After studying the portfolio, subjects were asked several questions regarding the applicant's qualifications, including How intelligent do you think she is? How flexible? How sympathetic would she be toward clients' problems? How much do you like her?

The key to the study is that the information given to different subjects differed in a number of details. For example, some subjects read portfolios showing that the applicant had finished second in her class in high school and was now an honor student in college, while others read that she had not yet decided whether to go to college; some saw a mention of the fact that the applicant was quite attractive, others learned nothing about her appearance; some read in the center director's report that the applicant had spilled a cup of coffee on the director's desk, while others saw no mention of such an incident; and some portfolios indicated that the applicant had been in a serious automobile accident, while others didn't. Some subjects were told they'd later meet the applicant, while others were not. These variable elements were shuffled in all possible combinations to create dozens of distinct scenarios. By studying the correlation of the facts the subjects were exposed to, and the judgments they made, researchers could compute mathematically the influence of each piece of information on the subjects' assessments. Their goal was to compare the actual influence of each factor to the subjects' perception of each factor's influence, and also to the predictions of outside observers who didn't know the subjects.

In order to understand what the subjects thought influenced them, after assessing the applicant, the subjects were polled with regard to each question: Did you judge the applicant's intelligence by her academic credentials? Were you swayed in your assessment of her likability by her physical attractiveness? Did the fact that she spilled a cup of coffee over the interviewer's desk affect your assessment of how sympathetic she'd be? And so on. Also, in order to find out what an outside observer would guess the influence of each factor would be, another group of volunteers ("outsiders") were recruited; they were not shown the portfolios but were simply asked to rate how much they thought each factor would influence a person's judgment.

The facts that were revealed about the applicant had been cleverly chosen. Some, such as the applicant's high grades, were factors that social norms dictate ought to exert a positive influence on those assessing the job application. The researchers expected both the subjects and the outsiders to name these factors as an influence. Other factors, such as the coffee-spilling incident and the anticipation of later meeting the applicant, were factors that social norms say nothing about in this regard. The researchers therefore expected the outsiders not to recognize their influence. However the researchers had chosen those factors because studies show that, contrary to the expectations dictated by the norms, they *do* have an effect on our judgment of people: an isolated pratfall such as the coffee-spilling incident tends to increase the likability of a generally competent-seeming person, and the anticipation of meeting an individual tends to improve your assessment of that individual's personality.[28] The crucial question was whether the subjects, upon self-reflection, would do better than the outsiders and recognize that they'd been swayed by those surprisingly influential factors.

When the researchers examined the subjects' and the outsiders' answers, they found that they showed impressive agreement, and that both were way off the mark. Both groups appeared to draw their conclusions about which factors were influential from the social-norms explanations, while ignoring the actual reasons. For example, both the subjects and the outsiders said the coffee-spilling incident would not affect their liking of the applicant, yet it had the greatest effect of all the factors. Both groups expected that the academic factor would have a significant effect on their liking the applicant, but its effect was nil. And both groups reported that the expectation of meeting the applicant would have no effect, but it did. In case after case, both groups were wrong about which factors would not affect them and which factors would. As psychological theory had predicted, the subjects had shown no greater insight into themselves than the outsiders had.

EVOLUTION DESIGNED THE human brain not to accurately understand itself but to help us survive. We observe ourselves and the world and make enough sense of things to get along. Some of us, interested in knowing ourselves more deeply—perhaps to make better life decisions, perhaps to live a richer life, perhaps out of curiosity—seek to get past our intuitive ideas of us. We can. We can use our conscious minds to study, to identify, and to pierce our cognitive illusions. By broadening our perspective to take into account how our minds operate, we can achieve a more enlightened view of who we are. But even as we grow to better understand ourselves, we should maintain our appreciation of the fact that, if our mind's natural view of the world is skewed, it is skewed for a reason.

I walked into an antiques store while on a trip to San Francisco one day, meaning to buy a beautiful vase in the window that was reduced from $100 to just $50. I walked out carrying a $2,500 Persian rug. To be precise, I'm not sure it was a $2,500 Persian rug; all I know is that $2,500 is what I paid for it. I wasn't in the market for a rug, I wasn't planning to spend $2,500 on a San Francisco souvenir, and I wasn't intending to lug home anything bigger than a bread box. I don't know why I did it, and none of the introspection I performed in the ensuing days turned up anything. But then again, there are no social norms regarding the purchase of Persian rugs on vacation whims. What I do know is that I like the way the rug looks in my dining room. I like it because it makes the room feel cozy, and its colors go well with the table and the walls. Or does it actually make the room look like a breakfast nook in a cheap hotel? Maybe the true reason I like it is that I'm not comfortable thinking that I spent $2,500 on an ugly rug to lay over my beautiful hardwood floor. That realization doesn't bother me; it gives me a greater appreciation of my unseen partner, my unconscious, always providing the support I need as I walk and stumble my way through life.

CHAPTER 10

Self

The secret of rulership is to combine a belief in one's own infallibility
with the power to learn from past mistakes. —GEORGE ORWELL

I N 2005 HURRICANE Katrina devastated the Gulf Coast of Louisiana
and Mississippi. More than a thousand people lost their lives, and hundreds of thousands of others were displaced. New Orleans was flooded,
with some parts of the city covered by fifteen feet of water. The U.S. government's response was, by all accounts, badly botched. Well, by almost
all accounts. When Michael Brown, the head of the Federal Emergency
Management Agency, was accused of mismanagement and a lack of leadership, and Congress convened a panel to investigate, did the inexperi-
enced Brown admit to any shortcomings? No, he said the poor response
was "clearly the fault of a lack of coordination and planning by Louisiana
governor Kathleen Blanco and New Orleans mayor Ray Nagin." In fact,
in his own mind, Brown seemed to be some sort of tragic, Cassandra-like
figure: "I predicted privately for several years," he said, "that we were going
to reach this point [of crisis] because of the lack of resources and the lack
of attention being paid."[1]

Perhaps in his heart Brown accepted more responsibility. Perhaps these public statements were simply an awkward attempt to plea-bargain the public accusations against him down from negligence to impotence. Disingenuousness is a little harder to argue in the case of O. J. Simpson, the former sports hero accused of murdering two people but acquitted in criminal court. Afterward, he couldn't seem to stay out of trouble. Finally, in 2007 he and a couple of buddies burst into a Las Vegas hotel room and seized sports memorabilia from dealers at gunpoint. At his sentencing, O.J. had a chance to apologize and ask the judge for leniency. He would certainly have had strong motive for a bit of either honest or phony self-criticism. But did he do the self-serving thing and, in an attempt to cut a few years off his sentence, express regret for behaving as a criminal? No, he stood his ground. His answer was sincere. He was sorry for his actions, he said, but he believed he had done nothing wrong. Even with years of prison at stake, Simpson felt the need to justify himself.

The stronger the threat to feeling good about yourself, it seems, the greater the tendency to view reality through a distorting lens. In his classic book *How to Win Friends and Influence People*, Dale Carnegie described the self-images of famous mobsters of the 1930s.[2] Dutch Schultz, who terrorized New York, wasn't shy about murder—and he certainly wouldn't have been diminished in the eyes of his colleagues in crime had he simply described himself as a man who had built a successful empire by killing people. Instead, he told a newspaper interviewer that he saw himself as a "public benefactor." Similarly, Al Capone, a purveyor of bootleg alcohol who was responsible for hundreds of killings, said, "I've spent the best years of my life giving people the lighter pleasures, helping them have a good time, and all I get is abuse, the existence of a hunted man." And when a notorious murderer named "Two Gun" Crowley was sentenced to the electric chair for killing a policeman who had asked for his driver's license, he didn't express sadness over taking another man's life. Rather, he complained, "This is what I get for defending myself."

Do we really believe the enhanced versions of ourselves that we offer up to our audiences? Do we manage to convince ourselves that our corporate strategy was brilliant even though revenue has plummeted, that we deserve our $50 million exit package when the company we led lost twenty times that amount in the three years we ran it, that we argued the case brilliantly, though our client got the chair, or that we are only social smokers, though we go through the same pack a day whether we see another human being or not? How accurately do we perceive ourselves?

Consider a survey of nearly one million high school seniors.[3] When asked to judge their ability to get along with others, 100 percent rated themselves as at least average, 60 percent rated themselves in the top 10 percent, and 25 percent considered themselves in the top 1 percent. And when asked about their leadership skills, only 2 percent assessed themselves as being below average. Teachers aren't any more realistic: 94 percent of college professors say they do above-average work.[4]

Psychologists call this tendency for inflated self-assessment the "above-average effect," and they've documented it in contexts ranging from driving ability to managerial skills.[5] In engineering, when professionals were asked to rate their performance, between 30 percent and 40 percent put themselves in the top 5 percent.[6] In the military, officers' assessments of their leadership qualities (charisma, intellect, and so on) are far rosier than assessments of them made by their subordinates and superiors.[7] In medicine, doctors' assessments of their interpersonal skill are far higher than the ratings they received from their patients and supervisors, and their estimates of their own knowledge are far higher than objective tests bear out.[8] In one study, in fact, physicians who diagnosed their patients as having pneumonia reported an average of 88 percent confidence in that diagnosis but proved correct only 20 percent of the time.[9]

This kind of inflation is equally the rule in the corporate world. Most business executives think their company is more likely to succeed than the typical company in their business, because it's theirs,[10] and CEOs display overconfidence when entering into new markets or embarking on risky projects.[11] One result of this is that when companies acquire other firms, they typically pay 41 percent more for the target firm's stock than its current price, feeling they can run it more profitably, while the combined value of the merging firms usually falls, indicating that impartial observers feel otherwise.[12]

Stock pickers, too, are overly optimistic about their ability to choose winners. Overconfidence can even lead otherwise savvy and rational investors to think they can predict when a stock market move will occur despite the fact that, on an intellectual level, they believe otherwise. In fact, in a survey conducted by economist Robert Schiller after the crash on Black Monday in October 1987, about one-third of investors claimed that they had a "pretty good idea when a rebound" would occur, though few, when asked, could offer an explicit theory to back up their confidence in predicting the market's future.[13]

Ironically, people tend to recognize that inflated self-assessment and overconfidence can be a problem—but only in others.[14] That's right, we even overestimate our ability to resist overestimating our abilities. What's going on?

IN 1959, THE social psychologist Milton Rokeach gathered three psychiatric patients to live together in Ypsilanti State Hospital in Michigan.[15] Each of the patients believed he was Jesus Christ. Since at least two of them had to be wrong, Rokeach wondered how they would process this idea. There were precedents. In a famous seventeenth-century case a fellow named Simon Morin was sent to a madhouse for making the same claim. There he met another Jesus and "was so struck with the folly of his companion that he acknowledged his own." Unfortunately, he subsequently reverted to his original belief and, like Jesus, ended up being killed—in this case, burned at the stake for blasphemy. No one was burned in Ypsilanti. One patient, like Morin, relinquished his belief; the second saw the others as mentally ill, but not himself; and the third managed to dodge the issue completely. So in this case, two out of the three patients managed to hang on to a self-image at odds with reality. The disconnect may be less extreme, but the same could be said to be true even of many of us who don't believe we can walk on water. If we probed—or, in many cases, simply bothered to pay attention—most of us would notice that our self-image and the more objective image that others have of us are not quite in sync.

By the time we were two, most of us had a sense of ourselves as social agents.[16] Around the time we learned that diapers are not a desirable fashion statement, we began to actively engage with adults to construct visions of our own past experiences. By kindergarten, we were able to do that without adult help. But we had also learned that people's behavior is motivated by their desires and beliefs. From that time onward, we've had to reconcile the person we would like to be with the person whose thoughts and actions we live with each moment of every day.

I've talked a lot about how research psychologists reject much of Freudian theory, but one idea Freudian therapists and experimental psychologists agree on today is that our ego fights fiercely to defend its honor. This agreement is a relatively recent development. For many decades, research psychologists thought of people as detached observers who assess events and then apply reason to discover truth and decipher the nature of the social world.[17] We were said to gather data on ourselves and to build our self-images based on generally good and accurate inferences. In that traditional view, a well-adjusted person was thought to be like a scientist of the self, whereas an individual whose self-image was clouded by illusion was regarded as vulnerable to, if not already a victim of, mental illness. Today, we know that the opposite is closer to the truth. Normal and healthy individuals—students, professors, engineers, lieutenant colonels, doctors, business executives—tend to think of themselves as not just competent but proficient, even if they aren't.

Doesn't the business executive, noting that her department keeps missing its numbers, question her own abilities? Or the lieutenant colonel, noting that he can't seem to shed that prefix, wonder whether he's fit to be a colonel? How do we convince ourselves that we've got talent and that when the promotion goes to the other guy, it's only because the boss was misguided?

As the psychologist Jonathan Haidt put it, there are two ways to get at the truth: the way of the scientist and the way of the lawyer. Scientists gather evidence, look for regularities, form theories explaining their observations, and test them. Attorneys begin with a conclusion they want to convince others of and then seek evidence that supports it, while also attempting to discredit evidence that doesn't. The human mind is designed to be both a scientist and an attorney, both a conscious seeker of objective truth and an unconscious, impassioned advocate for what we *want* to believe. Together these approaches vie to create our worldview.

Believing in what you desire to be true and then seeking evidence to justify it doesn't seem to be the best approach to everyday decisions. For example, if you're at the races, it is rational to bet on the horse you believe is fastest, but it doesn't make sense to believe a horse is fastest because you bet on it. Similarly, it makes sense to choose a job you believe is appealing, but it's irrational to believe a job is appealing because you've accepted the offer. Still, even though in each case the latter approach doesn't make rational sense, it is the irrational choice that would probably make you happier. And the mind generally seems to opt for happy. In both these instances, the research indicates, it is the latter choice that people are likely to make.[18] The "causal arrow" in human thought processes consistently tends to point from belief to evidence, not vice versa.[19]

As it turns out, the brain is a decent scientist but an absolutely *outstanding* lawyer. The result is that in the struggle to fashion a coherent, convincing view of ourselves and the rest of the world, it is the impassioned advocate that usually wins over the truth seeker. We've seen in earlier chapters how the unconscious mind is a master at using limited data to construct a version of the world that appears realistic and complete to its partner, the conscious mind. Visual perception, memory, and even emotion are all constructs, made of a mix of raw, incomplete, and sometimes conflicting data. We use the same kind of creative process to generate our self-image. When we paint our picture of self, our attorney-like unconscious blends fact and illusion, exaggerating our strengths, minimizing our weaknesses, creating a virtually Picassoesque series of distortions in which some parts have been blown up to enormous size (the parts we like) and others shrunk to near invisibility. The rational scientists of our conscious minds then innocently admire the self-portrait, believing it to be a work of photographic accuracy.

Psychologists call the approach taken by our inner advocate "motivated reasoning." Motivated reasoning helps us to believe in our own goodness and competence, to feel in control, and to generally see ourselves in an overly positive light. It also shapes the way we understand and interpret our environment, especially our social environment, and it helps us justify our preferred beliefs. Still, it isn't possible for 40 percent to squeeze into the top 5 percent, for 60 percent to squeeze into the top decile, or for 94 percent to be in the top half, so convincing ourselves of our great worth is not always an easy task. Fortunately, in accomplishing it, our minds have a great ally, an aspect of life whose importance we've encountered before: ambiguity. Ambiguity creates wiggle room in what may otherwise be inarguable truth, and our unconscious minds employ that wiggle room to build a narrative of ourselves, of others, and of our environment that makes the best of our fate, that fuels us in the good times, and gives us comfort in the bad.

WHAT DO YOU see when you look at the figure below? On first glance, you will see it as either a horse or a seal, but if you keep looking, after a while you will see it as the other creature. And once you've seen it both ways, your perception tends to automatically alternate between the two animals. The truth is, the figure is both and it is neither. It is just a suggestive assemblage of lines, a sketch that, like your character, personality, and talents, can be interpreted in different ways.

Attention, Perception & Psychophysics 4, no. 3 (1968), p. 191, "Ambiguity of Form: Old and New," by Gerald H. Fisher, Fig. 3.2, copyright © 1968 by the Psychonomics Society. Reprinted with kind permission from Springer Science+Business Media B.V.

. Earlier I said that ambiguity opened the door to stereotyping, to misjudging people we don't know very well. It also opens the door to misjudging ourselves. If our talents and expertise, our personality and character were all defined by scientific measurement and carved into inalterable stone tablets, it would be difficult to maintain a biased image of who we are. But our characteristics are more like the horse/seal image, open to differing interpretations.

How easy is it for us to tailor reality to fit our desires? David Dunning has spent years pondering questions like that. A social psychologist at Cornell University, he has devoted much of his professional career to studying how and when people's perception of reality is shaped by their preferences. Consider the horse/seal image. Dunning and a colleague loaded it onto a computer, recruited dozens of subjects, and provided motivation for them to see it as either a horse or a seal.[20] Here is how it worked: The scientists told their subjects that they would be assigned to drink one of two liquids. One was a glass of tasty orange juice. The other was a "health smoothie" that looked and smelled so vile that a number of subjects dropped out rather than face the possibility of tasting it. The participants were told that the identity of the beverage they were to drink would be communicated to them via the computer, which would flash a figure—the image above—on the screen for one second. One second is generally not enough time for a person to see the image both ways, so each subject would see either just a horse or just a seal.[21]

That's the key to the experiment, for half the subjects were told that if the figure was a "farm animal," they were to drink the juice and if it was a "sea creature," they were to drink the smoothie; the other half were told the reverse. Then, after the subjects had viewed the image, the researchers asked them to identify the animal they'd seen. If the students' motivations biased their perceptions, the unconscious minds of the subjects who were told that farm animal equals orange juice would bias them toward seeing a horse. Similarly, the unconscious minds of those told that farm animal equals disgusting smoothie would bias them toward seeing the seal. And that's just what happened: among those hoping to see a farm animal, 67 percent reported seeing a horse, while among those hoping to see a sea creature, 73 percent identified a seal.

Dunning's study was certainly persuasive about the impact of motivation on perception, but the ambiguity at hand was very clear and simple. Everyday life experiences, by contrast, present issues far more complex than deciding what animal you're looking at. Talent at running a business or a military unit, the ability to get along with people, the desire to act ethically, and myriad other traits that define us are all complicated qualities. As a result, our unconscious can choose from an entire smorgasbord of interpretations to feed our conscious mind. In the end we feel we are chewing on the facts, though we've actually been chomping on a preferred conclusion.

Biased interpretations of ambiguous events are at the heart of some of our most heated arguments. In the 1950s, a pair of psychology professors, one from Princeton, the other from Dartmouth, decided to see if, even a year after the event, Princeton and Dartmouth students would be capable of objectivity about an important football game.[22] The game in question was a brutal match in which Dartmouth played especially rough but Princeton came out on top. The scientists showed a group of students from each school a film of the match and asked them to take note of every infraction they spotted, specifying which were "flagrant" or "mild." Princeton students saw the Dartmouth team commit more than twice as many infractions as their own team, while Dartmouth students counted about an equal number on both sides. Princeton viewers rated most of the Dartmouth fouls as flagrant but few of their own as such, whereas the Dartmouth viewers rated only a few of their own infractions as flagrant but half of Princeton's. And when asked if Dartmouth was playing intentionally rough or dirty, the vast majority of the Princeton fans said "yes," while the vast majority of the Dartmouth fans who had a definite opinion said "no." The researchers wrote, "The same sensory experiences emanating from the football field, transmitted through the visual mechanism to the brain . . . gave rise to different experiences in different people. . . . There is no such 'thing' as a game existing 'out there' in its own right which people merely 'observe.' "

I like that last quote because, though it was written about football, it seems to be true about the game of life in general. Even in my field, science, in which objectivity is worshipped, it is often clear that people's views of the evidence are highly correlated to their vested interests. For example, in the 1950s and '60s a debate raged about whether the universe had had a beginning or whether it had always been in existence. One camp supported the big bang theory, which said that the cosmos began in a manner indicated by the theory's name. The other camp believed in the steady state theory, the idea that the universe had always been around, in more or less the same state that it is in today. In the end, to any disinterested party, the evidence landed squarely in support of the big bang theory, especially after 1964, when the afterglow of the big bang was serendipitously detected by a pair of satellite communications researchers at Bell Labs. That discovery made the front page of the *New York Times*, which proclaimed that the big bang had won out. What did the steady state researchers proclaim? After three years, one proponent finally accepted it with the words "The universe is in fact a botched job, but I suppose we shall have to make the best of it." Thirty years later, another leading steady state theorist, by then old and silver-haired, still believed in a modified version of his theory.[23]

The little research that has been done by scientists on scientists shows that it isn't uncommon for scientists to operate as advocates rather than impartial judges, especially in the social sciences, in which there is greater ambiguity than in the physical sciences. For example, in one study, advanced graduate students at the University of Chicago were asked to rate research reports dealing with issues on which they already had an opinion.[24] Unbeknownst to the volunteers, the research reports were all phony. For each issue, half the volunteers saw a report presenting data that supported one side, while the other half saw a report in which the data supported the opposite camp. But it was only the numbers that differed—the research methodology and presentation were identical in both cases.

When asked, most subjects denied that their assessment of the research depended on whether the data supported their prior opinion. But they were wrong. The researcher's analysis showed that they had indeed judged the studies that supported their beliefs to be more methodologically sound and clearly presented than the otherwise identical studies that opposed their beliefs—and the effect was stronger for those with strong prior beliefs.[25] I'm not saying that claims of truth in science are a sham—they aren't. History has repeatedly shown that the better theory eventually wins. That's why the big bang triumphed and the steady state theory died, and no one even remembers cold fusion. But it is also true that scientists with an investment in an established theory sometimes stubbornly cling to their old beliefs. Sometimes, as the economist Paul Samuelson wrote, "science advances funeral by funeral."[26]

Because motivated reasoning is unconscious, people's claims that they are unaffected by bias or self-interest can be sincere, even as they make decisions that are in reality self-serving. For example, many physicians think they are immune to monetary influence, yet recent studies show that accepting industry hospitality and gifts has a significant subliminal effect on patient-care decisions.[27] Similarly, studies have shown that research physicians with financial ties to pharmaceutical manufacturers are significantly more likely than independent reviewers to report findings that support the sponsor's drugs and less likely to report unfavorable findings; that investment managers' estimates of the probabilities of various events are significantly correlated to the perceived desirability of those events; that auditors' judgments are affected by the incentives offered; and that, at least in Britain, half the population believes in heaven, but only about a quarter believes in hell.[28]

Recent brain-imaging studies are beginning to shed light on how our brains create these unconscious biases. They show that when assessing emotionally relevant data, our brains *automatically* include our wants and dreams and desires.[29] Our internal computations, which we believe to be objective, are not really the computations that a detached computer would make but, rather, are implicitly colored by who we are and what we are after. In fact, the motivated reasoning we engage in when we have a personal stake in an issue proceeds via a different physical process within the brain than the cold, objective analysis we carry out when we don't. In particular, motivated reasoning involves a network of brain regions that are not associated with "cold" reasoning, including the orbitofrontal cortex and the anterior cingulate cortex—parts of the limbic system—and the posterior cingulate cortex and precuneus, which are also activated when one makes emotionally laden moral judgments.[30] That's the *physical* mechanism for how our brains manage to deceive us. But what is the *mental* mechanism? What techniques of subliminal reasoning do we employ to support our preferred worldviews?

OUR CONSCIOUS MINDS are not chumps. So if our unconscious minds distorted reality in some clumsy and obvious way, we would notice and we wouldn't buy into it. Motivated reasoning won't work if it stretches credulity too far, for then our conscious minds start to doubt and the self-delusion game is over. That there are limits to motivated reasoning is critically important, for it is one thing to have an inflated view of your expertise at making lasagna and it is quite another to believe you can leap tall buildings in a single bound. In order for your inflated self-image to serve you well, to have survival benefits, it must be inflated to just the right degree and no further. Psychologists describe this balance by saying that the resulting distortion must maintain the "illusion of objectivity." The talent we are blessed with in this regard is the ability to justify our rosy images of ourselves through credible arguments, in a way that does not fly in the face of obvious facts. What tools do our unconscious minds use to shape our cloudy, ambiguous experience into the clear and distinctly positive vision of the self that we wish to see?

One method is reminiscent of an old joke about a Catholic and a Jew—both white—and a black man, all of whom die and approach the gates of heaven. The Catholic says, "I was a good man all my life, but I suffered a lot of discrimination. What do I have to do to get into heaven?"

"That's easy," says God. "All you have to do to enter heaven is spell one word."

"What's that?" the Catholic asks.

"God," answers the Lord.

The Catholic spells it out, G-O-D, and is let in. Then the Jew approaches. He, too, says, "I was a good man." And then he adds, "And it wasn't easy—I had to deal with discrimination all my life. What do I have to do to get into heaven?"

God says, "That's easy. All you have to do is spell one word."

"What's that?" the Jew asks.

"God," answers the Lord.

The Jew says, "G-O-D," and he, too, is let in. Then the black man approaches and says that he was kind to everyone, although he faced nasty discrimination because of the color of his skin.

God says, "Don't worry, there is no discrimination here."

"Thank you," says the black man. "So how do I get into heaven?"

"That's easy," says God. "All you have to do is spell one word!"

"What's that?" the black man asks.

"Czechoslovakia," answers the Lord.

The Lord's method of discrimination is classic, and our brains employ it often: when information favorable to the way we'd like to see the world tries to enter the gateway of our mind we ask that it spell "God," but when unfavorable information comes knocking, we make it spell "Czechoslovakia."

For example, in one study volunteers were given a strip of paper to test whether they had a serious deficiency of an enzyme called TAA, which would make them susceptible to a variety of serious pancreas disorders.[31]

The researchers told them to dip the strip of paper in a bit of their saliva and wait ten to twenty seconds to see if the paper turned green. Half the subjects were told that if the strip turned green it meant they had *no* enzyme deficiency, while the other half were told that if it turned green it meant they *had* the dangerous deficiency. In reality, no such enzyme exists, and the strip was ordinary yellow construction paper, so none of the subjects were destined to see it change color. The researchers watched as their subjects performed the test. Those who were motivated to see no change dipped the paper, and when nothing happened, they quickly accepted the happy answer and decided the test was complete. But those motivated to see the paper turn green stared at the strip for an extra thirty seconds, on average, before accepting the verdict. What's more, over half of these subjects engaged in some sort of retesting behavior. One subject redipped the paper twelve times, like a child nagging its parents. *Can you turn green? Can you? Please? Please?*

Those subjects may seem silly, but we all dip and redip in an effort to bolster our preferred views. People find reasons to continue supporting their preferred political candidates in the face of serious and credible accusations of wrongdoing or ignorance but take thirdhand hearsay about an illegal left turn as evidence that the candidate of the other party ought to be banned from politics for life. Similarly, when people want to believe in a scientific conclusion, they'll accept a vague news report of an experiment somewhere as convincing evidence. And when people don't want to accept something, the National Academy of Sciences, the American Association for the Advancement of Science, the American Geophysical Union, the American Meteorological Society, and a thousand unanimous scientific studies can all converge on a single conclusion, and people will still find a reason to disbelieve.

That's exactly what happened in the case of the inconvenient and costly issue of global climate change. The organizations I named above, plus a thousand academic articles on the topic, were unanimous in concluding that human activity is responsible, yet in the United States more than half the people have managed to convince themselves that the science of global warming is not yet settled.[32] Actually, it would be difficult to get all those organizations and scientists to agree on anything short of a declaration stating that Albert Einstein was a smart fellow, so their consensus reflects the fact that the science of global warming is *very much* settled. It's just not good news. To a lot of people, the idea that we are descended from apes is also not good news. So they have found ways not to accept that fact, either.

When someone with a political bias or vested interest sees a situation differently than we do, we tend to think that person is deliberately mis-interpreting the obvious to justify their politics or to bring about some personal gain. But through motivated reasoning each side finds ways to justify its favored conclusion and discredit the other, while maintaining a belief in its own objectivity. And so those on both sides of important issues may sincerely think that theirs is the only rational interpretation. Consider the following research on the death penalty. People who either supported or opposed capital punishment on the theory that it deterred crime (or didn't) were shown two phony studies. Each study employed a different statistical method to prove its point. Let's call them method A and method B. For half the subjects, the study that used method A concluded that capital punishment works as a deterrent, and the study that used method B concluded that it doesn't. The other subjects saw studies in which the conclusions were reversed. If people were objective, those on both sides would agree that either method A or method B was the best approach regardless of whether it supported or undermined their prior belief (or they'd agree that it was a tie). But that's not what happened. Subjects read-ily offered criticisms such as "There were too many variables," "I don't think they have complete enough collection of data," and "The evidence given is relatively meaningless." But both sides lauded whatever method supported their belief and trashed whatever method did not. Clearly, it was the reports' conclusions, not their methods, that inspired these analyses.[33]

Exposing people to well-reasoned arguments both pro– and anti–death penalty did not engender understanding for the other point of view. Rather, because we poke holes in evidence we dislike and plug holes in evidence we like, the net effect in these studies was to amplify the intensity of the disagreement. A similar study found that, after viewing identical samples of major network television coverage of the 1982 massacre in Beirut, both pro-Israeli and pro-Arab partisans rated the programs, and the networks, as being biased against their side.[34] There are critical lessons in this research. First, we should keep in mind that those who disagree with us are not necessarily duplicitous or dishonest in their refusal to acknowledge the obvious errors in their thinking. More important, it would be enlightening for all of us to face the fact that our own reasoning is often not so perfectly objective, either.

ADJUSTING OUR STANDARDS for accepting evidence to favor our preferred conclusions is but one instrument in the subliminal mind's motivated reasoning tool kit. Other ways we find support for our worldviews (including our view of ourselves) include adjusting the importance we assign to various pieces of evidence and, sometimes, ignoring unfavorable evidence altogether. For example, ever notice how, after a win, sports fans crow about their team's great play, but after a loss they often ignore the quality of play and focus on Lady Luck or the referees?[35] Similarly, executives in public companies pat themselves on the back for good outcomes but suddenly recognize the importance of random environmental factors when performance is poor.[36] It can be hard to tell whether those attempts to put a spin on a bad outcome are sincere, and the result of unconscious motivated reasoning, or are conscious and self-serving.

One situation in which that ambiguity is not an issue is scheduling. There is no good reason to offer unrealistic promises with regard to deadlines, because in the end you'll be required to back up those promises by delivering the goods. Yet contractors and businesses often miss their deadlines even when there are financial penalties for doing so, and studies show that motivated reasoning is a major cause of those miscalculations. It turns out that when we calculate a completion date, the method we think we follow in arriving at it is to break the project down into the necessary steps, estimate the time required for each step, and put it all together. But research shows that, instead, our minds often work backward. That is, the desired target date exerts a great and unconscious influence on our estimate of the time required to complete each of the intermediate steps. In fact, studies show that our estimates of how long it will take to finish a task depend directly on how invested we are in the project's early completion.[37]

If it's important for a producer to get the new PlayStation game done in the next two months, her mind will find reasons to believe that the programming and quality-assurance testing will be more problem-free than ever before. Likewise, if we need to get three hundred popcorn balls made in time for Halloween, we manage to convince ourselves that having the kids help on our kitchen assembly line will go smoothly for the first time in the history of our family. It is because we make these decisions, and sincerely believe they are realistic, that all of us, whether we are throwing a dinner party for ten people or building a new jet fighter, regularly create overly optimistic estimates of when we can finish the project.[38] In fact, the U.S. General Accounting Office estimated that when the military purchased equipment involving new technology, it was delivered on schedule and within budget just 1 percent of the time.[39]

In the last chapter I mentioned that research shows that employers often aren't in touch with the real reasons they hire someone. An interviewer may like or dislike an applicant because of factors that have little to do with the applicant's objective qualifications. They may both have attended the same school or both be bird-watchers. Or perhaps the applicant reminds the interviewer of a favorite uncle. For whatever reason, once the interviewer makes a gut-level decision, her unconscious often employs motivated reasoning to back that intuitive inclination. If she likes the applicant, without realizing her motivation she will tend to assign high importance to areas in which the applicant excels and take less seriously those in which the applicant falls short.

In one study, participants considered applications from a male and a female candidate for the job of police chief. That's a stereotypically male position, so the researchers postulated that the participants would favor the male applicant and then unwittingly narrow the criteria by which they judged the applicants to those that would support that decision. Here is how the study worked: There were two types of résumés. The experimenters designed one to portray a streetwise individual who was poorly educated and lacking in administrative skills. They designed the other to reflect a well-educated and politically connected sophisticate who had little street smarts. Some participants were given a pair of résumés in which the male applicant had the streetwise résumé and the female was the sophisticate. Others were given a pair of résumés in which the man's and the woman's strong points were reversed. The participants were asked not just to make a choice but to explain it.

The results showed that when the male applicant had the streetwise résumé, the participants decided street smarts were important for the job and selected him, but when the male applicant had the sophisticate's résumé, they decided that street smarts were overrated and also chose the male. They were clearly making their decisions on the basis of gender, and not on the streetwise-versus-sophisticated distinction, but they were just as clearly unaware of doing so. In fact, when asked, none of the subjects mentioned gender as having influenced them.[40]

Our culture likes to portray situations in black and white. Antagonists are dishonest, insincere, greedy, evil. They are opposed by heroes who are the opposite in terms of those qualities. But the truth is, from criminals to greedy executives to the "nasty" guy down the street, people who act in ways we abhor are usually convinced that they are right.

The power of vested interest in determining how we weigh the evidence in social situations was nicely illustrated in a series of experiments in which researchers randomly assigned volunteers to the role of plaintiff or defendant in a mock lawsuit based on a real trial that occurred in Texas.[41] In one of those experiments, the researchers gave both sides documents regarding the case, which involved an injured motorcyclist who was suing the driver of an automobile that had collided with him. The subjects were told that in the actual case, the judge awarded the plaintiff an amount between $0 and $100,000. They were then assigned to represent one side or the other in mock negotiations in which they were given a half hour to fashion their own version of a settlement. The researchers told the subjects they'd be paid based on their success in those negotiations. But the most interesting part of the study came next: the subjects were also told they could earn a cash bonus if they could *guess*—within $5,000—what the judge *actually* awarded the plaintiff.

In making their guesses, it was obviously in the subjects' interest to ignore whether they were playing the role of plaintiff's or defendant's advocate. They'd have the greatest chance at winning the cash bonus if they assessed the payout that would be fair, based solely on the law and the evidence. The question was whether they could maintain their objectivity.

On average, the volunteers assigned to represent the plaintiff's side estimated that the judge would dictate a settlement of nearly $40,000, while the volunteers assigned to represent the defendant put that number at only around $20,000. Think of it: $40,000 versus $20,000. If, despite the financial reward offered for accurately guessing the size of a fair and proper settlement, subjects artificially assigned to different sides of a dispute disagree by 100 percent, imagine the magnitude of *sincere* disagreement between actual attorneys representing different sides of a case, or opposing negotiators in a bargaining session. The fact that we assess information in a biased manner and are unaware we are doing so can be a real stumbling block in negotiations, even if both sides sincerely seek a fair settlement.

Another version of the experiment, created around the scenario of that same lawsuit, investigated the reasoning mechanism the subjects employed to reach their conflicting conclusions. In that study, at the end of the bargaining session, the researchers asked the volunteers to explicitly comment on each side's arguments, to make concrete judgments on issues like Does ordering an onion pizza via cell phone affect one's driving? Does a single beer an hour or two before getting on a motorcycle impair safety? As in the police chief résumé example, subjects on both sides tended to assign more importance to the factors that favored their desired conclusion than to the factors favoring their opponent. These experiments suggest that, as they were reading the facts of the case, the subjects' knowledge that they would be taking one side or the other affected their judgment in a subtle and unconscious manner that trumped any motivation to analyze the situation fairly.

To further probe that idea, in another variant on the experiment, researchers asked volunteers to assess the accident information *before* being told which side they would be representing. Then the subjects were assigned their roles and asked to evaluate the appropriate award, again with the promise of a cash bonus if they came close. The subjects had thus weighed the evidence while still unbiased, but made their guess about the award after the cause for bias had been established. In this situation, the discrepancy in the assessments fell from around $20,000 to just $7,000, a reduction of nearly two-thirds. Moreover, the results showed that due to the subjects' having analyzed the data before taking sides in the dispute, the proportion of times the plaintiff's and defendant's advocates failed to come to an agreement within the allotted half hour fell from 28 percent to just 6 percent. It's a cliché, but the experience of walking in the other side's shoes does seem to be the best way to understand their point of view.

As these studies suggest, the subtlety of our reasoning mechanisms allows us to maintain our illusions of objectivity even while viewing the world through a biased lens. Our decision-making processes bend but don't break our usual rules, and we perceive ourselves as forming judgments in a bottom-up fashion, using data to draw a conclusion, while we are in reality deciding top-down, using our preferred conclusion to shape our analysis of the data. When we apply motivated reasoning to assessments about ourselves, we produce that positive picture of a world in which we are all above average. If we're better at grammar than arithmetic, we give linguistic knowledge more weight in our view of what is important, whereas if we are good at adding but bad at grammar, we think language skills just aren't that crucial.[42] If we are ambitious, determined, and persistent, we believe that goal-oriented people make the most effective leaders; if we see ourselves as approachable, friendly, and extroverted, we feel that the best leaders are people-oriented.[43]

We even recruit our memories to brighten our picture of ourselves. Take grades, for example. A group of researchers asked ninety-nine college freshmen and sophomores to think back a few years and recall the grades they had received for high school classes in math, science, history, foreign language study, and English.[44] The students had no incentive to lie because they were told that their recollections would be checked against their high school registrars' records, and indeed all signed forms giving their permission. Altogether, the researchers checked on the students' memories of 3,220 grades. A funny thing happened. You'd think that the handful of years that had passed would have had a big effect on the students' grade recall, but they didn't. The intervening years didn't seem to affect the students' memories very much at all—they remembered their grades from their freshman, sophomore, junior, and senior years all with the same accuracy, about 70 percent. And yet there *were* memory holes. What made the students forget? It was not the haze of years but the haze of poor performance: their accuracy of recall declined steadily from 89 percent for A's to 64 percent for B's, 51 percent for C's, and 29 percent for D's. So if you are ever depressed over being given a bad evaluation, cheer up. Chances are, if you just wait long enough, it'll improve.

MY SON NICOLAI, now in tenth grade, received a letter the other day. The letter was from a person who used to live in my household but no longer exists. That is, the letter was written by Nicolai himself, but four years earlier. Though the letter had traveled very little in space, it had traveled very far in time, at least in the time of a young child's life. He had written the letter in sixth grade as a class assignment. It was a message from an eleven-year-old Nicolai asked to speak to the fifteen-year-old Nicolai of the future. The class's letters had been collected and held those four years by his wonderful English teacher, who eventually mailed them to the adolescents her sixth-grade children had become.

What was striking about Nicolai's letter was that it said, "Dear Nicolai . . . you want to be in the NBA. I look forward to playing basketball on the middle school seventh and eighth grade team, and then in high school, where you are now in your second year." But Nicolai did not make the team in seventh grade; nor did he make it in eighth grade. Then, as his luck would have it, the coach who passed him over for those teams also turned up as the freshman coach in high school, and again declined to pick Nicolai for the team. That year, only a handful of the boys who tried out were turned away, making the rejection particularly bitter for Nicolai. What's remarkable here is not that Nicolai wasn't smart enough to know when to give up but that through all those years he maintained his dream of playing basketball, to the extent that he put in five hours a day one summer practicing alone on an empty court. If you know kids, you understand that if a boy continues to insist that someday he will be in the NBA but year after year fails to make even his local school team, it will not be a plus for his social life. Kids might like to tease a loser, but they *love* teasing a loser for whom winning would have been everything. And so, for Nicolai, maintaining his belief in himself came at some cost.

The story of Nicolai's basketball career is not over. At the end of ninth grade, his school's new junior varsity coach saw him practicing day after day, sometimes until it was so dark he could barely see the ball. He invited Nicolai to practice with the team that summer. This fall he finally made the team. In fact, he is the team captain.

I've mentioned the successes of Apple computer a couple of times in this book, and much has been made of Apple cofounder Steve Jobs's ability to create what has come to be called a "reality distortion field," which allowed him to convince himself and others that they could accomplish whatever they set their mind to. But that reality distortion field was not just his creation; it is also Nicolai's, and—to one degree or another—it is a gift of everyone's unconscious mind, a tool built upon our natural propensity to engage in motivated reasoning.

There are few accomplishments, large or small, that don't depend to some degree on the accomplisher believing in him- or herself, and the greatest accomplishments are the most likely to rely on that person being not only optimistic but unreasonably optimistic. It's not a good idea to believe you are Jesus, but believing you can become an NBA player—or, like Jobs, come back from the humiliating defeat of being ejected from your own company, or be a great scientist or author or actor or singer—may serve you very well indeed. Even if it doesn't end up turning out to be true in the details of what you accomplish, belief in the self is an ultimately positive force in life. As Steve Jobs said, "You can't connect the dots looking forward; you can only connect them looking backwards. So you have to trust that the dots will somehow connect in your future."[45] If you believe the dots will connect down the road, it will give you the confidence to follow your heart, even when it leads you off the well-worn path.

I've attempted, in writing this book, to illuminate the many ways in which a person's unconscious mind serves them. For me, the extent to which my inner unknown self guides my conscious mind came as a great surprise. An even greater surprise was the realization of how lost I would be without it. But of all the advantages our unconscious provides, it is this one that I value most. Our unconscious is at its best when it helps us create a positive and fond sense of self, a feeling of power and control in a world full of powers far greater than the merely human. The artist Salvador Dalí once said, "Every morning upon awakening, I experience a supreme pleasure: that of being Salvador Dalí, and I ask myself, wonderstruck, what prodigious thing will he do today, this Salvador Dalí?"[46] Dalí may have been a sweet guy or he may have been an insufferable egomaniac, but there is something wonderful about his unrestrained and unabashedly optimistic vision of his future.

The psychological literature is full of studies illustrating the benefits— both personal and social—of holding positive "illusions" about ourselves.[47] Researchers find that when they induce a positive mood, by whatever means, people are more likely to interact with others and more likely to help others. Those feeling good about themselves are more cooperative in bargaining situations and more likely to find a constructive solution to their conflicts. They are also better problem solvers, more motivated to succeed, and more likely to persist in the face of a challenge. Motivated reasoning enables our minds to defend us against unhappiness, and in the process it gives us the strength to overcome the many obstacles in life that might otherwise overwhelm us. The more of it we do, the better off we tend to be, for it seems to inspire us to strive to become what we think we are. In fact, studies show that the people with the most accurate self-perceptions tend to be moderately depressed, suffer from low self-esteem, or both.[48] An overly positive self-evaluation, on the other hand, is normal and healthy.[49]

I imagine that, fifty thousand years ago, anyone in their right mind looking toward the harsh winters of northern Europe would have crawled into a cave and given up. Women seeing their children die from rampant infections, men watching their women die in childbirth, human tribes suffering drought, flood, and famine must have found it difficult to keep courageously marching forward. But with so many seemingly insurmountable barriers in life, nature provided us with the means to create an unrealistically rosy attitude about overcoming them—which helps us do precisely that.

As you confront the world, unrealistic optimism can be a life vest that keeps you afloat. Modern life, like our primitive past, has its daunting obstacles. The physicist Joe Polchinski wrote that when he started to draft his textbook on string theory, he expected that the project would take one year. It took him ten. Looking back, had I had a sober assessment of the time and effort required to write this book, or to become a theoretical physicist, I would have shrunk before both endeavors. Motivated reasoning and motivated remembering and all the other quirks of how we think about ourselves and our world may have their downsides, but when we're facing great challenges—whether it's losing a job, embarking on a course of chemotherapy, writing a book, enduring a decade of medical school, internship, and residency, spending the thousands of practice hours necessary to become an accomplished violinist or ballet dancer, putting in years of eighty-hour weeks to establish a new business, or starting over in a new country with no money and no skills—the natural optimism of the human mind is one of our greatest gifts.

Before my brothers and I were born, my parents lived in a small flat on the North Side of Chicago. My father worked long hours sewing clothes in a sweatshop, but his meager income left my parents unable to make the rent. Then one night my father came home excited and told my mother they were looking for a new seamstress at work, and that he had gotten her the job. "You start tomorrow," he said. It sounded like a propitious move, since this would almost double their income, keep them off beggars' row, and give them the comfort of spending far more time together. There was only one drawback: my mother didn't sew. Before Hitler invaded Poland, before she lost everyone and everything, before she became a refugee in a strange land, my mother had been a child of wealth. Sewing wasn't anything a teenage girl in her family had needed to learn.

And so my future parents had a little discussion. My father told my mother he could teach her. They would work at it all night, and in the morning they'd take the train to the shop together and she'd do a passable job. Anyway, he was very fast and could cover for her until she got the hang of it. My mother considered herself clumsy and, worse, too timid to go through with such a scheme. But my father insisted that she was capable and brave. She was a survivor just as he was, he told her. And so they talked, back and forth, about which qualities truly defined my mother.

We choose the facts that we want to believe. We also choose our friends, lovers, and spouses not just because of the way we perceive them but because of the way they perceive us. Unlike phenomena in physics, in life, events can often obey one theory or another, and what actually happens can depend largely upon which theory we choose to believe. It is a gift of the human mind to be extraordinarily open to accepting the theory of ourselves that pushes us in the direction of survival, and even happiness. And so my parents did not sleep that night, while my father taught my mother how to sew.

Acknowledgments

Caltech is one of the world's leading centers of neuroscience, and I am lucky to count one of Caltech's shining lights, Christof Koch, among my good friends. In 2006, just a few years after the birth of the field of social neuroscience, I began speaking to Christof about a possible book on the unconscious mind. He invited me into his lab as a guest, and for much of the next five years I observed as Christof, his students and postdocs, and fellow faculty members, especially Ralph Adolphs, Antonio Rangel, and Mike Tyszka, studied the human mind. Over those years, I read and digested more than eight hundred academic research papers. I sat in on seminars on subjects such as the neuroscience of memory, concept cells in the human visual system, and the cortical structures that allow us to identify faces. I volunteered for experiments in which fMRI images were made of my brain as I looked at photos of junk food, and as I listened to strange sounds projected into my ear. I took courses such as the wonderful "Brains, Minds, and Society," "The Neurobiology of Emotion," and "The Molecular Basis of Behavior." I attended conferences on topics such as "The Biological Origins of Human Group Behavior." And, with few exceptions, I attended the weekly Koch lab lunches, where I feasted on great food, and listened to discussions of the latest cutting-edge advances and gossip in neuroscience. Through it all, Christof and his colleagues in the Caltech neuroscience program have been generous with their time, inspiring with their passion, and patient with their explanations. I think neither Christof nor I could have imagined, when I first approached him, that he would be investing as much effort as he did teaching neuroscience to a physicist. I owe this book to his mentorship and generosity of spirit.

As always, I would also like to thank Susan Ginsburg, my agent, friend, critic, advocate, and cheerleader extraordinaire, and my editor Edward Kastenmeier for his steady guidance, patience, and clear view of the book's vision. And to their colleagues, Dan Frank, Stacy Testa, Emily Giglierano, and Tim O'Connell, for their advice, support, and problem-solving skills. I'd also like to thank my wonderful copy editor, Bonnie Thompson, for keeping me in line. Finally, thanks to those who read and commented on parts of the book. To Donna Scott, my wife and in-house editor, who read version after version and always provided honest and very perceptive input, and never threw the manuscript at me, no matter how many drafts I asked her to read; to Beth Rashbaum, whose sage editorial advice I also treasure; to Ralph Adolphs, who over many a beer gave profound input regarding the scientific content; and to all those other friends and colleagues who read part or all of the manuscript and provided useful suggestions and input. They include: Christof, Ralph, Antonio, Mike, Michael Hill, Mili Milosavljevic, Dan Simons, Tom Lyon, Seth Roberts, Kara Witt, Heather Berlin, Mark Hillery, Cynthia Harrington, Rosemary Macedo, Fred Rose, Todd Doersch, Natalie Roberge, Alexei Mlodinow, Jerry Webman, Tracey Alderson, Martin Smith, Richard Cheverton, Catherine Keefe, and Patricia McFall. And finally to my family, for their love and support, and for all the times they held dinner an extra hour or two until I got home.

Notes

PROLOGUE

1. Joseph W. Dauben, "Peirce and the History of Science," in *Peirce and Contemporary Thought*, ed. Kenneth Laine Ketner (New York: Fordham University Press, 1995), 146–49.

2. Charles Sanders Peirce, "Guessing," *Hound and Horn* 2 (1929): 271.

3. Ran R. Hassin et al., eds., *The New Unconscious* (Oxford: Oxford University Press, 2005), 77–78.

4. T. Sebeok with J. U. Sebeok, "You Know My Method," in Thomas A. Sebeok, *The Play of Musement* (Bloomington: Indiana University Press, 1981), 17–52.

5. Carl Jung, ed., *Man and His Symbols* (London: Aldus Books, 1964), 5.

6. Thomas Naselaris et al., "Bayesian Reconstruction of Natural Images from Human Brain Activity," *Neuron* 63 (September 24, 2009): 902–15.

7. Kevin N. Ochsner and Matthew D. Lieberman, "The Emergence of Social Cognitive Neuroscience," *American Psychologist* 56, no. 9 (September 2001): 717–28.

1. THE NEW UNCONSCIOUS

1. Yael Grosjean et al., "A Glial Amino-Acid Transporter Controls Synapse Strength and Homosexual Courtship in *Drosophila*," *Nature Neuroscience* 1 (January 11, 2008): 54–61.

2. Ibid.

3. Boris Borisovich Shtonda and Leon Avery, "Dietary Choice in *Caenorhabditis elegans*," *Journal of Experimental Biology* 209 (2006): 89–102.

4. S. Spinelli et al., "Early Life Stress Induces Long-Term Morphologic Changes in Primate Brain," *Archives of General Psychiatry* 66, no. 6 (2009): 658–65; Stephen J. Suomi, "Early Determinants of Behavior: Evidence from Primate Studies," *British Medical Bulletin* 53, no. 1 (1997): 170–84.

5. David Galbis-Reig, "Sigmund Freud, MD: Forgotten Contributions to Neurology, Neuropathology, and Anesthesia," *Internet Journal of Neurology* 3, no. 1 (2004).

6. Timothy D. Wilson, *Strangers to Ourselves: Discovering the Adaptive Unconscious* (Cambridge, MA: Belknap Press, 2002), 5.

7. See "The Simplifier: A Conversation with John Bargh," *Edge*, http://www.edge.org/3rd_culture/bargh09/bargh09_index.html.

8. John A. Bargh, ed., *Social Psychology and the Unconscious: The Automaticity of Higher Mental Processes* (New York: Psychology Press, 2007), 1.

9. Scientists have found little evidence of the Oedipus complex or penis envy.

10. Heather A. Berlin, "The Neural Basis of the Dynamic Unconscious," *Neuropsychoanalysis* 13, no. 1 (2011): 5–31.

11. Daniel T. Gilbert, "Thinking Lightly About Others: Automatic Components of the Social Inference Process," in *Unintended Thought*, ed. James S. Uleman and John A. Bargh (New York: Guilford, 1989), 192; Ran R. Hassin et al., eds., *The New Unconscious* (New York: Oxford University Press, 2005), 5–6.

12. John F. Kihlstrom et al., "The Psychological Unconscious: Found, Lost, and Regained," *American Psychologist* 47, no. 6 (June 1992): 789.

13. John T. Jones et al., "How Do I Love Thee? Let Me Count the Js: Implicit Egotism and Interpersonal Attraction," *Journal of Personality and Social Psychology* 87, no. 5 (2004): 665–83. The particular states studied—Georgia, Tennessee, and Alabama—were chosen because of the unusual search capabilities provided by their statewide marriage databases.

14. N. J. Blackwood, "Self-Responsibility and the Self-Serving Bias: An fMRI Investigation of Causal Attributions," *Neuroimage* 20 (2003): 1076–85.

15. Brian Wansink and Junyong Kim, "Bad Popcorn in Big Buckets: Portion Size Can Influence Intake as Much as Taste," *Journal of Nutrition Education and Behavior* 37, no. 5 (September–October 2005): 242–45.

16. Brian Wansink, "Environmental Factors That Increase Food Intake and Consumption Volume of Unknowing Consumers," *Annual Review of Nutrition* 24 (2004): 455–79.

17. Brian Wansink et al., "How Descriptive Food Names Bias Sensory Perceptions in Restaurants," *Food and Quality Preference* 16, no. 5 (July 2005): 393–400; Brian Wansink et al., "Descriptive Menu Labels' Effect on Sales," *Cornell Hotel and Restaurant Administrative Quarterly* 42, no. 6 (December 2001): 68–72.

18. Norbert Schwarz et al., "When Thinking Is Difficult: Metacognitive Experiences as Information," in *Social Psychology of Consumer Behavior*, ed. Michaela Wänke (New York: Psychology Press, 2009), 201–23.

19. Benjamin Bushong et al., "Pavlovian Processes in Consumer Choice: The Physical Presence of a Good Increases Willingness-to-Pay," *American Economic Review* 100, no. 4 (2010): 1556–71.

20. Vance Packard, *The Hidden Persuaders* (New York: David McKay, 1957), 16.

21. Adrian C. North et al., "In-Store Music Affects Product Choice," *Nature* 390 (November 13, 1997): 132.

22. Donald A. Laird, "How the Consumer Estimates Quality by Subconscious Sensory Impressions," *Journal of Applied Psychology* 16 (1932): 241–46.

23. Robin Goldstein et al., "Do More Expensive Wines Taste Better? Evidence from a Large Sample of Blind Tastings," *Journal of Wine Economics* 3, no. 1 (Spring 2008): 1–9.

24. Hilke Plassmann et al., "Marketing Actions Can Modulate Neural Representations of Experienced Pleasantness," *Proceedings of the National Academy of Sciences of the United States of America* 105, no. 3 (January 22, 2008): 1050–54.

25. See, for instance, Morten L. Kringelbach, "The Human Orbitofrontal Cortex: Linking Reward to Hedonic Experience," *Nature Reviews: Neuroscience* 6 (September 2005): 691–702.

26. M. P. Paulus and L. R. Frank, "Ventromedial Prefrontal Cortex Activation Is Critical for Preference Judgments," *Neuroreport* 14 (2003): 1311–15; M. Deppe et al., "Nonlinear Responses Within the Medial Prefrontal Cortex Reveal When Specific Implicit Information Influences Economic Decision-Making," *Journal of Neuroimaging* 15 (2005): 171–82; M. Schaeffer et al., "Neural Correlates of Culturally Familiar Brands of Car Manufacturers," *Neuroimage* 31 (2006): 861–65.

27. Michael R. Cunningham, "Weather, Mood, and Helping Behavior: Quasi Experiments with Sunshine Samaritan," *Journal of Personality and Social Psychology* 37, no. 11 (1979): 1947–56.

28. Bruce Rind, "Effect of Beliefs About Weather Conditions on Tipping," *Journal of Applied Social Psychology* 26, no. 2 (1996): 137–47.

29. Edward M. Saunders Jr., "Stock Prices and Wall Street Weather," *American Economic Review* 83 (1993): 1337–45. See also Mitra Akhtari, "Reassessment of the Weather Effect: Stock Prices and Wall Street Weather," *Undergraduate Economic Review* 7, no. 1 (2011), http://digitalcommons.iwu.edu/uer/vol7/iss1/19.

30. David Hirshleiter and Tyler Shumway, "Good Day Sunshine: Stock Returns and the Weather," *Journal of Finance* 58, no. 3 (June 2003): 1009–32.

2. SENSES PLUS MIND EQUALS REALITY

1. Ran R. Hassin et al., eds., *The New Unconscious* (Oxford: Oxford University Press, 2005), 3.

2. Louis Menand, *The Metaphysical Club* (New York: Farrar, Straus and Giroux, 2001), 258.

3. Donald Freedheim, *Handbook of Psychology*, vol. 1 (Hoboken, NJ: Wiley, 2003), 2.

4. Alan Kim, "Wilhelm Maximilian Wundt," *Stanford Encyclopedia of Phi-*

losophy, http://plato.stanford.edu/entries/wilhelm-wundt/ (2006); Robert S. Harper, "The First Psychology Laboratory," *Isis* 41 (July 1950): 158–61.

5. Quoted in E. R. Hilgard, *Psychology in America: A Historical Survey* (Orlando: Harcourt Brace Jovanovich, 1987), 37.

6. Menand, *The Metaphysical Club,* 259–60.

7. William Carpenter, *Principles of Mental Physiology* (New York: D. Appleton and Company, 1874), 526 and 539.

8. Menand, *The Metaphysical Club,* 159.

9. M. Zimmerman, "The Nervous System in the Context of Information Theory," in *Human Physiology,* ed. R. F. Schmidt and G. Thews (Berlin: Springer, 1989), 166–73. Quoted in Ran R. Hassin et al., eds., *The New Unconscious,* 82.

10. Christof Koch, "Minds, Brains, and Society" (lecture at Caltech, Pasadena, CA, January 21, 2009).

11. R. Toro et al., "Brain Size and Folding of the Human Cerebral Cortex," *Cerebral Cortex* 18, no. 10 (2008): 2352–57.

12. Alan J. Pegna et al., "Discriminating Emotional Faces Without Primary Visual Cortices Involves the Right Amygdala," *Nature Neuroscience* 8, no. 1 (January 2005): 24–25.

13. P. Ekman and W. P. Friesen, *Pictures of Facial Affect* (Palo Alto: Consulting Psychologists Press, 1975).

14. See http://www.moillusions.com/2008/12/who-says-we-dont-have-barack-obama.html; accessed March 30, 2009. Contact: vurdlak@gmail.com.

15. See, e.g., W. T. Thach, "On the Specific Role of the Cerebellum in Motor Learning and Cognition: Clues from PET Activation and Lesion Studies in Man," *Behavioral and Brain Sciences* 19 (1996): 411–31.

16. Beatrice de Gelder et al., "Intact Navigation Skills After Bilateral Loss of Striate Cortex," *Current Biology* 18, no. 24 (2008): R1128–29.

17. Benedict Carey, "Blind, Yet Seeing: The Brain's Subconscious Visual Sense," *New York Times,* December 23, 2008.

18. Christof Koch, *The Quest for Consciousness* (Englewood, CO: Roberts, 2004), 220.

19. Ian Glynn, *An Anatomy of Thought* (Oxford: Oxford University Press, 1999), 214.

20. Ronald S. Fishman, "Gordon Holmes, the Cortical Retina, and the Wounds of War," *Documenta Ophthalmologica* 93 (1997): 9–28.

21. L. Weiskrantz et al., "Visual Capacity in the Hemianopic Field Following a Restricted Occipital Ablation," *Brain* 97 (1974): 709–28; L. Weiskrantz, *Blindsight: A Case Study and Its Implications* (Oxford: Clarendon, 1986).

22. N. Tsuchiya and C. Koch, "Continuous Flash Suppression Reduces Negative Afterimages," *Nature Neuroscience* 8 (2005): 1096–101.

23. Yi Jiang et al., "A Gender- and Sexual Orientation–Dependent Spatial Attentional Effect of Invisible Images," *Proceedings of the National Academy of Sciences of the United States of America* 103, no. 45 (November 7, 2006): 17048–52.

24. I. Kohler, "Experiments with Goggles," *Scientific American* 206 (1961): 62–72.

25. Richard M. Warren, "Perceptual Restoration of Missing Speech Sounds," *Science* 167, no. 3917 (January 23 1970): 392–93.

26. Richard M. Warren and Roselyn P. Warren, "Auditory Illusions and Confusions," *Scientific American* 223 (1970): 30–36.

27. This study was reported in Warren and Warren, "Auditory Illusions and Confusions" and was referred to in other studies but apparently was never published.

3. REMEMBERING AND FORGETTING

1. Jennifer Thompson-Cannino and Ronald Cotton with Erin Torneo, *Picking Cotton* (New York: St. Martin's, 2009); see also the transcript of "What Jennifer Saw," *Frontline*, show 1508, February 25, 1997.

2. Gary L. Wells and Elizabeth A. Olsen, "Eyewitness Testimony," *Annual Review of Psychology* 54 (2003): 277–91.

3. G. L. Wells, "What Do We Know About Eyewitness Identification?" *American Psychologist* 48 (May 1993): 553–71.

4. See the project website, http://www.innocenceproject.org/understand/ Eyewitness-Misidentification.php.

5. Erica Goode and John Schwartz, "Police Lineups Start to Face Fact: Eyes Can Lie," *New York Times*, August 28, 2011. See also Brandon Garrett, *Convicting the Innocent: Where Criminal Prosecutors Go Wrong* (Cambridge, MA: Harvard University Press, 2011).

6. Thomas Lundy, "Jury Instruction Corner," *Champion Magazine* (May–June 2008): 62.

7. Daniel Schacter, *Searching for Memory: The Brain, the Mind, and the Past* (New York: Basic Books, 1996), 111–12; Ulric Neisser, "John Dean's Memory: A Case Study," in *Memory Observed: Remembering in Natural Contexts*, ed. Ulric Neisser (San Francisco: Freeman, 1982), 139–59.

8. Loftus and Ketcham, *Witness for the Defense*.

9. B. R. Hergenhahn, *An Introduction to the History of Psychology*, 6th ed. (Belmont, CA: Wadsworth, 2008), 348–50; "H. Münsterberg," in Allen Johnson and Dumas Malone, eds., *Dictionary of American Biography*, base set (New York: Charles Scribner's Sons, 1928–36).

10. H. Münsterberg, *On the Witness Stand: Essays on Psychology and Crime* (New York: Doubleday, 1908).

11. Ibid. For the significance of Münsterberg's work, see Siegfried Ludwig

Sporer, "Lessons from the Origins of Eyewitness Testimony Research in Europe," *Applied Cognitive Psychology* 22 (2008): 737–57.

12. For a capsule summary of Münsterberg's life and work, see D. P. Schultz and S. E. Schultz, *A History of Modern Psychology* (Belmont, CA: Wadsworth, 2004), 246–52.

13. Michael T. Gilmore, *The Quest for Legibility in American Culture* (Oxford: Oxford University Press, 2003), 11.

14. H. Münsterberg, *Psychotherapy* (New York: Moffat, Yard, 1905), 125.

15. A. R. Luria, *The Mind of a Mnemonist: A Little Book About a Vast Memory*, trans. L. Solotaroff (New York: Basic Books, 1968); see also Schachter, *Searching for Memory*, 81, and Gerd Gigerenzer, *Gut Feelings* (New York: Viking, 2007), 21–23.

16. John D. Bransford and Jeffery J. Franks, "The Abstraction of Linguistic Ideas: A Review," *Cognition* 1, no. 2–3 (1972): 211–49.

17. Arthur Graesser and George Mandler, "Recognition Memory for the Meaning and Surface Structure of Sentences," *Journal of Experimental Psychology: Human Learning and Memory* 104, no. 3 (1975): 238–48.

18. Schacter, *Searching for Memory*, 103; H. L. Roediger III and K. B. McDermott, "Creating False Memories: Remembering Words Not Presented in Lists," *Journal of Experimental Psychology: Learning, Memory, and Cognition* 21 (1995): 803–14.

19. Private conversation, September 24, 2011. See also Christopher Chabris and Daniel Simons, *The Invisible Gorilla* (New York: Crown, 2009), 66–70.

20. For detailed summaries of Bartlett's life and his work on memory, see H. L. Roediger, "Sir Frederic Charles Bartlett: Experimental and Applied Psychologist," in *Portraits of Pioneers in Psychology*, vol. 4, ed. G. A. Kimble and M. Wertheimer (Mahwah, NJ: Erlbaum, 2000), 149–61, and H. L. Roediger, E. T. Bergman, and M. L. Meade, "Repeated Reproduction from Memory," in *Bartlett, Culture and Cognition*, ed. A. Saito (London, UK: Psychology Press, 2000), 115–34.

21. Sir Frederick Charles Bartlett, *Remembering: A Study in Experimental and Social Psychology* (Cambridge, UK: Cambridge University Press, 1932), 68.

22. Friedrich Wulf, "Beiträge zur Psychologie der Gestalt: VI. Über die Veränderung von Vorstellungen (Gedächtniss und Gestalt)," *Psychologische Forschung* 1 (1922): 333–75; G. W. Allport, "Change and Decay in the Visual Memory Image," *British Journal of Psychology* 21 (1930): 133–48.

23. Bartlett, *Remembering*, 85.

24. Ulric Neisser, *The Remembering Self: Construction and Accuracy in the Self-Narrative* (Cambridge, UK: Cambridge University Press, 1994), 6; see also Elizabeth Loftus, *The Myth of Repressed Memory: False Memories and Allegations of Sexual Abuse* (New York: St. Martin's Griffin, 1996), 91–92.

25. R. S. Nickerson and M. J. Adams, "Long-Term Memory for a Common Object," *Cognitive Psychology* 11 (1979): 287–307.

26. For example, Lionel Standing et al., "Perception and Memory for Pictures:

Single-Trial Learning of 2500 Visual Stimuli," *Psychonomic Science* 19, no. 2 (1970): 73–74, and K. Pezdek et al., "Picture Memory: Recognizing Added and Deleted Details," *Journal of Experimental Psychology: Learning, Memory, and Cognition* 14, no. 3 (1988): 468; quoted in Daniel J. Simons and Daniel T. Levin, "Change Blindness," *Trends in the Cognitive Sciences* 1, no. 7 (October 1997): 261–67.

27. J. Grimes, "On the Failure to Detect Changes in Scenes Across Saccades," in *Perception*, ed. K. Atkins, vol. 2 of Vancouver Studies in Cognitive Science (Oxford: Oxford University Press, 1996), 89–110.

28. Daniel T. Levin and Daniel J. Simons, "Failure to Detect Changes to Attended Objects in Motion Pictures," *Psychonomic Bulletin & Review* 4, no. 4 (1997): 501–6.

29. Daniel J. Simons and Daniel T. Levin, "Failure to Detect Changes to People During a Real-World Interaction," *Psychonomic Bulletin & Review* 5, no. 4 (1998): 644–48.

30. David G. Payne et al., "Memory Illusions: Recalling, Recognizing, and Recollecting Events That Never Occurred," *Journal of Memory and Language* 35 (1996): 261–85.

31. Kimberly A. Wade et al., "A Picture Is Worth a Thousand Lies: Using False Photographs to Create False Childhood Memories," *Psychonomic Bulletin & Review* 9, no. 3 (2002): 597–602.

32. Elizabeth F. Loftus, "Planting Misinformation in the Human Mind: A 30-Year Investigation of the Malleability of Memory," *Learning & Memory* 12 (2005): 361–66.

33. Kathryn A. Braun et al., "Make My Memory: How Advertising Can Change Our Memories of the Past," *Psychology and Marketing* 19, no. 1 (January 2002): 1–23, and Elizabeth Loftus, "Our Changeable Memories: Legal and Practical Implications," *Nature Reviews Neuroscience* 4 (March 2003): 231–34.

34. Loftus, "Our Changeable Memories," and Shari R. Berkowitz et al., "Pluto Behaving Badly: False Beliefs and Their Consequences," *American Journal of Psychology* 121, no. 4 (Winter 2008): 643–60.

35. S. J. Ceci et al., "Repeatedly Thinking About Non-events," *Consciousness and Cognition* 3 (1994) 388–407; S. J. Ceci et al, "The Possible Role of Source Misattributions in the Creation of False Beliefs Among Preschoolers," *International Journal of Clinical and Experimental Hypnosis*, 42 (1994), 304–20.

36. I. E. Hyman and F. J. Billings, "Individual Differences and the Creation of False Childhood Memories," *Memory* 6, no. 1 (1998): 1–20.

37. Ira E. Hyman et al, "False Memories of Childhood Experiences," *Applied Cognitive Psychology* 9 (1995): 181–97.

4. THE IMPORTANCE OF BEING SOCIAL

1. J. Kiley Hamlin et al., "Social Evaluation by Preverbal Infants," *Nature* 450 (November 22, 2007): 557–59.

2. James K. Rilling, "A Neural Basis for Social Cooperation," *Neuron* 35, no. 2 (July 2002): 395–405.

3. Stanley Schachter, *The Psychology of Affiliation* (Palo Alto, CA: Stanford University Press, 1959).

4. Naomi I. Eisenberger et al., "Does Rejection Hurt? An fMRI Study of Social Exclusion," *Science* 10, no. 5643 (October 2003): 290–92.

5. C. Nathan DeWall et al., "Tylenol Reduces Social Pain: Behavioral and Neural Evidence," *Psychological Science* 21 (2010): 931–37.

6. James S. House et al., "Social Relationships and Health," *Science* 241 (July 29, 1988): 540–45.

7. Richard G. Klein, "Archeology and the Evolution of Human Behavior," *Evolutionary Anthropology* 9 (2000): 17–37; Christopher S. Henshilwood and Curtis W. Marean, "The Origin of Modern Human Behavior: Critique of the Models and Their Test Implication," *Current Anthropology* 44, no. 5 (December 2003): 627–51; and L. Brothers, "The Social Brain: A Project for Integrating Primate Behavior and Neurophysiology in a New Domain," *Concepts in Neuroscience* 1 (1990): 27–51.

8. Klein, "Archeology and the Evolution of Human Behavior," and Henshilwood and Marean, "The Origin of Modern Human Behavior."

9. F. Heider and M. Simmel, "An Experimental Study of Apparent Behavior," *American Journal of Psychology* 57 (1944): 243–59.

10. Josep Call and Michael Tomasello, "Does the Chimpanzee Have a Theory of Mind? 30 Years Later," *Cell* 12, no. 5 (2008): 187–92.

11. J. Perner and H. Wimmer, " 'John Thinks That Mary Thinks That . . . ': Attribution of Second-Order Beliefs by 5- to 10-Year-Old Children," *Journal of Experimental Child Psychology* 39 (1985): 437–71, and Angeline S. Lillard and Lori Skibbe, "Theory of Mind: Conscious Attribution and Spontaneous Trait Inference," in *The New Unconscious*, ed. Ran R. Hassin et al. (Oxford: Oxford University Press, 2005), 277–78; see also Matthew D. Lieberman, "Social Neuroscience: A Review of Core Processes," *Annual Review of Psychology* 58 (2007): 259–89.

12. Oliver Sacks, *An Anthropologist on Mars* (New York: Knopf, 1995), 272.

13. Robin I. M. Dunbar, "The Social Brain Hypothesis," *Evolutionary Anthropology: Issues, News, and Reviews* 6, no. 5 (1998): 178–90.

14. Ibid.

15. R. A. Hill and R. I. M. Dunbar, "Social Network Size in Humans," *Human Nature* 14, no. 1 (2003): 53–72, and Dunbar, "The Social Brain Hypothesis."

16. Robin I. M. Dunbar, *Grooming, Gossip and the Evolution of Language* (Cambridge, MA: Harvard University Press, 1996).

17. Stanley Milgram, "The Small World Problem," *Psychology Today* 1, no. 1 (May 1967): 61–67, and Jeffrey Travers and Stanley Milgram, "An Experimental Study of the Small World Problem," *Sociometry* 32, no. 4 (December 1969): 425–43.

18 Peter Sheridan Dodds et al., "An Experimental Study of Search in Global Networks," *Science* 301 (August 8, 2003): 827–29.

19. James P. Curley and Eric B. Keveme, "Genes, Brains and Mammalian Social Bonds," *Trends in Ecology and Evolution* 20, no. 10 (October 2005).

20. Patricia Smith Churchland, "The Impact of Neuroscience on Philosophy," *Neuron* 60 (November 6, 2008): 409–11, and Ralph Adolphs, "Cognitive Neuroscience of Human Social Behavior," *Nature Reviews* 4 (March 2003): 165–78.

21. K. D. Broad et al., "Mother-Infant Bonding and the Evolution of Mammalian Social Relationships," *Philosophical Transactions of the Royal Society B* 361 (2006): 2199–214.

22. Thomas R. Insel and Larry J. Young, "The Neurobiology of Attachment," *Nature Reviews Neuroscience* 2 (February 2001): 129–33.

23. Larry J. Young et al., "Anatomy and Neurochemistry of the Pair Bond," *Journal of Comparative Neurology* 493 (2005): 51–57.

24. Churchland, "The Impact of Neuroscience on Philosophy."

25. Zoe R. Donaldson and Larry J. Young, "Oxytocin, Vasopressin, and the Neurogenetics of Sociality," *Science* 322 (November 7, 2008): 900–904.

26. Ibid.

27. Larry J. Young, "Love: Neuroscience Reveals All," *Nature* 457 (January 8, 2009): 148; Paul J. Zak, "The Neurobiology of Trust," *Scientific American* (June 2008): 88–95; Kathleen C. Light et al., "More Frequent Partner Hugs and Higher Oxytocin Levels are Linked to Lower Blood Pressure and Heart Rate in Premenopausal Women," *Biological Psychiatry* 69, no. 1 (April 2005): 5–21; and Karten M. Grewen et al., "Effect of Partner Support on Resting Oxytocin, Cortisol, Norepinephrine and Blood Pressure Before and After Warm Personal Contact," *Psychosomatic Medicine* 67 (2005): 531–38.

28. Michael Kosfeld et al., "Oxytocin Increases Trust in Humans," *Nature* 435 (June 2, 2005): 673–76; Paul J. Zak et al., "Oxytocin Is Associated with Human Trustworthiness," *Hormones and Behavior* 48 (2005): 522–27; Angeliki Theodoridou, "Oxytocin and Social Perception: Oxytocin Increases Perceived Facial Trustworthiness and Attractiveness," *Hormones and Behavior* 56, no. 1 (June 2009): 128–32; and Gregor Domes et al., "Oxytocin Improves 'Mind-Reading' in Humans," *Biological Psychiatry* 61 (2007): 731–33.

29. Donaldson and Young, "Oxytocin, Vasopressin, and the Neurogenetics of Sociality."

30. Hassin et al., eds., *The New Unconscious*, 3–4.

31. Ibid., and Timothy D. Wilson, *Strangers to Ourselves: Discovering the Adaptive Unconscious* (Cambridge, MA: Belknap, 2002), 4.

32. Ellen Langer et al., "The Mindlessness of Ostensibly Thoughtful Action: The Role of 'Placebic' Information in Interpersonal Interaction," *Journal of Personality and Social Psychology* 36, no. 6 (1978): 635–42, and Robert P. Abelson, "Psycho-

logical Status of the Script Concept," *American Psychologist* 36, no. 7 (July 1981): 715–29.

33. William James, *The Principles of Psychology* (New York: Henry Holt, 1890), 97–99.

34. C. S. Roy and C. S. Sherrington, "On the Regulation of the Blood-Supply of the Brain," *Journal of Physiology* (London) 11 (1890): 85–108.

35. Tim Dalgleish, "The Emotional Brain," *Nature Reviews Neuroscience* 5, no. 7 (2004): 582–89; see also Colin Camerer et al., "Neuroeconomics: How Neuroscience Can Inform Economics," *Journal of Economic Literature* 43, no. 1 (March 2005): 9–64.

36. Lieberman, "Social Neuroscience."

37. Ralph Adolphs, "Cognitive Neuroscience of Human Social Behavior," *Nature Reviews* 4 (March 2003): 165–78.

38. Lieberman, "Social Neuroscience."

39. Bryan Kolb and Ian Q. Whishaw, *An Introduction to Brain and Behavior* (New York: Worth, 2004), 410–11.

40. R. Glenn Northcutt and Jon H. Kaas, "The Emergence and Evolution of Mammalian Neocortex," *Trends in Neuroscience* 18, no. 9 (1995): 373–79, and Jon H. Kaas, "Evolution of the Neocortex," *Current Biology* 21, no. 16 (2006): R910–14.

41. Nikos K. Logothetis, "What We Can Do and What We Cannot Do with fMRI," *Nature* 453 (June 12, 2008): 869–78. By the first research article employing fMRI, Logothetis meant the first employing fMRI that could be done without injections of contrast agents, which are impractical because they complicate the experimental procedure and inhibit the ability of researchers to recruit volunteers.

42. Lieberman, "Social Neuroscience."

5. READING PEOPLE

1. See Edward T. Heyn, "Berlin's Wonderful Horse," *New York Times*, September 4, 1904; " 'Clever Hans' Again," *New York Times*, October 2, 1904; "A Horse—and the Wise Men," *New York Times*, July 23, 1911; and "Can Horses Think? Learned Commission Says 'Perhaps,' " *New York Times*, August 31, 1913.

2. B. Hare et al., "The Domestication of Social Cognition in Dogs," *Science* 298 (November 22, 2002): 1634–36; Brian Hare and Michael Tomasello, "Human-like Social Skills in Dogs?" *Trends in Cognitive Sciences*, 9, no. 9 (2005): 440–44; and Á. Miklósi et al., "Comparative Social Cognition: What Can Dogs Teach Us?" *Animal Behavior* 67 (2004): 995–1004.

3. Monique A. R. Udell et al., "Wolves Outperform Dogs in Following Human Social Cues," *Animal Behavior* 76 (2008): 1767–73.

4. Jonathan J. Cooper et al., "Clever Hounds: Social Cognition in the Domestic Dog (*Canis familiaris*)," *Applied Animal Behavioral Science* 81 (2003): 229–44,

and A. Whiten and R. W. Byrne, "Tactical Deception in Primates," *Behavioral and Brain Sciences* 11 (2004): 233–73.

5. Hare, "The Domestication of Social Cognition in Dogs," 1634, and E. B. Ginsburg and L. Hiestand, "Humanity's Best Friend: The Origins of Our Inevitable Bond with Dogs," in *The Inevitable Bond: Examining Scientist-Animal Interactions*, ed. H. Davis and D. Balfour (Cambridge: Cambridge University Press, 1991), 93–108.

6. Robert Rosenthal and Kermit L. Fode, "The Effect of Experimenter Bias on the Performance of the Albino Rat," *Behavioral Science* 8, no. 3 (1963): 183–89; see also Robert Rosenthal and Lenore Jacobson, *Pygmalion in the Classroom: Teacher Expectation and Pupils' Intellectual Development* (New York: Holt, Rinehart, and Winston, 1968), 37–38.

7. L. H. Ingraham and G. M. Harrington, "Psychology of the Scientist: XVI. Experience of E as a Variable in Reducing Experimenter Bias," *Psychological Reports* 19 (1966): 455–461.

8. Robert Rosenthal and Kermit L. Fode, "Psychology of the Scientist: V. Three Experiments in Experimenter Bias," *Psychological Reports* 12 (April 1963): 491–511.

9. Rosenthal and Jacobson, *Pygmalion in the Classroom*, 29.

10. Ibid.

11. Robert Rosenthal and Lenore Jacobson, "Teacher's Expectancies: Determinants of Pupil's IQ Gains," *Psychological Reports* 19 (August 1966): 115–18.

12. Simon E. Fischer and Gary F. Marcus, "The Eloquent Ape: Genes, Brains and the Evolution of Language," *Nature Reviews Genetics* 7 (January 2006): 9–20.

13. L. A. Petitto and P. F. Marentette, "Babbling in the Manual Mode: Evidence for the Ontology of Language," *Science* 251 (1991): 1493–96, and S. Goldin-Meadow and C. Mylander, "Spontaneous Sign Systems Created by Deaf Children in Two Cultures," *Nature* 391 (1998): 279–81.

14. Charles Darwin, *The Autobiography of Charles Darwin* (1887, repr. New York: Norton, 1969), 141; see also Paul Ekman, "Introduction," in *Emotions Inside Out: 130 Years After Darwin's "The Expression of the Emotions in Man and Animals"* (New York: Annals of the N.Y. Academy of Science, 2003), 1–6.

15. For example, J. Bulwer, *Chirologia; or, The Natural Language of the Hand* (London: Harper, 1644); C. Bell, *The Anatomy and Philosophy of Expression as Connected with the Fine Arts* (London: George Bell, 1806); and G. B. Duchenne de Boulogne, *Mécanismes de la Physionomie Humaine, ou Analyse Électrophysiologique de l'Expression des Passions* (Paris: Baillière, 1862).

16. Peter O. Gray, *Psychology* (New York: Worth, 2007), 74–75.

17. Antonio Damasio, *Descartes' Error: Emotion, Reason, and the Human Brain* (New York: Putnam, 1994), 141–42.

18. Quoted in Mark G. Frank et al., "Behavioral Markers and Recognizability

of the Smile of Enjoyment," *Journal of Personality and Social Psychology* 64, no. 1 (1993): 87.

19. Ibid., 83–93.

20. Charles Darwin, *The Expression of the Emotions in Man and Animals* (1872; repr. New York: D. Appleton, 1886), 15–17.

21. James A. Russell, "Is There Universal Recognition of Emotion from Facial Expression? A Review of the Cross-Cultural Studies," *Psychological Bulletin* 115, no. 1 (1994): 102–41.

22. See Ekman's Afterword in Charles Darwin, *The Expression of the Emotions in Man and Animals* (1872; repr. Oxford: Oxford University Press, 1998), 363–93.

23. Paul Ekman and Wallace V. Friesen, "Constants Across Cultures in the Face and Emotion," *Journal of Personality and Social Psychology* 17, no. 2 (1971): 124–29.

24. Paul Ekman, "Facial Expressions of Emotion: An Old Controversy and New Findings," *Philosophical Transactions of the Royal Society of London B* 335 (1992): 63–69. See also Rachel E. Jack et al., "Cultural Confusions Show That Facial Expressions Are Not Universal," *Current Biology* 19 (September 29, 2009): 1543–48. That study found results that, despite the paper's title, were "consistent with previous observations," although East Asians confused fear and disgust with surprise and anger in Western faces more often than Westerners themselves did.

25. Edward Z. Tronick, "Emotions and Emotional Communication in Infants," *American Psychologist* 44, no. 2 (February 1989): 112–19.

26. Dario Galati et al., "Voluntary Facial Expression of Emotion: Comparing Congenitally Blind with Normally Sighted Encoders," *Journal of Personality and Social Psychology* 73, no. 6 (1997): 1363–79.

27. Gary Alan Fine et al., "Couple Tie-Signs and Interpersonal Threat: A Field Experiment," *Social Psychology Quarterly* 47, no. 3 (1984): 282–86.

28. Hans Kummer, *Primate Societies* (Chicago: Aldine-Atherton, 1971).

29. David Andrew Puts et al., "Dominance and the Evolution of Sexual Dimorphism in Human Voice Pitch," *Evolution and Human Behavior* 27 (2006): 283–96; Joseph Henrich and Francisco J. Gil-White, "The Evolution of Prestige: Freely Conferred Deference as a Mechanism for Enhancing the Benefits of Cultural Transmission," *Evolution and Human Behavior* 22 (2001): 165–96.

30. Allan Mazur et al., "Physiological Aspects of Communication via Mutual Gaze," *American Journal of Sociology* 86, no. 1 (1980): 50–74.

31. John F. Dovidio and Steve L. Ellyson, "Decoding Visual Dominance: Attributions of Power Based on Relative Percentages of Looking While Speaking and Looking While Listening," *Social Psychology Quarterly* 45, no. 2 (1982): 106–13.

32. R. V. Exline et al., "Visual Behavior as an Aspect of Power Role Relationships," in *Advances in the Study of Communication and Affect*, vol. 2, ed. P. Pliner et al. (New York: Plenum, 1975), 21–52.

33. R. V. Exline et al., "Visual Dominance Behavior in Female Dyads: Situational and Personality Factors," *Social Psychology Quarterly* 43, no. 3 (1980): 328–36.

34. John F. Dovidio et al., "The Relationship of Social Power to Visual Displays of Dominance Between Men and Women," *Journal of Personality and Social Psychology* 54, no. 2 (1988): 233–42.

35. S. Duncan and D. W. Fiske, *Face-to-Face Interaction: Research, Methods, and Theory* (Hillsdale, NJ: Erlbaum, 1977), and N. Capella, "'Controlling the Floor in Conversation," in *Multichannel Integrations of Nonverbal Behavior*, ed. A. W. Siegman and S. Feldstein (Hillsdale, NJ: Erlbaum, 1985), 69–103.

36. A. Atkinson et al., "Emotion Perception from Dynamic and Static Body Expressions in Point-Light and Full-Light Displays," *Perception* 33 (2004): 717–46; "Perception of Emotion from Dynamic Point-Light Displays Represented in Dance," *Perception* 25 (1996): 727–38; James E. Cutting and Lynn T. Kozlowski, "Recognizing Friends by Their Walk: Gait Perception Without Familiarity Cues," *Bulletin of the Psychonomic Society* 9, no. 5 (1977): 353–56; and James E. Cutting and Lynn T. Kozlowski, "Recognizing the Sex of a Walker from a Dynamic Point-Light Display," *Perception and Psychophysics* 21, no. 6 (1977): 575–80.

37. S. H. Spence, "The Relationship Between Social-Cognitive Skills and Peer Sociometric Status," *British Journal of Developmental Psychology* 5 (1987): 347–56.

38. M. A. Bayes, "Behavioral Cues of Interpersonal Warmth," *Journal of Consulting and Clinical Psychology* 39, no. 2 (1972): 333–39.

39. J. K. Burgoon et al., "Nonverbal Behaviors, Persuasion, and Credibility," *Human Communication Research* 17 (Fall 1990): 140–69.

40. A. Mehrabian and M. Williams, "Nonverbal Concomitants of Perceived and Intended Persuasiveness," *Journal of Personality and Social Psychology* 13, no. 1 (1969): 37–58.

41. Starkey Duncan Jr., "Nonverbal Communication," Psychological Bulletin 77, no. 2 (1969): 118–37.

42. Harald G. Wallbott, "Bodily Expression of Emotion," *European Journal of Social Psychology* 28 (1998): 879–96; Lynn A. Streeter et al., "Pitch Changes During Attempted Deception," *Journal of Personality and Social Psychology* 35, no. 5 (1977): 345–50; Allan Pease and Barbara Pease, *The Definitive Book of Body Language* (New York: Bantam, 2004); Bella M. DePaulo, "Nonverbal Behavior and Self Presentation," *Psychological Bulletin* 11, no. 2 (1992): 203–43; Judith A. Hall et al., "Nonverbal Behavior and the Vertical Dimension of Social Relations: A Meta-analysis," *Psychological Bulletin* 131, no. 6 (2005): 898–924; and Kate Fox, *SIRC Guide to Flirting: What Social Science Can Tell You About Flirting and How to Do It*, published online by the Social Issues Research Centre, http://www.sirc.org/index.html.

6. JUDGING PEOPLE BY THEIR COVERS

1. Grace Freed-Brown and David J. White, "Acoustic Mate Copying: Female Cowbirds Attend to Other Females' Vocalizations to Modify Their Song Preferences," *Proceedings of the Royal Society B* 276 (2009): 3319–25.

2. Ibid.

3. C. Nass et al., "Computers Are Social Actors," *Proceedings of the ACM CHI 94 Human Factors in Computing Systems Conference* (Reading, MA: Association for Computing Machinery Press, 1994), 72–77; C. Nass et al., "Are Computers Gender Neutral?" *Journal of Applied Social Psychology* 27, no. 10 (1997): 864–76; and C. Nass and K. M. Lee, "Does Computer-Generated Speech Manifest Personality? An Experimental Test of Similarity-Attraction," *CHI Letters* 2, no. 1 (April 2000): 329–36.

4. When we speak with someone we surely react to the content of their speech. But we also react, both consciously and unconsciously, to nonverbal qualities of the person that delivers it. By removing that person from the interaction, Nass and his colleagues focused on their subjects' automatic reaction to the human voice. But maybe that's not what was happening. Maybe the subjects were really responding to the physical box, the machine, and not the voice. There is no way, through pure logic, to know which it was, since both choices are equally inappropriate. So the researchers performed another experiment, in which they mixed things up. Some of the students in these experiments made their evaluations on computers that were not the machines that had tutored them but had the same voice. Others made their evaluations on the same computer that had taught them but had a different voice for the evaluation phase. The results showed that it was indeed the voice that the students were responding to, and not the physical machine.

5. Byron Reeves and Clifford Nass, *The Media Equation: How People Treat Computers, Television, and New Media Like Real People and Places* (Cambridge: Cambridge University Press, 1996), 24.

6. Sarah A. Collins, "Men's Voices and Women's Choices," *Animal Behavior* 60 (2000): 773–80.

7. David Andrew Puts et al., "Dominance and the Evolution of Sexual Dimorphism in Human Voice Pitch," *Evolution and Human Behavior* 27 (2006): 283–96.

8. David Andrew Puts, "Mating Context and Menstrual Phase Affect Women's Preferences for Male Voice Pitch," *Evolution and Human Behavior* 26 (2005): 388–97.

9. R. Nathan Pepitone et al., "Women's Voice Attractiveness Varies Across the Menstrual Cycle," *Evolution and Human Behavior* 29, no. 4 (2008): 268–74.

10. Collins, "Men's Voices and Women's Choices." Larger species produce lower-pitched vocalizations than smaller ones, but within a (mammal) species, that is not the case. Recently, however, a number of studies have indicated that the timbre or higher-frequency harmonics called the formant might be a more reliable indicator, at least of height. See Drew Rendall et al., "Lifting the Curtain on the Wizard of Oz: Biased Voice-Based Impressions of Speaker Size," *Journal of Experimental Psychology: Human Perception and Performance* 33, no. 5 (2007): 1208–19.

11. L. Bruckert et al., "Women Use Voice Parameters to Assess Men's Characteristics," *Proceedings of the Royal Society B* 273 (2006): 83–89.

12. C. L. Apicella et al., "Voice Pitch Predicts Reproductive Success in Male Hunter-Gatherers," *Biology Letters* 3 (2007): 682–84.

13. Klaus R. Scherer et al., "Minimal Cues in the Vocal Communication of Affect: Judging Emotions from Content-Masked Speech," *Journal of Paralinguistic Research* 1, no. 3 (1972): 269–85.

14. William Apple et al., "Effects of Speech Rate on Personal Attributions," *Journal of Personality and Social Psychology* 37, no. 5 (1979): 715–27.

15. Carl E. Williams and Kenneth N. Stevens, "Emotions and Speech: Some Acoustical Correlates," *Journal of the Acoustical Society of America* 52, no. 4, part 2 (1972): 1238–50, and Scherer et al., "Minimal Cues in the Vocal Communication of Affect."

16. Sally Feldman, "Speak Up," *New Humanist* 123, no. 5 (September–October, 2008).

17. N. Guéguen, "Courtship Compliance: The Effect of Touch on Women's Behavior," *Social Influence* 2, no. 2 (2007): 81–97.

18. M. Lynn et al., "Reach Out and Touch Your Customers," *Cornell Hotel & Restaurant Quarterly* 39, no. 3 (June 1998): 60–65; J. Hornik, "Tactile Stimulation and Consumer Response," *Journal of Consumer Research* 19 (December 1992): 449–58; N. Guéguen and C. Jacob, "The Effect of Touch on Tipping: An Evaluation in a French Bar," *Hospitality Management* 24 (2005): 295–99; N. Guéguen, "The Effect of Touch on Compliance with a Restaurant's Employee Suggestion," *Hospitality Management* 26 (2007): 1019–23; N. Guéguen, "Nonverbal Encouragement of Participation in a Course: The Effect of Touching," *Social Psychology of Education* 7, no. 1 (2003): 89–98; J. Hornik and S. Ellis, "Strategies to Secure Compliance for a Mall Intercept Interview," *Public Opinion Quarterly* 52 (1988): 539–51; N. Guéguen and J. Fischer-Lokou, "Tactile Contact and Spontaneous Help: An Evaluation in a Natural Setting," *The Journal of Social Psychology* 143, no. 6 (2003): 785–87.

19. C. Silverthorne et al., "The Effects of Tactile Stimulation on Visual Experience," *Journal of Social Psychology* 122 (1972): 153–54; M. Patterson et al., "Touch, Compliance, and Interpersonal Affect," *Journal of Nonverbal Behavior* 10 (1986): 41–50; and N. Guéguen, "Touch, Awareness of Touch, and Compliance with a Request," *Perceptual and Motor Skills* 95 (2002): 355–60.

20. Michael W. Krauss et al., "Tactile Communication, Cooperation, and Performance: An Ethological Study of the NBA," *Emotion* 10, no. 5 (October 2010): 745–49.

21. India Morrison et al., "The Skin as a Social Organ," *Experimental Brain Research*, published online September 22, 2009; Ralph Adolphs, "Conceptual Challenges and Directions for Social Neuroscience," *Neuron* 65, no. 6 (March 25, 2010): 752–67.

22. Ralph Adolphs, interview by author, November 10, 2011.

23. Morrison et al., "The Skin as a Social Organ."

24. R. I. M. Dunbar, "The Social Role of Touch in Humans and Primates:

Behavioral Functions and Neurobiological Mechanisms," *Neuroscience and Bio-behavioral Reviews* 34 (2008): 260–68.

25. Matthew J. Hertenstein et al., "The Communicative Functions of Touch in Humans, Nonhuman Primates, and Rats: A Review and Synthesis of the Empirical Research," *Genetic, Social, and General Psychology Monographs* 132, no. 1 (2006): 5–94.

26. The debate scenario is from Alan Schroeder, *Presidential Debates: Fifty Years of High-Risk TV*, 2nd ed. (New York: Columbia University Press, 2008).

27. Sidney Kraus, *Televised Presidential Debates and Public Policy* (Mahwah, NJ: Erlbaum, 2000), 208–12. Note that Kraus incorrectly states that the Southern Governors' Conference was in Arizona.

28. James N. Druckman, "The Power of Televised Images: The First Kennedy-Nixon Debate Revisited," *Journal of Politics* 65, no. 2 (May 2003): 559–71.

29. Shawn W. Rosenberg et al., "The Image and the Vote: The Effect of Candidate Presentation on Voter Preference," *American Journal of Political Science* 30, no. 1 (February 1986): 108–27, and Shawn W. Rosenberg et al., "Creating a Political Image: Shaping Appearance and Manipulating the Vote," *Political Behavior* 13, no. 4 (1991): 345–66.

30. Alexander Todorov et al., "Inferences of Competence from Faces Predict Election Outcomes," *Science* 308 (June 10, 2005): 1623–26.

31. It is interesting to note that while this is quite clear in photographs of Darwin, his nose seems to have been minimized in paintings.

32. Darwin Correspondence Database, http://www.darwinproject.ac.uk/entry 3235.

33. Charles Darwin, *The Autobiography of Charles Darwin* (1887; repr. Rockville, MD.: Serenity, 2008), 40.

7. SORTING PEOPLE AND THINGS

1. David J. Freedman et al., "Categorical Representation of Visual Stimuli in the Primate Prefrontal Cortex," *Science* 291 (January 2001): 312–16.

2. Henri Tajfel and A. L. Wilkes, "Classification and Quantitative Judgment," *British Journal of Psychology* 54 (1963): 101–14; Oliver Corneille et al., "On the Role of Familiarity with Units of Measurement in Categorical Accentuation: Tajfel and Wilkes (1963) Revisited and Replicated," *Psychological Science* 13, no. 4 (July 2002): 380–83.

3. Robert L. Goldstone, "Effects of Categorization on Color Perception," *Psychological Science* 6, no. 5 (September 1995): 298–303.

4. Joachim Krueger and Russell W. Clement, "Memory-Based Judgments About Multiple Categories: A Revision and Extension of Tajfel's Accentuation Theory," *Journal of Personality and Social Psychology* 67, no. 1 (July 1994): 35–47.

5. Linda Hamilton Krieger, "The Content of Our Categories: A Cognitive Bias Approach to Discrimination and Equal Employment Opportunity," *Stanford Law Review* 47, no. 6 (July 1995): 1161–248.

6. Elizabeth Ewen and Stuart Ewen, *Typecasting: On the Arts and Sciences of Human Inequality* (New York: Seven Stories, 2008).

7. Ibid.

8. Ibid.

9. The image is from Giambattista della Porta, *De Humana Physiognomonia Libri IIII.* From the website of the National Library of Medicine: http://www.nlm.nih.gov/exhibition/historicalanatomies/porta_home.html. According to http://steven poke.com/giambattista-della-porta-de-humana-physiognomonia-1586: "I found these images at the Historical Anatomies on the Web exhibition which is part of the US National Library of Medicine which has over 70,000 images available online."

10. Darrell J. Steffensmeier, "Deviance and Respectability: An Observational Study of Shoplifting," *Social Forces* 51, no. 4 (June 1973): 417–26; see also Kenneth C. Mace, "The 'Overt-Bluff' Shoplifter: Who Gets Caught?" *Journal of Forensic Psychology* 4, no. 1 (December 1972): 26–30.

11. H. T. Himmelweit, "Obituary: Henri Tajfel, FBPsS," *Bulletin of the British Psychological Society* 35 (1982): 288–89.

12. William Peter Robinson, ed., *Social Groups and Identities: Developing the Legacy of Henri Tajfel* (Oxford: Butterworth-Heinemann, 1996), 3.

13. Ibid.

14. Henri Tajfel, *Human Groups and Social Categories* (Cambridge: Cambridge University Press, 1981).

15. Robinson, ed., *Social Groups and Identities*, 5.

16. Krieger, "The Content of Our Categories."

17. Anthony G. Greenwald et al., "Measuring Individual Differences in Implicit Cognition: The Implicit Association Test," *Journal of Personality and Social Psychology* 74, no. 6 (1998): 1464–80; see also Brian A. Nosek et al., "The Implicit Association Test at Age 7: A Methodological and Conceptual Review," in *Automatic Processes in Social Thinking and Behavior*, ed. J. A. English (New York: Psychology Press, 2007), 265–92.

18. Elizabeth Milne and Jordan Grafman, "Ventromedial Prefrontal Cortex Lesions in Humans Eliminate Implicit Gender Stereotyping," *Journal of Neuroscience* 21 (2001): 1–6.

19. Gordon W. Allport, *The Nature of Prejudice* (Cambridge: Addison-Wesley, 1954), 20–23.

20. Ibid., 4–5.

21. Joseph Lelyveld, *Great Soul: Mahatma Gandhi and His Struggle with India* (New York: Knopf, 2011).

22. Ariel Dorfman, "Che Guevara: The Guerrilla," *Time*, June 14, 1999.

23. Marian L. Tupy, "Che Guevara and the West," Cato Institute: Commentary (November 10, 2009).

24. Krieger, "The Content of Our Categories," 1184. Strangely, the woman lost her case. Her lawyers appealed, but the appeals court upheld the verdict, dismissing the statement as a "stray remark."

25. Millicent H. Abel and Heather Watters, "Attributions of Guilt and Punishment as Functions of Physical Attractiveness and Smiling," *Journal of Social Psychology* 145, no. 6 (2005): 687–702; Michael G. Efran, "The Effect of Physical Appearance on the Judgment of Guilt, Interpersonal Attraction, and Severity of Recommended Punishment in a Simulated Jury Task," *Journal of Research in Personality* 8, no. 1 (June 1974): 45–54; Harold Sigall and Nancy Ostrove, "Beautiful but Dangerous: Effects of Offender Attractiveness and Nature of the Crime on Juridic Judgment," *Journal of Personality and Social Psychology* 31, no. 3 (1975): 410–14; Jochen Piehl, "Integration of Information in the Courts: Influence of Physical Attractiveness on Amount of Punishment for a Traffic Offender," *Psychological Reports* 41, no. 2 (October 1977): 551–56; and John E. Stewart II, "Defendant's Attractiveness as a Factor in the Outcome of Criminal Trials: An Observational Study," *Journal of Applied Psychology* 10, no. 4 (August 1980): 348–61.

26. Rosaleen A. McCarthy and Elizabeth K. Warrington, "Visual Associative Agnosia: A Clinico-Anatomical Study of a Single Case," *Journal of Neurology, Neurosurgery, and Psychiatry* 49 (1986): 1233–40.

8. IN-GROUPS AND OUT-GROUPS

1. Muzafer Sherif et al., *Intergroup Conflict and Cooperation: The Robbers Cave Experiment* (Norman: University of Oklahoma Press, 1961).

2. L. Keeley, *War Before Civilization* (Oxford: Oxford University Press, 1996).

3. N. Chagnon, *Yanomamo* (Fort Worth: Harcourt, 1992).

4. Blake E. Ashforth and Fred Mael, "Social Identity Theory and the Organization," *Academy of Management Review* 14, no. 1 (1989): 20–39.

5. Markus Brauer, "Intergroup Perception in the Social Context: The Effects of Social Status and Group Membership on Perceived Out-Group Homogeneity," *Journal of Experimental Social Psychology* 37 (2001): 15–31.

6. K. L. Dion, "Cohesiveness as a Determinant of Ingroup-Outgroup Bias," *Journal of Personality and Social Psychology* 28 (1973): 163–71, and Ashforth and Mael, "Social Identity Theory."

7. Charles K. Ferguson and Harold H. Kelley, "Significant Factors in Overevaluation of Own-Group's Product," *Journal of Personaliity and Social Psychology* 69, no. 2 (1064): 223–28.

8. Patricia Linville et al., "Perceived Distributions of the Characteristics of In-Group and Out-Group Members: Empirical Evidence and a Computer Simulation," *Journal of Personality and Social Psychology* 57, no. 2 (1989): 165–88, and Bernadette Park and Myron Rothbart, "Perception of Out-Group Homogeneity and Levels of Social Categorization: Memory for the Subordinate Attributes of In-Group and Out-Group Members," *Journal of Personality and Social Psychology* 42, no. 6 (1982): 1051–68.

9. Park and Rothbart, "Perception of Out-Group Homogeneity."

10. Margaret Shih et al., "Stereotype Susceptibility: Identity Salience and Shifts in Quantitative Performance," *Psychological Science* 10, no. 1 (January 1999): 80–83.

11. Noah J. Goldstein and Robert B. Cialdini, "Normative Influences on Consumption and Conservation Behaviors," in *Social Psychology and Consumer Behavior*, ed. Michaela Wänke (New York: Psychology Press, 2009), 273–96.

12. Robert B. Cialdini et al., "Managing Social Norms for Persuasive Impact," *Social Influence* 1, no. 1 (2006): 3–15.

13. Marilyn B. Brewer and Madelyn Silver, "Ingroup Bias as a Function of Task Characteristics," *European Journal of Social Psychology* 8 (1978): 393–400.

14. Ashforth and Mael, "Social Identity Theory."

15. Henri Tajfel, "Experiments in Intergroup Discrimination," *Scientific American* 223 (November 1970): 96–102, and H. Tajfel et al., "Social Categorization and Intergroup Behavior," *European Journal of Social Psychology* 1, no. 2 (1971): 149–78.

16. Sherif et al., *Intergroup Conflict and Cooperation*, 209.

17. Robert Kurzban et al., "Can Race be Erased? Coalitional Computation and Social Categorization," *Proceedings of the National Academy of Sciences* 98, no. 26 (December 18, 2001): 15387–92.

9. FEELINGS

1. Corbett H. Thigpen and Hervey Cleckley, "A Case of Multiple Personalities," *Journal of Abnormal and Social Psychology* 49, no. 1 (1954): 135–51.

2. Charles E. Osgood and Zella Luria, "A Blind Analysis of a Case of Multiple Personality Using the Semantic Differential," *Journal of Abnormal and Social Psychology* 49, no. 1 (1954): 579–91.

3. Nadine Brozan, "The Real Eve Sues to Film the Rest of Her Story," *New York Times*, February 7, 1989.

4. Piercarlo Valdesolo and David DeSteno, "Manipulations of Emotional Context Shape Moral Judgment," *Psychological Science* 17, no. 6 (2006): 476–77.

5. Steven W. Gangestad et al., "Women's Preferences for Male Behavioral Displays Change Across the Menstrual Cycle," *Psychological Science* 15, no. 3 (2004): 203–7, and Kristina M. Durante et al., "Changes in Women's Choice of Dress Across

the Ovulatory Cycle: Naturalistic and Laboratory Task-Based Evidence," *Personality and Social Psychology Bulletin* 34 (2008): 1451–60.

6. John F. Kihlstrom and Stanley B. Klein, "Self-Knowledge and Self-Awareness," *Annals of the New York Academy of Sciences* 818 (December 17, 2006): 5–17, and Shelley E. Taylor and Jonathan D. Brown, "Illusion and Well-Being: A Social Psychological Perspective on Mental Health," *Psychological Bulletin* 103, no. 2 (1988): 193–210.

7. H. C. Kelman, "Deception in Social Research," *Transaction* 3 (1966): 20–24; see also Steven J. Sherman, "On the Self-Erasing Nature of Errors of Prediction," *Journal of Personality and Social Psychology* 39, no. 2 (1980): 211–21.

8. E. Grey Dimond et al., "Comparison of Internal Mammary Artery Ligation and Sham Operation for Angina Pectoris," *American Journal of Cardiology* 5, no. 4 (April 1960): 483–86; see also Walter A. Brown, "The Placebo Effect," *Scientific American* (January 1998): 90–95.

9. William James, "What Is an Emotion?" *Mind* 9, no. 34 (April 1884): 188–205.

10. Tor D. Wager, "The Neural Bases of Placebo Effects in Pain," *Current Directions in Psychological Science* 14, no. 4 (2005): 175–79, and Tor D. Wager et al., "Placebo-Induced Changes in fMRI in the Anticipation and Experience of Pain," *Science* 303 (February 2004): 1162–67.

11. James H. Korn, "Historians' and Chairpersons' Judgments of Eminence Among Psychologists," *American Psychologist* 46, no. 7 (July 1991): 789–92.

12. William James to Carl Strumpf, February 6, 1887, in *The Correspondence of William James*, vol. 6, ed. Ignas K. Skrupskelis and Elizabeth M. Berkeley (Charlottesville: University Press of Virginia, 1992), 202.

13. D. W. Bjork, *The Compromised Scientist: William James in the Development of American Psychology* (New York: Columbia University Press, 1983), 12.

14. Henry James, ed., *The Letters of William James* (Boston: Little, Brown, 1926), 393–94.

15. Stanley Schachter and Jerome E. Singer, "Cognitive, Social, and Physiological Determinants of Emotional State," *Psychological Review* 69, no. 5 (September 1962): 379–99.

16. Joanne R. Cantor et al., "Enhancement of Experienced Sexual Arousal in Response to Erotic Stimuli Through Misattribution of Unrelated Residual Excitation," *Journal of Personality and Social Psychology* 32, no. 1 (1975): 69–75.

17. See http://www.imdb.com/title/tt0063013/.

18. Donald G. Dutton and Arthur P. Aron, "Some Evidence for Heightened Sexual Attraction Under Conditions of High Anxiety," *Journal of Personality and Social Psychology* 30, no. 4 (1974): 510–17.

19. Fritz Strack et al., "Inhibiting and Facilitating Conditions of the Human Smile: A Nonobtrusive Test of the Facial Feedback Hypothesis," *Journal of Personal-*

ity and Social Psychology 54, no. 5 (1988): 768–77, and Lawrence W. Barsalou et al., "Social Embodiment," *Psychology of Learning and Motivation* 43 (2003): 43–92.

20. Peter Johansson et al., "Failure to Detect Mismatches Between Intention and Outcome in a Simple Decision Task," *Science* 310 (October 7, 2005): 116–19.

21. Lars Hall et al., "Magic at the Marketplace: Choice Blindness for the Taste of Jam and the Smell of Tea," *Cognition* 117, no. 1 (October 2010): 54–61.

22. Wendy M. Rahm et al., "Rationalization and Derivation Processes in Survey Studies of Political Candidate Evaluation," *American Journal of Political Science* 38, no. 3 (August 1994): 582–600.

23. Joseph LeDoux, *The Emotional Brain: The Mysterious Underpinnings of Emotional Life* (New York: Simon and Schuster, 1996), 32–33, and Michael Gazzaniga, "The Split Brain Revisited," *Scientific American* 279, no. 1 (July 1998): 51–55.

24. Oliver Sacks, *The Man Who Mistook His Wife for a Hat* (New York: Simon and Schuster, 1998), 108–11.

25. J. Haidt, "The Emotional Dog and Its Rational Tail: A Social Intuitionist Approach to Moral Judgment," *Psychological Review* 108, no. 4 (2001): 814–34.

26. Richard E. Nisbett and Timothy DeCamp Wilson, "Telling More Than We Can Know: Verbal Reports on Mental Processes," *Psychological Review* 84, no. 3 (May 1977): 231–59.

27. Richard E. Nisbett and Timothy DeCamp Wilson, "Verbal Reports About Causal Influences on Social Judgments: Private Access Versus Public Theories," *Journal of Personality and Social Psychology* 35, no. 9 (September 1977): 613–24; see also Nisbett and Wilson, "Telling More Than We Can Know."

28. E. Aronson et al., "The Effect of a Pratfall on Increasing Personal Attractiveness," *Psychonomic Science* 4 (1966): 227–28, and M. J. Lerner, "Justice, Guilt, and Veridicial Perception," *Journal of Personality and Social Psychology* 20 (1971): 127–35.

10. SELF

1. Robert Block, "Brown Portrays FEMA to Panel as Broken and Resource-Starved," *Wall Street Journal*, September 28, 2005.

2. Dale Carnegie, *How to Win Friends and Influence People* (New York: Simon and Schuster, 1936), 3–5.

3. College Board, *Student Descriptive Questionnaire* (Princeton, NJ: Educational Testing Service, 1976–77).

4. P. Cross, "Not Can but Will College Teaching Be Improved?" *New Directions for Higher Education* 17 (1977): 1–15.

5. O. Svenson, "Are We All Less Risky and More Skillful Than Our Fellow Driver?" *Acta Psychologica* 47 (1981): 143–48, and L. Larwood and W. Whittaker, "Managerial Myopia: Self-Serving Biases in Organizational Planning," *Journal of Applied Psychology* 62 (1977): 194–98.

6. David Dunning et al., "Flawed Self-Assessment: Implications for Health, Education, and the Workplace," *Psychological Science in the Public Interest* 5, no. 3 (2004): 69–106.

7. B. M Bass and F. J Yamarino, "Congruence of Self and Others' Leadership Ratings of Naval Officers for Understanding Successful Performance," *Applied Psychology* 40 (1991): 437–54.

8. Scott R. Millis et al., "Assessing Physicians' Interpersonal Skills: Do Patients and Physicians See Eye-to-Eye?" *American Journal of Physical Medicine & Rehabilitation* 81, no. 12 (December 2002): 946–51, and Jocelyn Tracey et al., "The Validity of General Practitioners' Self Assessment of Knowledge: Cross Sectional Study," *BMJ* 315 (November 29, 1997): 1426–28.

9. Dunning et al., "Flawed Self-Assessment."

10. A. C. Cooper et al., "Entrepreneurs' Perceived Chances for Success," *Journal of Business Venturing* 3 (1988): 97–108, and L. Larwood and W. Whittaker, "Managerial Myopia: Self-Serving Biases in Organizational Planning," *Journal of Applied Psychology* 62 (1977): 194–98.

11. Dunning et al., "Flawed Self-Assessment," and David Dunning, *Self-Insight: Roadblocks and Detours on the Path to Knowing Thyself* (New York: Psychology Press, 2005), 6–9.

12. M. L. A. Hayward and D. C. Hambrick, "Explaining the Premiums Paid for Large Acquisitions: Evidence of CEO Hubris," *Administrative Science Quarterly* 42 (1997): 103–27, and U. Malmendier and G. Tate, "Who Makes Acquisitions? A Test of the Overconfidence Hypothesis," *Stanford Research Paper 1798* (Palo Alto, CA: Stanford University, 2003).

13. T. Odean, "Volume, Volatility, Price, and Profit When All Traders Are Above Average," *Journal of Finance* 8 (1998): 1887–934. For Schiller's survey, see Robert J. Schiller, *Irrational Exuberance* (New York: Broadway Books, 2005), 154–55.

14. E. Pronin et al., "The Bias Blind Spot: Perception of Bias in Self Versus Others," *Personality and Social Psychology Bulletin* 28 (2002): 369–81; Emily Pronin, "Perception and Misperception of Bias in Human Judgment," *Trends in Cognitive Sciences* 11, no. 1 (2006): 37–43, and J. Friedrich, "On Seeing Oneself as Less Self-Serving Than Others: The Ultimate Self-Serving Bias?" *Teaching of Psychology* 23 (1996): 107–9.

15. Vaughan Bell et al., "Beliefs About Delusions," *Psychologist* 16, no. 8 (August 2003): 418–23, and Vaughan Bell, "Jesus, Jesus, Jesus," *Slate* (May 26, 2010).

16. Dan P. McAdams, "Personal Narratives and the Life Story," in *Handbook of Personality: Theory and Research*, ed. Oliver John et al. (New York: Guilford, 2008), 242–62.

17. F. Heider, *The Psychology of Interpersonal Relations* (New York: Wiley, 1958).

18. Robert E. Knox and James A. Inkster, "Postdecision Dissonance at Post Time," *Journal of Personality and Social Psychology* 8, no. 4 (1968): 319–23, and

Edward E. Lawler III et al., "Job Choice and Post Decision Dissonance," *Organizational Behavior and Human Performance* 13 (1975): 133–45.

19. Ziva Kunda, "The Case for Motivated Reasoning," *Psychological Bulletin* 108, no. 3 (1990): 480–98; see also David Dunning, "Self-Image Motives and Consumer Behavior: How Sacrosanct Self-Beliefs Sway Preferences in the Marketplace," *Journal of Consumer Psychology* 17, no. 4 (2007): 237–49.

20. Emily Balcetis and David Dunning, "See What You Want To See: Motivational Influences on Visual Perception," *Journal of Personality and Social Psychology* 91, no. 4 (2006): 612–25.

21. To be certain they weren't actually seeing both animals, the researchers also employed an eye-tracking system capable of identifying, from unconscious eye movements, how the subjects really were interpreting the figure.

22. Albert H. Hastorf and Hadley Cantril, "They Saw a Game: A Case Study," *Journal of Abnormal and Social Psychology* 49 (1954): 129–34.

23. George Smoot and Keay Davidson, *Wrinkles in Time: Witness to the Birth of the Universe* (New York: Harper Perennial, 2007), 79–86.

24. Jonathan J. Koehler, "The Influence of Prior Beliefs on Scientific Judgments of Evidence Quality," *Organizational Behavior and Human Decision Processes* 56 (1993): 28–55.

25. See Koehler's article for a discussion of this behavior from the Bayesian point of view.

26. Paul Samuelson, *The Collected Papers of Paul Samuelson* (Boston: MIT Press, 1986), 53. He was paraphrasing Max Planck, who said, "It is not that old theories are disproved, it is just that their supporters die out." See Michael Szenberg and Lall Ramrattan, eds., *New Frontiers in Economics* (Cambridge, UK: Cambridge University Press, 2004), 3–4.

27. Susan L. Coyle, "Physician-Industry Relations. Part 1: Individual Physicians," *Annals of Internal Medicine* 135, no. 5 (2002): 396–402.

28. Ibid.; Karl Hackenbrack and Mark W. Wilson, "Auditors' Incentives and Their Application of Financial Accounting Standards," *Accounting Review* 71, no. 1 (January 1996): 43–59; Robert A. Olsen, "Desirability Bias Among Professional Investment Managers: Some Evidence from Experts," *Journal of Behavioral Decision Making* 10 (1997): 65–72; and Vaughan Bell et al., "Beliefs About Delusions," *Psychologist* 16, no. 8 (August 2003): 418–23.

29. Drew Westen et al., "Neural Bases of Motivated Reasoning: An fMRI Study of Emotional Constraints on Partisan Political Judgment in the 2004 U.S. Presidential Election," *Journal of Cognitive Neuroscience* 18, no. 11 (2006): 1947–58.

30. Ibid.

31. Peter H. Ditto and David F. Lopez, "Motivated Skepticism: Use of Differential Decision Criteria for Preferred and Nonpreferred Conclusions," *Journal of Personality and Social Psychology* 63, no. 4: 568–84.

32. Naomi Oreskes, "The Scientific Consensus on Climate Change," *Science*

306 (December 3, 2004): 1686, and Naomi Oreskes and Erik M. Conway, *Merchants of Doubt* (New York: Bloomsbury, 2010), 169–70.

33. Charles G. Lord et al., "Biased Assimilation and Attitude Polarization: The Effects of Prior Theories on Subsequently Considered Evidence," *Journal of Personality and Social Psychology* 37, no. 11 (1979): 2098–109.

34. Robert P. Vallone et al., "The Hostile Media Phenomenon: Biased Perception and Perceptions of Media Bias in Coverage of the Beirut Massacre," *Journal of Personality and Social Psychology* 49, no. 3 (1985): 577–85.

35. Daniel L. Wann and Thomas J. Dolan, "Attributions of Highly Identified Sports Spectators," *Journal of Social Psychology* 134, no. 6 (1994): 783–93, and Daniel L. Wann and Thomas J. Dolan, "Controllability and Stability in the Self-Serving Attributions of Sport Spectators," *Journal of Social Psychology* 140, no. 2 (1998): 160–68.

36. Stephen E. Clapham and Charles R. Schwenk, "Self-Serving Attributions, Managerial Cognition, and Company Performance," *Strategic Management Journal* 12 (1991): 219–29.

37. Ian R. Newby-Clark et al., "People Focus on Optimistic Scenarios and Disregard Pessimistic Scenarios While Predicting Task Completion Times," *Journal of Experimental Psychology: Applied* 6, no. 3 (2000): 171–82.

38. David Dunning, "Strangers to Ourselves?" *Psychologist* 19, no. 10 (October 2006): 600–604; see also Dunning et al., "Flawed Self-Assessment."

39. R. Buehler et al., "Inside the Planning Fallacy: The Causes and Consequences of Optimistic Time Predictions," in *Heuristics and Biases: The Psychology of Intuitive Judgment*, ed. T. Gilovitch et al. (Cambridge, UK: Cambridge University Press, 2002), 251–70.

40. Eric Luis Uhlmann and Geoffrey L. Cohen, "Constructed Criteria," *Psychological Science* 16, no. 6 (2005): 474–80.

41. Regarding all the experiments in this series, see Linda Babcock and George Loewenstein, "Explaining Bargaining Impasse: The Role of Self-Serving Biases," *Journal of Economic Perspectives* 11, no. 1 (Winter 1997): 109–26. See also Linda Babcock et al., "Biased Judgments of Fairness in Bargaining," *American Economic Review* 85, no. 5 (1995): 1337–43, and the authors' other related work cited in Babcock and Loewenstein.

42. Shelley E. Taylor and Jonathan D. Brown, "Illusion and Well-Being: A Social Psychological Perspective on Mental Health," *Psychological Bulletin* 103, no. 2 (1988): 193–210.

43. David Dunning et al., "Self-Serving Prototypes of Social Categories," *Journal of Personality and Social Psychology* 61, no. 6 (1991): 957–68.

44. Harry P. Bahrick et al., "Accuracy and Distortion in Memory for High School Grades," *Psychological Science* 7, no. 5 (September 1996): 265–71.

45. Steve Jobs, Stanford University commencement address, 2005.

46. Stanley Meisler, "The Surreal World of Salvador Dalí," *Smithsonian Magazine* (April 2005).

47. Taylor and Brown, "Illusion and Well-Being"; Alice M. Isen et al., "Positive Affect Facilitates Creative Problem Solving," *Journal of Personality and Social Psychology* 52, no. 6 (1987): 1122–31; and Peter J. D. Carnevale and Alice M. Isen, "The Influence of Positive Affect and Visual Access on the Discovery of Integrative Solutions in Bilateral Negotiations," *Organizational Behavior and Human Decision Processes* 37 (1986): 1–13.

48. Taylor and Brown, "Illusion and Well-Being," and Dunning, "Strangers to Ourselves?"

49. Taylor and Brown, "Illusion and Well-Being."

Index

Page numbers in *italics* refer to illustrations.

Index

split-, 189–90
stress-sensitive regions of, 15
structure of, 6–8, 33, 100–4
subliminal level of, 187–8
surgery on, 99
traumatic experiences and, 14–15
unconscious, 91–2, 97–9, 187–8
vertebrate, 33, 101
visual cortex of, 6–8, 30, 35–51, 102
brain stem, 16
"brand-appreciation" module, 25
brand names, 24–5
Brazil, 117–18, 180
Brown, Michael, 196–7
Browning, Elizabeth Barrett, 18
Buchenwald concentration camp, 122–3
Bugs Bunny, 76
bullet penetration, 41–2
burglaries, 59–63, 197
Burlington, N.C., 52–6
business executives, 58, 88, 198, 210–11
business negotiations, 58

Cadillac, 172
Caesar, Julius, 169
California, 55–6, 84, 140–2, 148–9, 195
Cambridge University, 68–9, 99–100
campaign flyers, 140–2
capital punishment, 209
Capone, Al, 197
cardiac surgeons, 179–80
Carnegie, Dale, 197
carotid artery, occluded, 159–60
Carpenter, William, 32, 33
cash bonuses, 212–13
categories, 145–60
cats, 85, 146–7
causal arrows, 201
CBS, 137–8
C. elegans (roundworm), 12–13
cerebellum, 16, 41
cerebral hemispheres, 36
cervix, and oxytocin, 95
chain letters, 90
Challenger explosion (1986), 69–70
chance, 4, 28, 210
change blindness, 72–4
character actors, 149–50
chatter, 126–7
cheating, 110
chemistry, brain, 92, 93–4, 99–100
chemistry, sexual, 186–7
Chesterton, G. K., 126
Chicago, University of, 205
children, 75–6, 80–1, 86, 87, 92–3, 95, 113–14, 120–1, 124, 161–5, 215, 217
Chile, 117–18
chimpanzees, 88, 116, 119–20
Christmas cards, 90

cigarette smoking, 84
circulatory system, 99–100, 159–60, 179–80
civilization, 8, 68–70, 96, 129–30
Clever Hans, 107–10, 114
clinical psychology, 31–2, 33, 59, 62, 68–70, 96, 99, 104, 180–3, 200
cliques, 89–90, 137
coaches, 136–7
Coca-Cola, 25
codes of conduct, 161–5
cognition, 15, 34–5, 96–9, 103–4
cognitive psychology, 96–9, 103–4
collective behavior, 26–9
colors, 23, 35, 147–8
color samples, 147–8
Columbia University, 183
communication, 34, 44–5, 58, 65–6, 74–5, 189, 234
see also language
communism, 138, 164
company names, 26–7
competitive behavior, 92–6, 161–5, 174–5
compressed images, 66
computers, 6–8, 7, 22, 34, 58–9, 66, 85, 88, 95, 97, 98, 104, 127–8, 132, 147, 165–6, 172, 203, 215–16, 236n
computer science, 34
concentration, mental, 34–5
concentration camps, 122–3, 152–3
conception, 131
confabulation, 190–1
Congress, U.S., 56–8, 140–2, 196
consciousness, 3–5, 8, 29, 30–5, 42–5, 91–2, 102–3, 200–1, 204–8, 210–16
consensus, 208–9
consonants, 48–50
"content-free" speech, 132–3
contracts, 88, 210–11
control groups, 169–70
Convicting the Innocent (Garrett), 55
cooperation, 80–2, 89–98, 110, 136–7, 161–5, 174–5
Cornell University, 72–4
corporations, 91
correlations, statistical, 27–9
cortex, 13, 83, 101
Cotton, Ronald, 53–6, 75
country clubs, 165
cowbirds, 126–7
crime, 52–63, 66, 170, 197
Crowley, "Two Gun," 197
cues, nonverbal, 43–4, 119–20, 135–7, 143–4
cultural norms, 117–18, 122, 191–5

Dalí, Salvador, 216
damages, lawsuit, 212–13
Dartmouth College, 204
Darwin, Charles, 142–3
databases, 6–8

Index

Federal Emergency Management Agency
  (FEMA), 196–7
fertility, 131
films, 119–20, 149–50, 177
financial crisis (2007–8), 28
fine motor movements, 102
First International Congress, 59
first-order intentionality, 87
fluency effect, 21–2, 26–7
fMRI (functional magnetic resonance
  imaging), 6–8, 7, 24, 25, 83, 100–4,
  232n
folk tales, 68–9
fonts, 21–2, 146, 149
food tastes, 20–6, 33
football, 204
"forced choice" experiment, 33, 38–40
fourth-order intentionality, 87–8
France, 135–6, 152–3
free will, 12–13, 181
Freiburg, University of, 59
frequencies, 132–3
Freud, Sigmund, 5, 16, 17, 33, 68, 96, 100, 104,
  180, 200
frontal lobe, 36, 91, 102, 121–3
fruit flies, 12, 13
functional magnetic resonance imaging
  (fMRI), 6–8, 7, 24, 25, 83, 100–4, 232n
fusiform area, 38–9

Gandhi, Mohandas K., 157
gangs, 161–5
gaps, information, 50–1
gaps, visual, 46–8, 49, 152
Gare d'Orsay, 153
Garrett, Brandon, 55
Gauldin, Mike, 53
gaze, 119–20, 121
gender stereotypes, 127–8, 151, 155–7, 158, 167,
  168, 169–70, 211–12
General Accounting Office, U.S., 211
General Motors (GM), 28
generic categories, 146
genetics, 54, 55, 95–6
Germany, 59–61, 107–10, 180–1
Gestalt, 69
gesture systems, 115
ghosts, 68–9
gifted students, 113–14
Gilbert, Daniel, 17
Girl on a Motorcycle, The, 186
global positioning system (GPS), 50, 85
global warming, 208–9
God, 207
Golan Heights, 44–5
gold chloride, 16
Goldwater, Barry, 141
Google, 172
government agencies, 91

grades, academic, 192–3, 194, 214, 215
grammar, 214
Grandin, Temple, 87
grand juries, 57
gratuities, 27–8
gravity, 6, 50
gray matter, 102
Great Britain, 134, 206
Great Depression, 141
Great Escape, The, 12
grooming, 89–90, 137
group affiliation, 84
group memories, 68–70
groups, 68–70, 84, 89–90, 122–3, 147–8,
  161–75
Guevara, Che, 157
guilt, 158–9

habitual thinking, 11–15
  see also programmed behavior
Hadza people, 131–2
Haidt, Jonathan, 200
hairdressers, 167, 168
Haldeman, H. R., 57
hamadryas baboons, 119–20
happiness, 117, 118, 184, 185
hard drives, 58–9
Harvard Psychological Laboratory, 31–2, 59, 62
Harvard University, 31–2, 59, 62, 67, 131–2,
  169–70, 180, 181
Hawking, Stephen, 79–80, 163
headaches, 176, 179, 187
head wounds, 41–2
hearing, 48–50
heart disease, 36–41, 77, 159–60, 179–80
heart rate, 184
heaven, 206
Hebrew language, 44–5
Helen of Troy, 38
hell, 206
"helper," 80–1
hemispheres, brain, 42, 189–90
hemorrhages, 36–7
Henry, Patrick, 81
Hewitt, Don, 138
high blood pressure, 84
high school students, 198, 214
hippocampus, 101, 103
hiring practices, 122, 132, 148–9, 192–4,
  211–12, 213
Hispanics, 148–9, 167
Hitler, Adolf, 218
Holocaust, 122–3, 152–3
hominids, 102, 114, 129–30, 163, 164
Homo erectus, 114
Homo habilis, 114
homosexuality, 44
hoof tapping, 108–9
horses, 107–10, 114, 200–3

Index

Index

Index

Index